C2 000003444584 EE

D1336589

FIX IT MANUAL

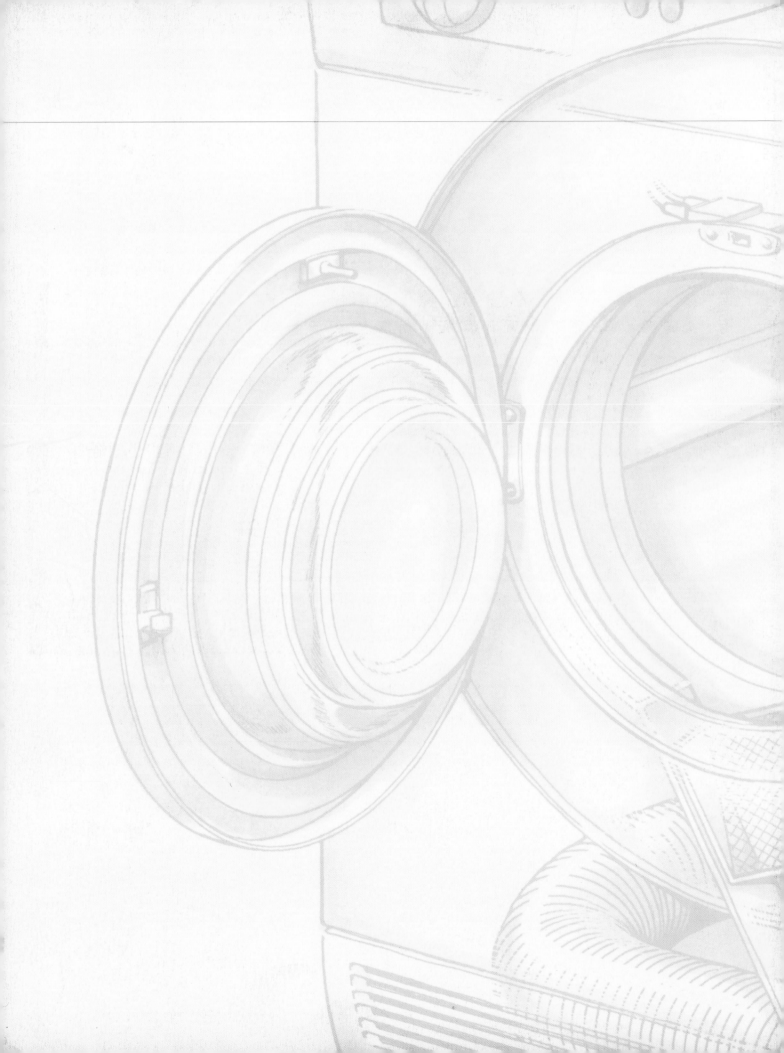

FIX IT MANUAL

Albert **Jackson**

Collins Fix It Manual
was created exclusively for
HarperCollins
by Jackson Day,
Greenwich, London.
The manual was conceived by
David Day, Simon Jennings and
Albert Jackson, trading as Inklink,
and is based on an original design
by Simon Jennings.

First published in 2003 by
Collins an imprint of
HarperCollins Publishers,
77–85 Fulham Palace Road, London
W6 8JB

Everything clicks at:
www.collins.co.uk

Author
Albert Jackson

**Technical consultant and
contributor**
Graham Dixon

Designer
Elizabeth Standley

Art director
Albert Jackson

Illustrator
Robin Harris

Editor
Peter Leek

Proofreader and indexer
Mary Morton

Studio photography
Colin Bowling
Britannia Studios

Albert Jackson
Jackson Day

For detailed photography credits,
see page 8.

Set construction
Simon Gilham

Additional consultants
Gregory Dixon
Computers

Geoff Hayman, Wireless Alarms
Alarm systems

For HarperCollins
Angela Newton – Managing editor
Alastair Laing – Editor
Luke Griffin – Design
Chris Gurney – Production

Copyright © 2003
HarperCollins Publishers

All rights reserved. No part of this
publication may be reproduced,
stored in a retrieval system or
transmitted in any form or by any
means, electronic, mechanical,
photocopying, recording or
otherwise, without prior written
permission of the copyright owner.

Albert Jackson asserts the moral
right to be identified as the author of
this work.

The CIP catalogue record for this
book is available from the
British Library

ISBN 000 4129938

Colour reproduction
Colourscan

Printed and bound by
Imago, Singapore

Care has been taken to ensure that the
information in this book is accurate and
up-to-date at the date of publication.
However, any information or advice
provided in this book is for guidance
purposes only and readers are responsible
for determining whether such information or
advice applies to their particular situation.
When using electrical equipment readers
should always follow the manufacturer's
instructions. The information and advice
contained in this book should not be relied
upon as statements or representations of
facts and no warranty is given as to the
accuracy of any information provided. It is
advised that this book should not be used
as an alternative to seeking expert advice.

All information contained in this book is
provided without responsibility on the part
of the authors and publishers and to the
full extent permissible by law. The authors
and publishers accept no liability for any
loss, damage or injury arising as a result of
any reliance (whether express or implied)
on the advice or information contained in
this book or arising in connection with any
DIY fix it projects.

**WARNING At all times readers should
ensure they read and follow with care any
safety instructions contained in this book.**

BIRMINGHAM LIBRARIES/BIB SERVICES	
WALMLEY	
Cypher	03.10.03
643.7	25.00

CONTENTS

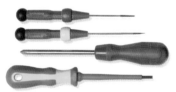

For **David**

INTRODUCTION

These days, when built-in obsolescence has become the norm, is there really any point in repairing anything? Now that mass production has brought prices down to an affordable level, mightn't it be less time-consuming and more economical to go out and buy a replacement? These are highly pertinent questions, which Collins Fix It Manual acknowledges and seeks to address.

If you're faced with the choice of paying a hefty repair bill or splashing out on a brand-new appliance, your first inclination may be to spend that little bit extra and treat yourself to the latest model. But perhaps your reaction would be different if you knew that it was perfectly feasible to get the errant appliance up and running again simply and quickly.

When a domestic appliance breaks down, most people experience annoyance and frustration – especially since the labour-saving appliances we rely on invariably quit at the most inconvenient moment. On top of that, it may prove impossible to get a service engineer to call for a week or more, and you then have to be on hand for most of the day. But the ultimate irritation is to discover that you could have got the machine working in next to no time – if only you had known what to do.

Inconvenience and economics aside, there is the environmental issue. Local authorities find themselves faced with an ever-growing mountain of discarded appliances. So much so that it has become necessary to introduce legislation in order to persuade manufacturers to make their products last longer, and to consider recycling components to cut down the enormous waste of resources. Today disposal has become such a problem that there are now strict regulations compelling us to take discarded appliances to designated sites in order to eliminate fly-tipping and prevent environmental contamination from some very unpleasant by-products.

Considerations such as these suggest that being able to fix things yourself is still worthwhile and rewarding, provided the repair isn't excessively demanding and won't take a disproportionate amount of time to complete.

The primary aim of this book is to highlight the easier ways of getting faulty appliances working again, without needing a lot of technical expertise. There's no guarantee you will be able to repair everything, and you will no doubt have to call on professional help from time to time. But, if you can't fix the problem yourself, you will at least have the advantage of being able to rule out some of the more obvious faults and will be better placed to discuss it with an expert.

And if, in the end, you come to the conclusion that buying a new appliance is the best course of action, then that too will be a better informed decision after reading Collins Fix It Manual.

ACKNOWLEDGMENTS

Graham Dixon

Special thanks are due to Graham Dixon for his unique contribution to this book. His expertise and practical skills and his unstinting support and enthusiasm for the project have been truly invaluable.

Sample products

The author and publisher are indebted to the companies and manufacturers who generously supplied samples of their products for photography and artist's reference:

Water softener

Culligan International (UK) Ltd
High Wycombe, Buckinghamshire

TV and radio reception equipment

Maxview Ltd
King's Lynn, Norfolk

Extractor fans
Venting kits

Oracstar Ltd
Brackmills, Northampton NN4

Power sharpener

Plasplugs Ltd
Burton-on-Trent, Staffordshire

Glassbreak detector

Pyronix Ltd
Rotherham, South Yorkshire

Test equipment

Rapitest – GET plc
London N11

Alarm systems

Wireless Alarms
Great Bookham, Surrey

Technical literature and advice

We are further indebted to the companies and associations who supplied technical literature and advice:

Ademco Microtech Ltd
East Kilbride, G74, Scotland

Aico Ltd
Oswestry, Shropshire

Black & Decker Ltd
Slough, Berkshire

British Security Industry Association Worcester, WR1

BSH Appliance Care
Milton Keynes, MK12

Culligan International (UK) Ltd
High Wycombe, Buckinghamshire

DeLonghi Ltd
Wellingborough, Northamptonshire

Electrolux Ltd
Luton, Bedfordshire

General Domestic Appliances Ltd
Peterborough, PE2

Gillette Group Ltd
Croydon, CR9

Hoover Ltd
Merthyr Tydfil, Mid Glamorgan

IntelliSense Ltd
Redditch, Worcestershire

Kenwood Ltd
Havant, Hampshire

Maxview Ltd
King's Lynn, Norfolk

Morphy Richards Ltd
Mexborough, South Yorkshire

Novar ED&S Ltd
Basildon, Essex

Pace Micro Technology plc
Saltaire, West Yorkshire

Panasonic UK Ltd
Bracknell, Berkshire

Philips DAP
London, CR9

Pyronix Ltd
Rotherham, South Yorkshire

Rapitest – GET plc
London N11

Robert Bosch Ltd
Uxbridge, Middlesex

Toshiba UK Ltd
Camberley, Surrey

UK Cleaning Products Industry
Haywards Heath, Sussex

Uniross Batteries Ltd
Nailsea, North Somerset

Visonic Ltd
Bedford, MK44

Wireless Alarms
Great Bookham, Surrey

Photography credits

With the following exceptions, all photographs in *Collins Fix It Manual* are by Albert Jackson.

Ben Jennings
10B; 11C; 12TL, TP; 16TL, R; 17T; 18R; 20TL, CL; 21B; 23; 24; 29; 47TL; 51TR; 56TL, C; 60CL, CR; 61; 75; 76–87; 121TR; 281TR; 284CL.

Neil Waving
11B; 14; 15TL, TR, BR; 18L; 19BR; 21R.

Complete – courtesy of Argos Ltd
26B; 32T; 33BR; 38BR; 39TL; 44T, B; 45; 46BR; 50TR; 51BR; 54; 60T; 66TR; 68TL, R; 70; 88; 90BR; 127; 164; 165T; 182L, BL, 188BR; 189, 198; 199TR; 200R; 202BC; 207R; 209; 210BL; 212T, B; 219BL; 220L, TR; 221TR; 228T; 231B; 234CL; 235B, BR; 238R; 240R; 244CL; 253L; 258; 259TR; 263L.

Colin Bowling
90TL; 92CR; 94CR; 95TL; 97BR; 103BR; 109BR; 112; 115BC; 116BL; 121TL; 124BC; 125BR; 128CR; 130BR; 13BL; 144TL; 147TR; 149TR; 153TR; 154TR; 155TR, BR; 160BR; 161BR; 162TR; 167R; 175BL; 178; 179; 180TL, BL, T; 181BR; 185CR; 186BR; 188L; 196CR; 199B; 20CB; 202TR; 210TL; 214; 222; 223; 224BR; 235T; 236; 239T; 240TL; 242BL; 246l, TR; 248R; 250; 251C; 254BL; 255T; 271L; 274BL; 276BL; 278; 279; 280TR, C; 286; 287.

In-Sink-Erator
136TL.

Culligan International (UK) Ltd
141.

Maxview Ltd
201R; 212CR.

Courtesy of Microsoft Corporation
236BR; 239CR; 240CL, BL; 242TL; 243BR; 244TL.

Key to photographic credits
L=Left, R=Right, T=Top, TL=Top left, TC=Top centre, TR=Top right, C=Centre, UC=Upper centre, CL=Centre left, CR=Centre right, LC=Lower centre, B=Bottom, BL=Bottom left, BC=Bottom centre, BR=Bottom right.

Please note
All products photographed for inclusion in this book are for aesthetic purposes only and were selected as representing typical examples of their type. It is not intended that the images accompanying the text should represent or identify any products as susceptible to malfunction. Inclusion of these products in this book is not intended to imply that they are defective as illustrated or at all.

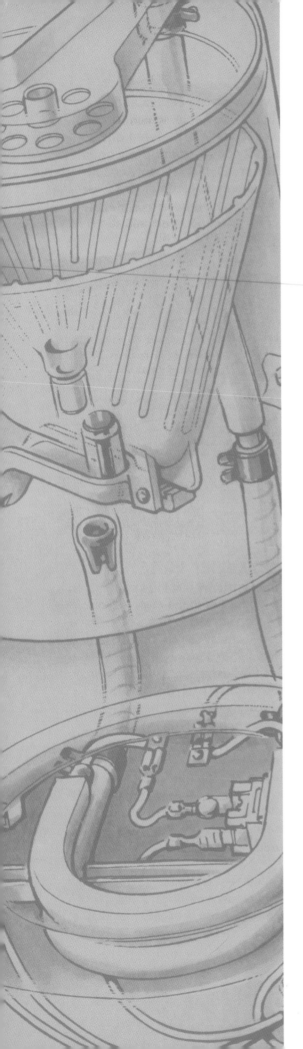

BEFORE
YOU START

A basic knowledge of how electricity and water are supplied and directed around your home is vital to being able to repair any appliance safely and effectively. Read this chapter thoroughly before you embark on any repairs involving electricity. It not only gives you all-important background knowledge and safety advice but will enable you to tackle – or at least rule out – those common faults that everyone encounters from time to time.

Above all:

- Never take risks with electricity and water – the combination can be fatal.

- Before you start to work on an appliance, always ensure that it has been unplugged or completely disconnected from the electrical supply.

- If you do not feel competent to tackle or complete a repair, get a qualified electrician or service engineer to undertake or continue the work.

- Remember that you will forfeit your rights if you attempt to service an appliance still under the manufacturer's guarantee.

How electricity works in your home

Electricity generated at the power station is delivered across country via overhead cables and finally reaches your home by way of your regional electricity company's main service cable, which terminates at your fuseboard. This is where the electricity, supplied at a standard 230 volts, is metered and diverted to the circuits that power all the light fittings and electrical appliances in your house or flat.

At the fuseboard, the service cable is connected to the 'cutout'. This contains the main service fuse, which prevents any serious fault in your wiring from affecting the supply of electricity to your neighbours. After the cutout comes the meter, which simply monitors your consumption of electricity. Two PVC-covered leads – one red and one black – run from the meter to the consumer unit, the heart of the electrical wiring in your home.

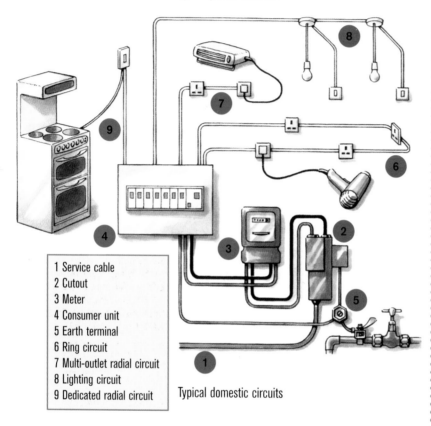

1 Service cable
2 Cutout
3 Meter
4 Consumer unit
5 Earth terminal
6 Ring circuit
7 Multi-outlet radial circuit
8 Lighting circuit
9 Dedicated radial circuit

Typical domestic circuits

How electricity is measured

Volts
Electric current is driven along conductors (cables or wires) by 'pressure' measured in volts. In this country, 230 volts (230V) is standard.

Watts
The amount of electricity used by an appliance when it is working is measured in watts. The wattage of a particular appliance is usually marked on its casing. One thousand watts (1000W) equals one kilowatt (1kW).

Amps
The flow of current needed to produce the wattage required by an appliance is measured in amps. Fuses and other electrical fittings are rated in amps – 13amp (13A), for example.

The consumer unit

Inside the consumer unit the incoming red cable is connected to the main isolating switch, which is used to turn off the entire supply of electricity to your home.

Connected to this switch is a row of individual fuse carriers or miniature circuit breakers (MCBs), each one serving a separate circuit that takes electricity to your wall sockets and fixed lighting and to individual appliances such as cookers and immersion heaters.

A fuse or MCB forms a weak link that bridges the gap between the main switch and each circuit. In the event of a serious fault on a circuit the link is broken, cutting off the supply of electricity.

Residual current devices

With most modern electrical installations, additional protection is usually provided in the form of a residual current device (RCD)

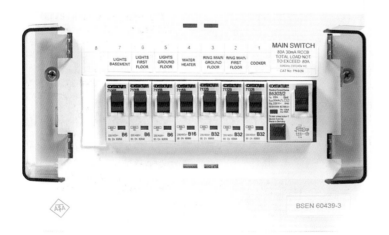

Modern consumer unit with miniature circuit breakers

Main isolating switch that incorporates an RCD

Residual current devices – left to right: wall socket with RCD, self-contained RCD and a plug-in RCD

Mains cables have a protective white or grey PVC sheathing that covers the three conductors

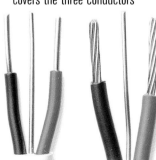

that cuts the supply of electricity as soon as it detects a fault on a circuit – in a fraction of the time it would take a fuse or MCB to operate.

A residual current device is often built into the consumer unit along with the main isolating switch, in order to safeguard the entire domestic installation. Also available are self-contained RCD units, which are especially suitable for incorporating into older installations in order to provide an up-to-date level of protection. Special wall sockets are made with integral RCDs that monitor appliances plugged into them. There are also RCDs that can be plugged into any standard socket outlet; this type of RCD is often used to provide a degree of protection for individual appliances, especially garden power tools.

If any appliance consistently causes an RCD to trip (switch off), get a qualified service engineer to test the appliance for low insulation. You can tell if an RCD is working efficiently by pressing its test button. Perform this test regularly.

Mains circuit cables

The cables that run from the fuse carriers or MCBs have three copper wires or conductors. A live or phase conductor, insulated with red PVC, takes electric current from the consumer unit to each socket outlet and appliance. The current returns to the consumer unit, completing the circuit, via a neutral wire insulated with black PVC.

Sandwiched between the live and neutral conductors is a bare wire, known as the earth wire, which provides the current with a direct route to the ground should a fault occur on the circuit. At each switch and socket outlet, the exposed earth wire is sleeved with green-and-yellow-striped PVC. This earth conductor is an essential safety measure aimed at preventing a dangerous condition existing on a circuit. When a fault occurs, the rapid flow of current to earth causes a protective device, such as a fuse or MCB, to cut the supply of electricity to the circuit.

Power failure

If there is a fault on a circuit or it is overloaded by having too many appliances plugged into it, the MCB protecting the circuit will trip (switch off); or if the circuit is protected by a fuse, the fuse will blow (melt). If an appliance suddenly stops working, first of all check to see if everything else on the circuit has stopped working, too. If so, go to your consumer unit and look for a blown fuse or tripped MCB.

RESETTING AN MCB

Inspect all the MCBs to see if there is one that has switched automatically to the 'off' position; or if they are the press-button type, check whether one of the buttons has popped out. If so:

1 Turn off the main isolating switch and reset the MCB by turning the toggle switch to the 'on' position or pressing the button back in.

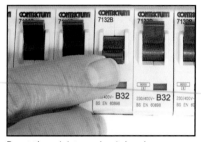

Reset the miniature circuit breaker

2 Turn the main switch on again.

3 If the same MCB trips immediately, unplug or switch off everything on the faulty circuit to make sure it is not simply overloaded, then reset the MCB as before.

4 If the MCB trips again, get an electrician to trace and rectify the fault on the circuit.

RESETTING AN RCD

If none of the MCBs have tripped, look at the main isolating switch and see if it is in the 'off' position. If it incorporates an RCD, that may have tripped before an earth fault could be detected by the relevant MCB.

Turn on the main isolating switch/RCD

Unplug all your appliances and turn on the main isolating switch. If the switch trips again as soon as you turn it on, there may be a fault with the permanent wiring of your house or flat – get expert advice.

If, however, the main isolating switch stays in the 'on' position, you can find out which appliance is causing the fault by plugging in each one in turn until the RCD in the main isolating switch trips again. Have the appliance you have just plugged in checked by a service engineer.

If you have a separate RCD wired into the installation, check that too.

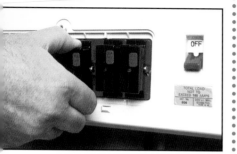

Turn off the main isolating switch before you pull out a fuse carrier

Replacing fuses

In older consumer units there may be a row of fuse carriers instead of MCBs. With fuses the faulty circuit is not obvious immediately, and you may have to inspect each fuse to find the one that has blown. However, if the circuits are labelled, you can usually pinpoint the circuit into which the suspect appliance is connected. Most appliances will be plugged into a power circuit, usually a ring circuit (also called a ring main). A large appliance, such as a cooker, electric shower or immersion heater, will be on its own individual radial circuit. Other circuits supply the fixed lighting.

Before you pull out a fuse carrier, turn off the main isolating switch. At the back of the carrier you will see either a cartridge fuse, similar to the ones found in three-pin plugs, or there will be a strip of fuse wire running between screw terminals at each end of the carrier.

It is important that the correct fuse wire or cartridge fuse is used for each type of circuit. Cartridge fuses are colour-coded and printed with the appropriate rating in amps. Fuse wire is wrapped around clearly labelled card. Consult the chart right to identify the correct rating when replacing fuses.

Replacing a cartridge fuse

The simplest way to check a suspect cartridge fuse is to replace it with a new one and see if that rectifies the problem. But if you want to test the fuse, place one of the probes of a continuity tester on the metal cap at each end of the fuse; then press the circuit-test button. If the tester's indicator is not activated, the fuse has blown.

1 Depending on the style of fuse carrier, either dismantle the carrier to gain access to the fuse or prise the fuse out of its spring clips.

2 Insert a new fuse and replace the carrier. Switch on the main isolating switch to restore the supply of electricity. If the fuse then blows, get expert advice.

Replacing fuse wire

Broken fuse wire is usually obvious, and there may be scorch marks on the fuse carrier. To check whether the fuse wire is broken, pull gently on the end of the wire with a small screwdriver.

Fuse wire and cartridge fuses

Fuse ratings

Type of circuit	Fuse rating	Fuse colour
Ring circuit	30amp	Red
Radial power circuit serving a floor area maximum 50sq m	30amp	Red
Radial power circuit serving a floor area maximum 20sq m	20amp	Yellow
Cooker	30amp	Red
Shower	45amp	Green
Immersion heater	15amp	Blue
Lighting circuit	5amp	White

Check a suspect cartridge fuse with a continuity tester

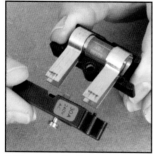

1 Dismantle the fuse carrier

Pull on the end to check wire

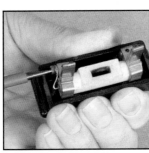

1 Loosen the screw terminal

2 Wrap wire round the terminal

Always remove the plug before servicing an appliance

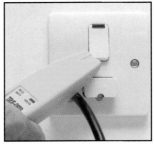

1 Aim the tester at the outlet

2 Then test the flex

1 Loosen the screw terminals and take out the pieces of broken wire.

2 Wrap one end of a new piece of correctly rated fuse wire clockwise around one terminal. Tighten the screw.

3 Attach the other end of the wire to the second terminal in the same way, making sure you don't stretch the wire taut – otherwise it may break when you tighten the screw.

4 Replace the fuse carrier and turn on the main switch. If the fuse then blows, get expert advice.

3 Tighten the screw terminal

Switching off the power

Before you service an appliance, pull its plug from the wall socket. Simply switching off at the socket is not sufficient. Keep the plug in view to ensure that no one puts it back into the socket while you are working.

Some appliances are wired permanently into a fused connection unit, flex outlet or cooker control unit – see pages 14 and 15. The safest way to isolate these appliances is to turn off the main isolating switch at the consumer unit. This cuts off the supply of electricity to every appliance and light fitting in your home.

This could be inconvenient if the power has to be turned off for a relatively long period. It is possible to isolate a single circuit by turning off the main isolating switch at the consumer unit and then removing the fuse carrier or switching off the MCB that is protecting the relevant circuit (circuits are usually labelled or listed inside the consumer unit). That particular circuit will then no longer be supplied with electricity even when you turn on the main isolating switch to restore power to the rest of your house or flat. As a precaution, tape a message to the consumer unit to ensure someone does not switch the

MCB on while you are working.

However, be doubly sure that the power is off by testing the outlet to which the appliance is connected, using a non-contact voltage tester you know to be working.

1 Following the manufacturer's instructions, aim the tester at the outlet, holding the tip of the tool against all parts of the faceplate.

2 Then aim the tester at the root of the flex where it leaves the outlet, rotating the tool around the flex so that you check from different angles.

In both cases, an audible warning or flashing light indicates that the appliance is not safe to work on and you should seek expert advice. Even if there is no warning, check the tester again on a circuit you know to be live before inspecting the appliance.

Then before you touch any component, as a final check that the power is off, remove the casing from the appliance and aim the tester at the internal terminal block to which the flex is connected.

If you are not certain an appliance is disconnected safely, get a service engineer to isolate and inspect it.

Sockets and electrical outlets

In order to use electricity, most domestic appliances have to be plugged into a 13amp wall socket. Portable appliances equipped with the necessary three-pin plug can draw current from any 13amp socket in your home. Larger appliances and ones fixed to the structure of the building are usually wired permanently into wall-mounted outlets designed to serve one appliance only. With any form of permanent wiring, where a plug cannot be removed, before an appliance is serviced it must be isolated by turning off the power at the consumer unit – see page 13.

Wall sockets

Wall sockets
There are various versions of the standard 13amp socket, including double and triple sockets designed to serve more than one appliance at the same time. Some sockets are fitted with a switch so that an appliance can be turned off without having to pull out the plug. However, you should not rely solely on switching off as a safe method of isolating an appliance that you intend to service – always remove the plug first.

Fused connection units
The flex from appliances such as extractor fans and cooker hoods is often connected to the house circuitry by means of a fused connection unit (FCU). Since there is no removable plug, the unit itself is fitted with a cartridge fuse to protect the appliance. There are switched and unswitched FCUs.

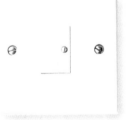

Unswitched and switched FCUs

CHECK OUT YOUR CIRCUITS

Before you contemplate making repairs to appliances, check all your sockets and fused connection units to see which circuits they are connected to. Switch off the appropriate MCB or remove the circuit fuse, then try each outlet in turn to see if it is supplying power. Make careful notes and keep them near your consumer unit.

Flexible-cord outlet

Flexible-cord outlets
It is not permitted to install wall sockets or fused connection units in bathrooms, but the flex from equipment such as a heated towel rail can be connected to a flex outlet. This simple unswitched device is wired to a length of buried cable that runs to a fused connection unit situated outside the bathroom.

Cooker control unit

Cooker control units

Ovens and hobs are wired to double-pole isolating switches called cooker control units. Some control units incorporate a single 13amp socket outlet.

Socket adapters

Plug-in adapters that allow you to power a number of appliances from a single socket are not recommended. The weight of several plugs can put a strain on internal socket connections and may lead to the type of poor-contact problems described below. The fact that you need to use an adapter probably indicates that you need more sockets. Ask an electrician for advice.

Have scorched sockets replaced

Faulty sockets

Sometimes problems with electrical appliances are caused by a faulty 13amp socket. The frequent inserting and removal of plugs can eventually lead to poor contact between the plug pins and connection points within the socket. Loose connections may result in intermittent faults and are a serious fire risk.

There are various clues that might lead you to suspect that a socket is suffering from this type of fault:
• scorching on the face of the socket or around the base of plug pins
• the plug or the face of the socket feels hot after use
• a pungent fishy smell
• radio or TV interference caused by arcing inside the socket
• frequent failure of plug fuses caused by overheating.

Sockets should be replaced if they display any of these symptoms; or if they have a cracked faceplate, or a switch that does not operate smoothly.

Any plug that has been used in a faulty socket should also be replaced.

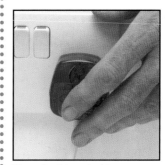

Plugs should not feel hot

Testing a socket

Although the fitting or replacement of sockets is outside the scope of this book, you may need to rule out the possibility that an appliance has stopped working as a result of faulty mains wiring. Indicators on a simple plug-in tester will tell you whether a socket is wired correctly. If the test suggests there is a fault, have the socket checked by an electrician.

Cracked sockets are dangerous

Simple plug-in socket tester

Three-pin plugs

Square-pin 13amp plugs are used for most portable electrical appliances. Although their style and construction vary slightly, all 13amp plugs work on a similar principle. Use only those plugs marked BS 1363, which guarantees that they are manufactured to exacting British Standards.

If your home is still fitted with the outmoded round-pin plugs and sockets, you should have your wiring tested and possibly replaced.

Many appliances are supplied with a moulded-on plug

Moulded-on plugs

Many new appliances are sold with a plug moulded onto the end of the flexible cord. This type of plug contains a small replaceable cartridge fuse within a retractable holder positioned between the pins. Moulded-on plugs cannot be dismantled, so if you ever need to replace one that is damaged, cut through the flex and fit a rewirable plug.

Rewirable plugs

Most 13amp plugs are rewirable and contain a replaceable cartridge fuse that is accessible by removing the plug's cover. Look for plugs with pins that are part-insulated. With this type, the insulation around the base of the pins prevents someone getting a shock from a plug that is partly pulled out of a socket.

Rewirable 13amp plug

Surge-protection plugs

Wired and fused like a standard 13amp plug, a surge-protection plug will protect vulnerable equipment such as computers, television sets and video recorders from potentially damaging surges of electricity. A mechanical indicator changes colour once the plug has been subjected to a high energy surge. In this event, you need to replace the plug. Inserting a surge-protection plug – even one not connected to flex – into a double socket protects equipment plugged into the same socket. This is especially handy if the appliance you want to safeguard is fitted with a moulded plug.

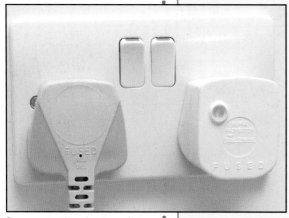

Surge-protection plug in socket

Cartridge fuses

The fuse in a plug is designed to blow if an appliance short-circuits or develops an earth fault. Use a red 3amp fuse for appliances rated up to 720W; and a brown 13amp fuse for appliances rated from 720W to 3kW. There are also 2, 5 and 10amp fuses, but they are hardly ever used for domestic appliances.

As a rule, don't insert a 13amp fuse – even temporarily – in a plug connected to an appliance rated at less than 720W. Although the appliance will work perfectly, a fault may go undetected. However, there are a few exceptions to this rule, such as some vacuum cleaners and television sets that are subjected to a brief surge of current at the moment of being switched on – always check the manufacturer's recommendations for these appliances before changing a fuse.

Take care to fit the appropriate cartridge fuse in a plug

Replacing a fuse

Loosen the large screw between the pins and remove the plug's cover. Carefully prise the old fuse from the spring clips, using the tip of a screwdriver. Insert a new fuse of the correct rating and replace the plug cover. If necessary, you can use a continuity tester to check that a fuse is working – see page 12.

In order to replace a fuse in a moulded-on plug, prise out the fuse carrier with a screwdriver and slide the fuse out sideways.

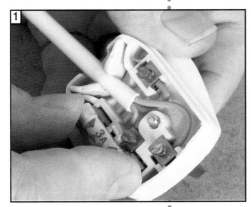

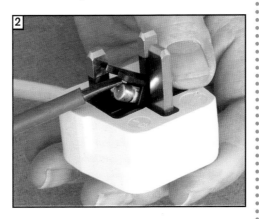

1 Push fuse into spring clips
2 Prise out the fuse carrier from a moulded-on plug

Replacing the fuse in a fused connection unit

With the power turned off at the consumer unit, loosen the retaining screw in the face of the fuse carrier. Pull the carrier from the FCU and take out the cartridge fuse. Having inserted a new fuse, replace the carrier and turn the power back on.

Slide a new fuse into the FCU

Three-core flex

Unkinkable braided flex

Coiled flex

Two-core flex

Sheathed flex lacking an earth conductor is used for double-insulated appliances. These appliances usually have moulded plastic casings that insulate the user from internal metal parts that could become live. Double-insulated appliances – which are always marked with a double-square symbol – do not need earthing.

Two-core flex

Flexible cord

Electricity flows to and from an appliance by means of a flexible cord, usually called flex. It is similar to mains cable in that it has copper conductors or 'cores', but the necessary flexibility is achieved by each conductor being made up from several thin wires twisted together. The three conductors are differentiated by colour-coded insulation:

- brown for live or phase
- blue for neutral
- green-and-yellow-striped for the earth conductor

Three-core flex

The three conductors are covered on the outside with PVC sheathing, which is usually white, black or grey. For safety, garden power tools are usually fitted with orange or red flex, which stands out against grass and foliage.

Special heat-resistant flex is required for the internal wiring of cookers and heaters.

Unkinkable braided flex

This type of flex is sometimes fitted to relatively high-wattage appliances, such as irons and kettles, whose flex must be able to withstand movement and wear during normal use. Reinforcing textile cords run parallel with the rubber-insulated conductors, and the protective rubber sheathing is bound on the outside with braided cotton.

Coiled flex

Some kettle manufacturers fit coiled PVC-sheathed flex instead of the braided version.

Flex sizes

Flex is rated according to the area of the cross section of its conductors, $0.5mm^2$ being the smallest size for normal domestic wiring. The size of the conductors is determined by how much current they can handle without overheating – so the flex must be matched to the wattage of the appliance.

Conductor	Current rating	Appliance
$0.5mm^2$	3amp	Light fittings up to 720W
$0.75mm^2$	6amp	Light fittings and appliances up to 1440W
$1.00mm^2$	10amp	Appliances up to 2400W
$1.25mm^2$	13amp	Appliances up to 3120W
$1.5mm^2$	15amp	Appliances up to 3600W

Storing flex

Careful storage helps prevent flex becoming tangled or kinked.

- Some appliances are fitted with flex that can be withdrawn into a storage compartment; always retract the flex slowly to prevent possible damage to plug connections.

- Wrap the long flex attached to garden tools around a purpose-made flex holder.

- Always leave an iron to cool down before you tidy up the flex and put the iron away.

Checking suspect plugs

Before you start trying to diagnose problems within the appliance itself, it pays to check the plug carefully. Some small fault within the plug is often enough to prevent an appliance working altogether. Whenever you have to change a plug's fuse, check for other potential problems (see far right) before you screw the cover back on.

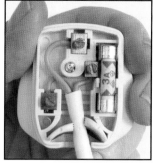

Correctly wired plug

Replacing a faulty plug

Don't fit a new plug onto flex that has burnt conductors or broken wire filaments. Crop the damaged end off the flex, cutting it back to a section of sound sheathing and insulation.

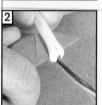

1 Slit the sheath lengthways, starting about 60mm (2¼in) from the end of the flex. Take care not to cut into the insulation covering the individual conductors.

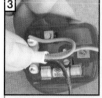

2 Peel the sheathing off the conductors and, bending it back over the knife blade, cut it off. If you are fitting braided flex (see opposite), wrap the cut end with insulating tape to prevent the braid fraying in use.

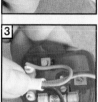

3 Lay the flex on the plug so that you can gauge the correct length for each of the conductors. They should take the direct route to their respective terminals – brown to live, blue to neutral, green-and-yellow to earth. If you're fitting two-core flex, the earth terminal remains unconnected – but make sure the earth-terminal is screwed down tight.

Using wire strippers, remove about 10mm (⅜in) of insulation from the end of each conductor, then twist the wire filaments together.

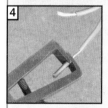

5 If you are wiring to post-type terminals, fold the bared end of the conductor (so that the end is doubled) and push it into the hole in the post. With the insulation running right up to the post, tighten the screw terminal.

6 If you are wiring to clamp-type terminals, wrap the bared end of each conductor clockwise around its terminal and screw down the clamp. Make sure all three terminals are tight and pull gently on each conductor to make sure it is held securely.

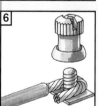

7 Tighten the cord clamp to grip the sheathing, then fit the appropriate cartridge fuse – see page 17. Replace the plug's cover and tighten the fixing screw.

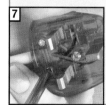

DISPOSING OF OLD PLUGS

Before you discard a damaged plug, bend one of its pins to prevent a child plugging it into a socket.

Correct wiring
Make sure the flex conductors are connected correctly – brown to live, blue to neutral, green-and-yellow to earth.

Loose connections
Tighten the screw terminals to make sure the connections are secure.

Visible wires
Make sure there are no exposed strands of wire. The insulation should butt up against the terminal to which the flex conductor is connected.

Wrong-length conductors
Each conductor should take the direct route to its terminal. Short wires that have been stretched may pull out of their terminals; long bunched-up conductors can prevent the plug cover fitting snugly.

Flex not clamped securely
The cord grip or clamp (right) should hold the sheathing – not just the insulated conductors.

Scorching
Scorch marks inside the plug indicate arcing caused by poor connections. Replace the plug.

Fuse
Make sure the fuse is correctly rated and that it is functioning – see page 17.

Damaged casing
A chipped or cracked casing is dangerous. Replace the plug.

CHECKING SUSPECT FLEX

Check flex for signs of damage or wear. Don't ignore minor wear and tear: if the flex is allowed to deteriorate, a dangerous situation could develop.

Damaged sheathing
Look for cuts and melted sections of PVC sheathing. Shorten the flex to remove the damaged section, or replace the flex completely.

Worn braid
Once the cotton cover on braided flex is worn, the sheathing and eventually the insulated conductors become vulnerable. Never just bind worn flex with insulating tape – replace the flex immediately.

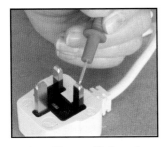

Testing with a moulded-on plug
As it is impossible to expose the internal terminals of a moulded-on plug, place the tester's probe on the plug pins when carrying out the continuity test described right. The live pin is bottom left when the pins are facing you. Make sure the fuse is working before you carry out the test.

Broken conductors

One or more of the flex's conductors can break as a result of wear. The best way to search for broken conductors is to subject the flex to a continuity test.

Testing for continuity

1 Pull out the plug and remove its cover, then dismantle just enough of the appliance's casing to expose the terminals to which the flex is connected. Be careful not to disturb internal wiring or components as you remove the casing.

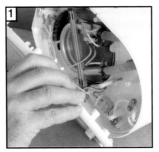

2 Place one probe of a continuity tester onto the plug's live terminal – that is, the terminal to which the brown conductor is attached. Place the tester's other probe on the live terminal in the appliance – the one connected to the other end of the brown conductor. If the tester's indicator is activated, that means the live conductor running between the two terminals is unbroken.

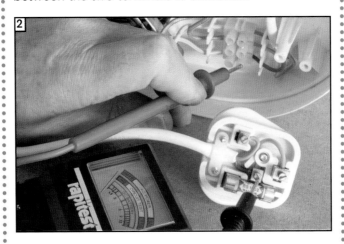

3 However, to check that there is not an inter-mittent fault, continue to hold both probes in place and ask someone to gently bend the flex back and forth, gradually working along the cord.

4 Perform the same test on the neutral terminals and, if an earth wire is present, on the earth terminals too. If the test reveals a break in any of the conductors, remove the damaged flex and replace it with new flex of the same size and type. If the break is near one end, you may be able to remove the damaged section by shortening the flex.

REPLACING THE FLEX

Before removing the old flex from the appliance's terminal block, make a note of the terminal connections – brown wire goes to live, blue to neutral, green-and-yellow to earth (if present).

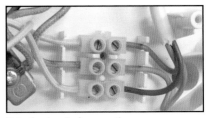

Note the terminal connections

If it is not obvious how the conductors are connected to the terminals, or the connections are soldered, replace the casing and have the appliance serviced by an expert.

1 Strip and prepare the ends of the conductors, as explained for wiring a plug. The conductors must be the same length as the originals and follow the same paths to their terminals.

2 If there's a protective cord support at the flex-entry point (see page 67), make sure you slide it onto the new flex before you attach its conductors to the terminals – brown to live, blue to neutral, green-and-yellow to earth.

3 Secure the sheathed part of the flex with the cord clamp, and test the flex again for continuity before you replace the appliance's casing.

4 Wire the other end of the new flex to the plug (see page 19). If the appliance is earthed, check there is a continuous path to earth (see page 22). Before using the appliance, plug it into a circuit protected by an RCD. Switch on and if the RCD trips, have the appliance tested by an expert.

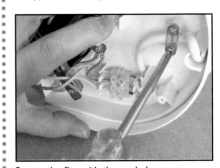

Secure the flex with the cord clamp

Flex connector

1 Strip back the sheathing

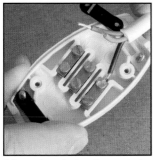

2 Insert bared wires in terminals

Extending a flex

Never be tempted to join two pieces of flex by binding their conductors together with insulating tape. This is a very dangerous practice. If a flexible cord is too short, either replace it completely with a longer piece of flex (see opposite) or extend it with a flex connector.

Fitting a flex connector

A flex connector is a simple fitting designed to join two lengths of flex permanently and safely. Never use a connector to join two-core flex to three-core flex.

1 Strip just enough sheathing from both pieces of flex for their conductors to reach the terminals – the sheathed part of the flex must be gripped by the cord clamp at each end of the fitting. Prepare the ends of all the conductors as described for wiring a plug – see page 19. When joining three-core flex, use the middle terminal for the earth conductor.

2 Insert the bared ends of the conductors into the terminals, ensuring there are no visible wires. Then tighten the terminal screws. Check that you have joined matching-colour conductors from both flexible cords to the same twin terminal.

3 Tighten the cord clamps, and check that the clamps and terminals fit snugly into the recesses moulded into the connector. Replace its cover.

Extension leads

When an appliance flex is too short to reach the nearest wall socket, you could plug it into an extension lead that has several metres of flex wound onto a drum fitted with a 13amp socket. Although it is possible to obtain 5amp extension leads, it makes sense to buy one rated at 13amps, which can be used to supply a wider range of appliances without overloading it. To prevent the flex overheating, it is important to unwind any extension lead fully before using it.

DETACHABLE FLEX CONNECTORS

If you don't want a permanent connection, you can extend the flex on a single appliance by using a lightweight two-part flex connector. Be sure to wire the same size flex to both parts of the connector; also, make sure you attach the part with the pins to the appliance, not to the 13amp plug. If you used the connector the other way round, the pins would become live – and dangerous – when the lead was plugged into a socket. Keep the flex attached to a power tool fairly short, so you can detach it quickly in an emergency.

Two-part flex connector

Trailing sockets

To power more than one appliance at once, use a trailing socket attached to a length of straight or coiled flex. Some of these sockets have built-in surge protectors. Make sure the electrical load does not exceed the rating of the plug (13amps).

Miniature trailing sockets, with special plugs, are designed to supply power from a single wall socket to a range of appliances, such as a computer and its ancillary equipment. However, although the socket itself is fused, the tiny plugs are not. This means that all the appliances attached to the socket could fail if just one of them develops a fault.

SAFETY WITH LARGER APPLIANCES

Never extend the flex of large appliances, such as washing machines and dishwashers. And don't plug them into an extension lead or trailing socket.

Basic fault finding

When servicing electrical appliances, you are likely to refer to this chapter frequently. Use the information to rule out the most basic faults (see right) before you proceed to diagnose faults within the appliance itself.

Safe working practices

• Always disconnect an appliance from the supply before you inspect or service it. If it has a plug, pull the plug out from the socket. If the appliance is connected to a fused connection unit, cooker control unit or flex outlet, switch off at the consumer unit, then remove the relevant fuse carrier or switch off the MCB – pages 11 to 13.

• Never handle electrical appliances, plugs, sockets or switches when your hands are wet.

• Take care when removing covers and panels – the internal edges of some appliances can be very sharp.

• Take care not to injure yourself when moving a heavy appliance, such as a washing machine.

• Always use correctly rated fuses and flex – see pages 12, 17 and 18.

• Don't run flex under carpets.

• Don't make temporary repairs, using insulating tape.

• Don't stretch a flex that is too short.

• Avoid using socket adapters.

• Don't run extension leads to electrical appliances in a bathroom.

• Don't overload extension leads or trailing sockets.

• Don't continue to use an appliance you know to be faulty.

• Take your time when servicing an appliance – check everything twice.

• Before putting any appliance back into service after working on it, test it by plugging it into a circuit protected by an RCD – see page 11. Then switch on, and if the RCD trips, have the appliance tested by a qualified service engineer.

• Don't take risks. If you are in doubt about anything, consult an electrician or have the appliance repaired by a service engineer.

APPLIANCE STOPS WORKING

• **Are other appliances on the same circuit still working?**
If not, check your consumer unit for blown fuse, tripped MCB, or tripped RCD.

• **Is the wall socket faulty?**
Check the socket with a plug-in tester.

• **Has the fuse blown?**
Check the fuse in the plug or fused connection unit.

• **Is the plug faulty?**
Check the plug for signs of damage or faulty wiring.

• **Has a conductor broken inside the flex?**
Subject the flex to a continuity test.

WORKS INTERMITTENTLY

• **Is the plug faulty?**
Check the plug for signs of damage or faulty wiring.

• **Has a conductor broken inside the flex?**
Subject the flex to a continuity test.

> **Appliance won't switch on**
> Before going through the check list above, make sure the appliance is plugged in and that the socket or fused connection unit is switched on.

Testing for a continuous earth path

Any appliance that is earthed should be tested to ensure there is a continuous path to earth. Apply one probe of a continuity tester to the earth pin of the plug (see right), and with the other probe touch any exposed metal component or an unpainted part of the metal casing. If there is a connection to earth, the tester's indicator will be activated. If it is not activated, have the appliance checked by a service engineer.

Also, don't use the appliance if the tester is activated when you perform the same test with a probe placed on either of the plug's other (live and neutral) pins.

This test is not applicable to double-insulated appliances (see page 18), because they do not have an earth connection in the plug.

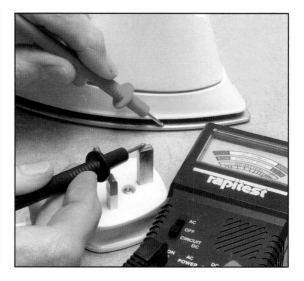

How water works in your home

Cold water is supplied under pressure to your home via the water company's service pipe. The company maintains a stopcock, usually in the street outside, so they can turn off the supply of water to the building. The service pipe terminates at your stopcock – a valve that allows you to turn off the water supply to your house or flat. From this point the water is fed around your home, using one of two systems.

TURNING OFF THE WATER

There are various points in every plumbing system where you can turn off the water to isolate part of the system so that it can be drained in order to repair a leak, service the taps or replace a float valve. However, servicing the main plumbing system lies outside the scope of this book.

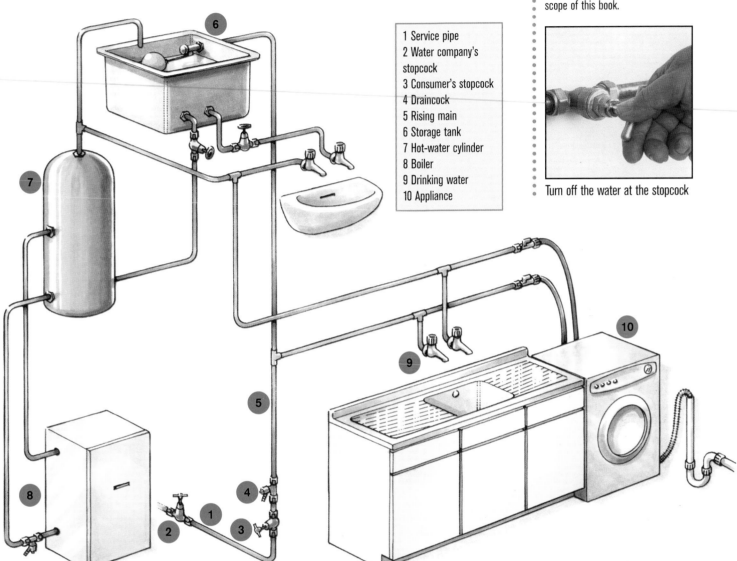

1 Service pipe
2 Water company's stopcock
3 Consumer's stopcock
4 Draincock
5 Rising main
6 Storage tank
7 Hot-water cylinder
8 Boiler
9 Drinking water
10 Appliance

Turn off the water at the stopcock

Stored-water system

The majority of homes, especially older properties, are likely to be plumbed with a stored-water system. From the stopcock, a pipe called the rising main runs directly to a storage tank in the loft. A branch pipe from the rising main takes water to the drinking tap in the kitchen. The same pipe usually feeds water to plumbed-in appliances, such as washing machines and dishwashers.

One pipe running from the storage tank feeds cold water to baths, washbasins and toilet cisterns. Another pipe from the same tank supplies cold water to the hot-water storage cylinder, where it is heated either by the central-heating boiler or an electric immersion heater. A pipe running from the top of the cylinder feeds hot water to taps and appliances throughout your house or flat.

Mains-fed system

With a mains-fed system, all the taps and appliances are fed by mains pressure – there is no storage tank. Water is heated by a combination boiler or an instantaneous multipoint heater and then fed to the hot taps and appliances. Some systems incorporate an unvented cylinder, which stores hot water but is fed from the mains.

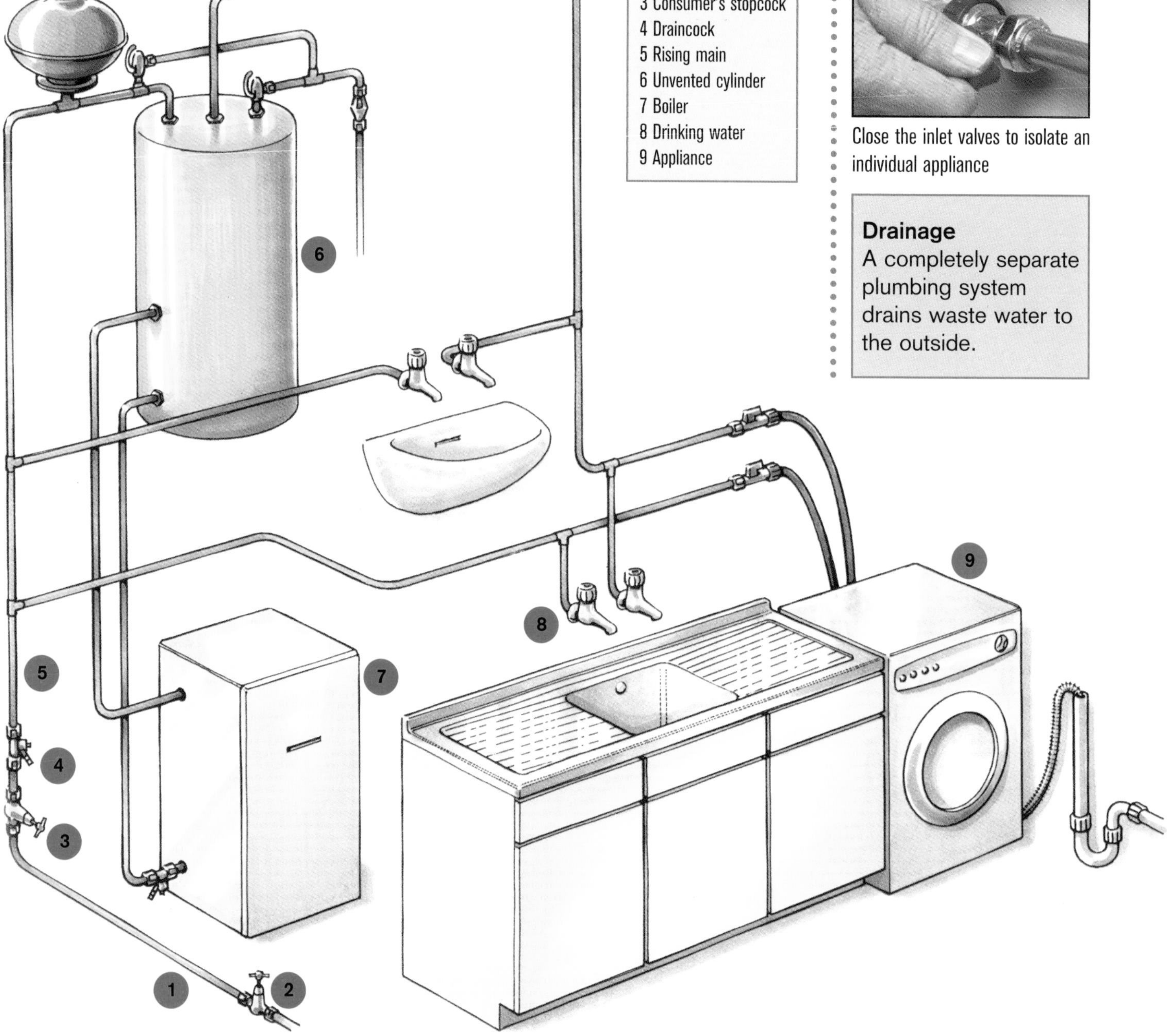

1 Service pipe
2 Water company's stopcock
3 Consumer's stopcock
4 Draincock
5 Rising main
6 Unvented cylinder
7 Boiler
8 Drinking water
9 Appliance

SERVICE VALVES

When servicing an individual appliance, such as a washing machine or dishwasher, simply turn off the hot and cold inlet valves, which are usually positioned directly behind the appliance or in an adjacent cupboard. Then all you have to do is empty the hoses into a bucket and drain the appliance itself.

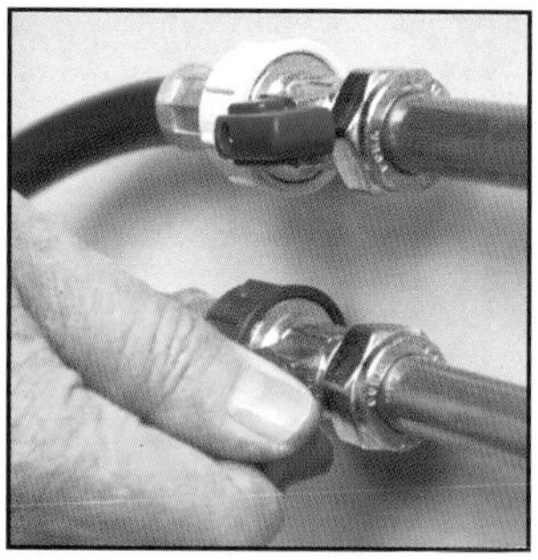

Close the inlet valves to isolate an individual appliance

Drainage

A completely separate plumbing system drains waste water to the outside.

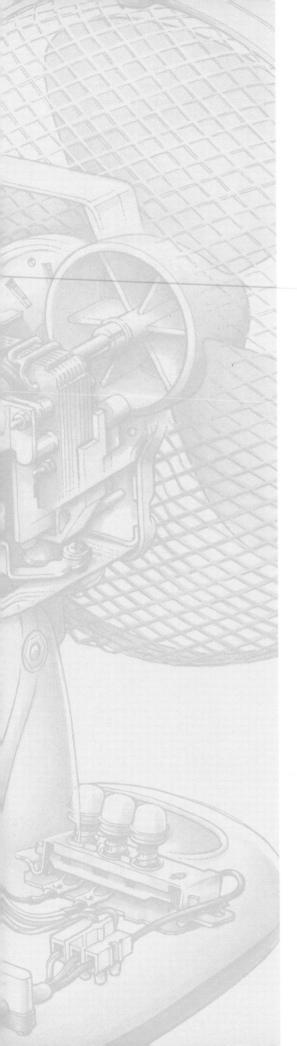

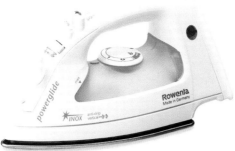

SMALL
APPLIANCES

Small electrical appliances are numerous and varied, and new models are introduced to the marketplace on a regular basis. The appliances described in this chapter represent typical examples of their type and are intended as a guide to how such appliances work.

Similarly, advice given on servicing and maintenance is not intended to cover every available model – and if your appliance differs substantially from the ones described in this chapter, then your safest option is to have it tested and repaired by a service engineer. If at any stage you are unsure about how to proceed, reassemble the appliance and take it to a service agent.

Don't use an appliance you know to be faulty; and don't put one back into service until it has been tested by being plugged into a circuit protected by an RCD or checked by a service engineer. Unless an appliance is double insulated, check that there is a continuous path to earth (see page 22) before you use it.

HAIRDRYERS

Hairdryers take a lot of punishment. They get left on the bedroom floor, knocked off the dressing table, and shaken continuously in normal use. It is no wonder, then, that they are often in need of attention. For safety's sake, it pays to give your hairdryer at least a cursory check for damage to the casing and flex before using the appliance.

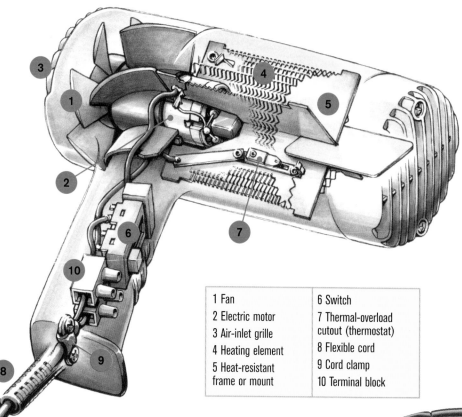

1 Fan	6 Switch
2 Electric motor	7 Thermal-overload cutout (thermostat)
3 Air-inlet grille	8 Flexible cord
4 Heating element	9 Cord clamp
5 Heat-resistant frame or mount	10 Terminal block

How it works

Your own hairdryer may look different from the examples shown here, but all hand-held hairdryers work on similar principles. A fan driven by an electric motor draws air through an inlet grille and blows it over a heater – an exposed wire element wrapped around a heat-resistant frame or mount. Some models have a removable filter that prevents hair and fluff passing through the air-inlet grille.

Many hairdryers have a combination of switches that not only turn the hairdryer on and off but also provide perhaps two or three heat settings and possibly two speed settings. Some models have a cool-air setting, which switches off the heater but leaves the fan turning.

A thermostat – thermal-overload cutout (TOC) – protects the element from overheating. The TOC automatically switches the heating element off if there is insufficient airflow over the element to dissipate the heat at a given rate. The TOC will usually reset automatically, so you should ascertain what caused it to operate before you use the hairdryer again – the dryer will usually resume working perfectly once it has cooled down. Because such recycling could leave the hairdryer in a dangerous condition, later models may be fitted with a thermal fuse, which prevents the appliance working even after it has cooled.

DISMANTLING THE CASING

The casing of a hairdryer usually splits into two halves, or the front section separates from the rear. Always unplug a hairdryer before you start to dismantle the casing.

The two sections are invariably held together with recessed screws. Some or all of these screws may require a special screwdriver or a modified flat-tip screwdriver. If the screws are different lengths, label them to make reassembly easier.

If the casing does not separate easily when the screws have been removed, look for hidden fixings. You may need to gently squeeze the edges of the casing to see if parts of it are held together with moulded plastic catches – but take care not to break or crack the casing, which would make the appliance unsafe to use. Having removed the fixing screws, lay the hairdryer on a table and carefully separate the two halves of the casing, so that you can make a mental note of how the various internal components relate to one another and how they fit into the casing. If necessary, draw a diagram. As with all double-insulated appliances (see page 18), it is important to replace all components and wiring in their original positions.

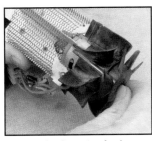
1 Check the fan spins freely

2 Replace wiring carefully

Looking after the flex
Inspect the flex regularly for signs of damaged sheathing. Check carefully for breaks where the flex enters the plug and hairdryer. Shorten or replace a damaged flex – see page 20.

It is bad practice to carry a hairdryer by its flex.

SMELL OF BURNING

There may be a smell of burning before the TOC or thermal fuse switches off the heater. If the smell persists after you've tried the following, have the appliance tested at a service centre.

Careless handling
When using your hairdryer, hold it by the handgrip to ensure you don't restrict the airflow by covering the intake with your hand.

Air intake blocked
A blockage may not be obvious from outside, so unplug the dryer, then dismantle the casing to remove hair packed behind the air-intake grille. Use a soft paintbrush to brush out dust and fluff.

1 Then check that the fan spins freely. If it doesn't, remove the fan and clear whatever is obstructing it – see page 28.

2 Make sure that all internal wiring – including heat-resistant sheathing – is intact, then reassemble the casing.

If your hairdryer has a removable filter, unscrew the rear section of the casing then take out the filter and use a soft brush to remove the accumulated fluff. Take care not to damage the fine filter.

Fluff on the heating element
Fluff that has been drawn through the air intake may be adhering to the heating element. Brush the element very gently with a soft paintbrush, teasing out the fluff without applying too much pressure.

NO HEAT

Fan turns but no heat is produced.

Heat turned off
Check that the switch is not on a cool-air setting.

Broken internal connections
With the appliance unplugged, inspect the wiring to ensure that the heater element is connected. Have an expert remake broken soldered connections – which must be able to carry the required current and withstand the temperatures generated by the appliance.

Don't restrict the airflow

Take out a removable filter

And clean it with a soft brush

Brush fluff from heating element

SAFETY FIRST

Before putting it back into service, test a hairdryer by plugging it into a circuit protected by an RCD – see page 11. Then switch on, and if the RCD trips have the appliance tested by a qualified service engineer.

Inspect the element for breaks

Place probe on each end of TOC

SAFETY FIRST

Don't use a hairdryer that has a cracked case.

Never connect a hairdryer to an extension lead in order to use the dryer in a bathroom.

Don't stretch the flex in order to reach a mirror.

Always unplug a hairdryer before you start to dismantle the casing.

Ensure the plug is wired correctly and that the appropriate fuse is fitted.

Broken or faulty heating element

A visual check may reveal a break in the wire element. If it appears intact, you could have it checked by a service engineer – but it may be more economical to buy a new hairdryer.

Faulty thermostat or blown thermal fuse

If the TOC or thermal fuse is accessible (it will normally be situated within the heating element), you may be able to check it with a continuity tester. These components are relatively cheap to replace. However, with some hairdryers it may be necessary to replace the heater along with the fuse or TOC, in which case replacement may not be economical.

FAN RUNS SLOWLY

There may also be a smell of burning because the fan is not creating sufficient airflow.

Restricted fan movement

Check to see if hair has wound around the fan shaft and is acting like a brake. Before you remove the fan make a note of its position on the shaft, so that you can replace it exactly.

1 If the fan is obstructed, it may be difficult to remove. You can usually ease it off its shaft by levering very carefully with the shaft of a screwdriver – but take care not to damage the fan or other components, which would make the hairdryer unsafe to use.

2 Tease out any hair that is packed behind the fan.

3 Then replace the fan and check that it spins freely.

4 Make sure all internal wiring is intact and that you have put back all the components in their original positions, then reassemble the casing.

Faulty plug or fuse

Check that the plug is wired correctly and replace a faulty fuse – see pages 17 and 19. If the fuse blows again as soon as you plug in and switch on, have the appliance checked at a service centre.

Power failure

If other appliances on the circuit have stopped working, check the consumer unit for a blown fuse or tripped MCB or RCD – see pages 11 and 12.

Broken flex conductor

This is a common fault. It pays to check that the outer sheathing on the flex is in good condition each time you use a hairdryer, and make sure it hasn't pulled out of the cord clamp inside the plug – see page 19.

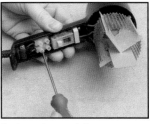

Replace damaged flex

To check a suspect flex for broken conductors, test it for continuity – see page 20. If possible replace damaged flex (see page 20), but leave soldered connections to an expert.

Loose connections

Inspect the internal wiring to ensure that there are no loose or broken connections. If soldered connections need repairing, take the dryer to a service centre.

Faulty on/off switch

It may be possible to check the switch with a continuity tester, but if the wiring is connected to the switch with soldered joints, it should be repaired by a service engineer, which may be too costly.

Faulty motor

A faulty electric motor should be checked by an expert, but may be uneconomical to repair or replace.

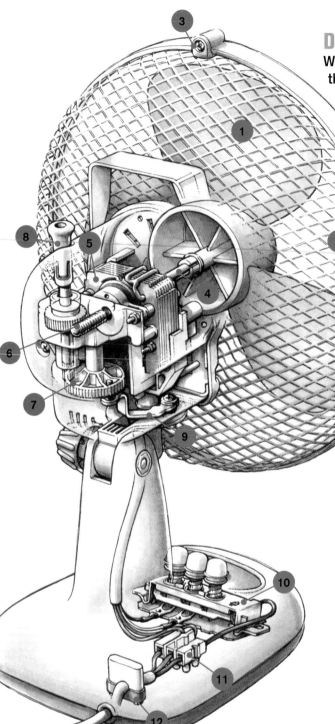

DESK FANS

Without the luxury of air conditioning, an electric fan is the only real option for keeping cool in hot weather. Desk fans are relatively simple and reliable appliances – but the moving components are subject to wear and, like so many portable appliances, they are often damaged as a result of careless handling. Similar fans mounted on a floor-standing pedestal are also available.

How it works

The fan assembly is mounted on a shaft driven directly by an electric motor. At the opposite end of the shaft is a worm drive connected by gearwheels to a cranked metal arm that causes the fan to swing gently from side to side, directing the airstream over a wide area. A selector is used to disengage the gearbox if the fan is to be used without oscillating. All but the very simplest fans have a two-speed switch.

The diameter of the average desk fan ranges from 175 to 300mm (7 to 12in), while floor-standing pedestal fans are somewhat larger.

Some desk fans are so inexpensive that they hardly warrant repairing – but since fans are usually easy to service, it's worth taking a little time to get one working again.

1 Fan blade	7 Gear assembly
2 Blade guard	8 Gearbox selector
3 Guard-fixing screw	9 Cranked arm
4 Drive shaft	10 Two-speed switch
5 Electric motor	11 Terminal block
6 Worm drive	12 Cord clamp

SAFETY FIRST

Don't leave a moving fan unattended where small children could insert objects or fingers through the guard.

Ensure the plug is wired correctly and that the appropriate fuse is fitted.

Never use a desk fan with the guard removed.

Always unplug a fan before attempting to service it.

When reassembling the appliance, always make sure the components and wiring are returned to their original locations.

Before putting it back into service, test a desk fan by plugging it into a circuit protected by an RCD – see page 11. Then switch on, and if the RCD trips have the appliance tested by a qualified service engineer.

SAFETY FIRST

When an appliance is earthed, you should always use a continuity tester to verify there is a continuous earth path before you put the appliance back into service – see page 22. In the case of the fan described here, the earth path was tested by placing one probe of a continuity tester on the earth pin of the plug, and the other probe on the electric motor and then the metal fan shaft.

1 Remove guard-fixing screw

1 Remove the rear cover

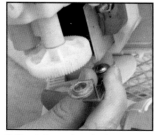

2 Check for a detached arm

FAN SOUNDS NOISY

Distorted or bent blades

A one-piece plastic fan is likely to distort if left near a strong heat source. Damaged fan blades may brush against the wire guard, creating noise and further damage to both blades and guard.

If you can obtain spare parts, remove the blade guard (see below) and ease the blade assembly off its shaft. The majority of one-piece fans are a snug push-fit onto a plain round shaft.

Bent wire guard

If a fan topples over or falls off the desk, the wire guard could be dented or flattened, fouling the blade assembly and possibly damaging it. The guard on your fan may have slightly different fixings from the ones described below.

1 The front half of the guard is removed easily, once the single screw fixing is detached.

2 If the rear half of the guard is damaged, pull the fan off its shaft to reveal the large plastic nut mounted behind. Unscrew this nut by hand to remove the guard.

3 Use your thumbs to press dents out of the guard, then reassemble the fan and guard in the reverse order. There will probably be locating lugs that ensure the two halves of the guard are orientated correctly.

FAN WON'T OSCILLATE

Cranked connecting arm detached

Dismantle the casing to see if the screws holding the arm in place have worked loose or fallen off.

1 To detach the rear cover, first remove any visible fixings. It may be necessary to pinch the sides of the cover to unlatch moulded-plastic clips.

2 Check to see if the metal arm is attached to the plastic gearwheel just below the gearbox.

3 Look for a missing screw inside the cover you have just removed. Reattach the arm and then replace the cover before testing the appliance.

2 Pull the fan off its shaft

3 Press dents out of the guard

3 Look for a screw in the cover

1 Check the selector moves freely

2 Lift out shaft and gearwheel

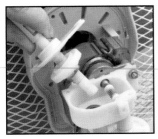

3 Redistribute lubrication

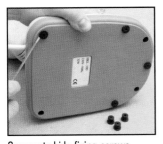

Grommets hide fixing screws

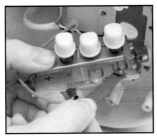

Clean dirty switch contacts

Oscillating action stuck

If the fan is not oscillating or the action is jerky, make sure the plastic gearwheels are meshing.

1 Check that the gearbox selector is moving up and down freely.

2 Take out the screw that holds the top of the gearbox in place, then lift out the shaft and main gearwheel.

3 Redistribute the lubrication, which may have migrated to the ends of the worm drive.

4 Reassemble the gearbox, ensuring the gears engage accurately; then replace the cover.

It may be impossible to obtain replacement parts for damaged gearwheels – in which case, your only option is to reassemble the gearbox and use the appliance as a fixed-position fan.

FAN OPERATES SPASMODICALLY

Faulty switch

On a typical desk fan, the switch is situated in the moulded base. The majority of fans have rubber or plastic feet or grommets to prevent them sliding on a smooth surface. The base-cover fixing screws are often concealed beneath these grommets.

1 If there are no obvious fixings, prise the grommets out of their locations with the tip of a small screwdriver or penknife.

2 Remove the screw fixings in order to detach the base cover and reveal the switch. A simple fan will have a basic two-speed switch. Spares may not be available for an inexpensive fan, but you can try servicing a faulty switch.

3 Check that the switch action is working smoothly, and clean corroded or pitted contacts with a folded strip of fine emery paper. Brush out the emery dust before replacing the switch.

4 Relocate the switch and check that all the wiring has been put back in its original location; then secure the base cover with the fixing screws.

FAN WON'T WORK AT ALL

Faulty plug or fuse

Check that the plug is wired correctly and replace a faulty fuse – see pages 17 and 19. If the fuse blows again as soon as you plug in, have the appliance checked at a service centre.

Power failure

If other appliances on the circuit have stopped working, inspect your consumer unit for a blown fuse or tripped MCB or RCD – see pages 11 and 12.

Broken flex conductor

Check the flex with a continuity tester – see page 20. Provided the flex is attached to screw terminals, replacing it with a new length of flex should be straightforward – see page 20.

Tighten earth connections

Loose connections

Check that internal wiring connections are secure, and fully tighten any earth connections. Check that there is a secure and positive connection to earth – see page 22.

Faulty switch

See left.

Faulty motor

Even if a replacement motor is obtainable, it's likely to cost almost as much as a new fan.

COFFEE MAKERS

A machine that makes a perfect cup of breakfast coffee, or brews a full jug while dessert is being served, is a convenience we take for granted these days. Only when the machine stops working do we realize how much we have come to rely on it.

1 Reservoir	9 Non-drip valve
2 Hose	10 Thermal fuse
3 Hose clip	11 Thermostat
4 Boiler tube	12 Switch
5 Heating element	13 Terminal block
6 Hotplate	14 Cord clamp
7 Hot-water outlet	15 Non-return valve
8 Filter holder	16 Spade connector

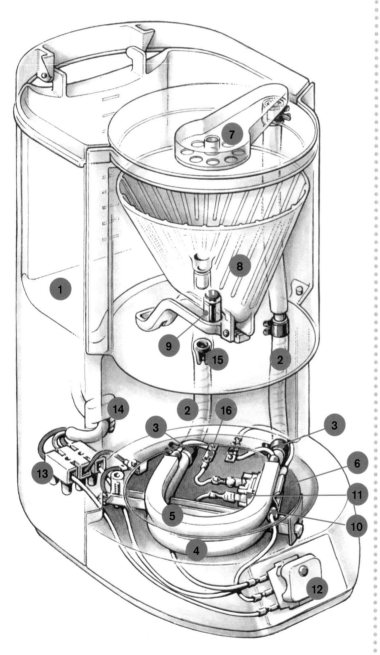

How it works

Even the most sophisticated coffee maker is simple in principle. All it has to do is pass heated water through ground coffee, then collect the brewed coffee in a jug and keep it warm until served.

This process starts by pouring the required amount of cold water into the machine's reservoir. From the base of the reservoir a flexible silicone tube runs to the base of the unit, where it is connected to a metal boiler tube. As the water passes along the boiler tube, it is heated rapidly by an electric element that is attached to the tube and the hotplate above. This heated water is carried to the top of the unit, where it trickles from an outlet mounted directly over a filter containing the ground coffee.

Having percolated through the grounds, the brewed coffee is collected in the jug standing on the hotplate. A simple non-drip valve mounted on the bottom of the filter holder prevents coffee running onto the hotplate if the jug is not in place to catch it.

This process is continuous until the reservoir is empty and all the water has passed through the boiler tube. A thermostat keeps the temperature at a level that will keep the jug of coffee warm. Should the unit overheat for any reason, a thermal fuse cuts the power to the element.

Neon indicator
All coffee makers have an indicator to tell you when the machine is switched on. This simple device is to remind you to switch off the appliance once the jug is empty.

Swing-out filter holder
An accessible filter holder makes it easier to remove used filters and to refill with fresh ground coffee.

SAFETY FIRST

Ensure the plug is wired correctly and that the appropriate fuse is fitted.

Check the flex regularly for signs of damage. If your machine has a flex-storage compartment, use it.

Don't use a machine that is leaking water or coffee. Unplug a leaking machine before mopping up spillage.

Always remove the plug from the socket before servicing a coffee maker.

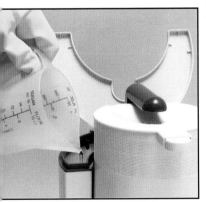

Fill the reservoir with descaler

Cleaning coffee makers

Before you brew coffee in a new machine, it pays to rinse the appliance first. The same goes for a coffee maker you haven't used for a long time.

Wash the permanent filter, jug and lid in hot soapy water, then rinse and dry them thoroughly. Do the same with the filter holder if it's detachable.

Assemble your coffee maker and fill the reservoir with fresh cold water, then switch on and let the water circulate through the machine. Throw the water away and repeat the process.

You can wipe the outside of your coffee maker with a clean damp cloth, but never immerse the machine in water.

Removing lime scale

If you live in a hard-water area, you need to decalcify your coffee maker every two to three months, using a proprietary descaler. You should read the manufacturer's instructions, but the procedure described below is typical for descalers available from supermarkets.

1 Fill the reservoir with descaler mixed according to the manufacturer's recommendations. Place the jug on the hotplate, but don't fit the filter.

2 Switch on and allow the agent to flow through the machine for one minute, then switch off and leave the descaler to work for about an hour.

3 Switch on again and allow the descaler to circulate and collect in the jug.

4 Empty the jug and rinse it, then fill the reservoir with fresh water and switch on again to flush out the machine. Flush the machine at least twice before using it to make coffee.

Using filtered water in your coffee maker will reduce the accumulation of lime scale and may improve the flavour of the coffee.

FILTERS
Most coffee makers are supplied with a filter that can be used over and over again. Made from plastic, stainless steel or even gilded metal mesh, these so-called permanent filters work perfectly well when new. However, unless you keep them scrupulously clean, they are not as hygienic as disposable paper filters. After a time, permanent filters tend to develop splits, allowing coffee grounds to drop through into the jug.

SERVING HOT COFFEE
In the past, coffee makers were designed to operate at relatively low temperatures. These appliances were unpopular with anyone who liked coffee with cold milk. Manufacturers have now eliminated this problem – but if you're stuck with a machine that will only produce luke-warm coffee, try warming the cups beforehand or use powdered coffee whitener instead of milk.

SAFETY FIRST

When reassembling your coffee maker, make sure the components and wiring are returned to their original locations.

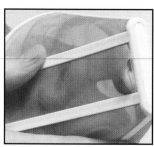

Look for splits close to the seams

COFFEE GROUNDS IN THE JUG

Split filter

A split filter will allow ground coffee to be flushed into the jug. Either buy a similar permanent filter from a service centre or change to disposable ones made from paper.

WEAK COFFEE

Incorrect measurement

Check the correct proportions of coffee and water recommended in your user's handbook.

Folded filter paper

If a paper filter is not positioned correctly, the first few drops of hot water may fold the paper over the grounds, preventing efficient percolation. Fit a new filter paper and try again.

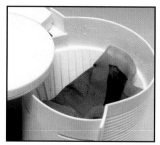

A folded filter makes weak coffee

APPLIANCE IS LEAKING COFFEE

Jug not on hotplate

The valve fitted to the base of the filter holder is designed to prevent coffee dripping onto the hotplate when you remove the jug. But if you've forgotten to return the jug to the hotplate before switching on, the valve may not hold back the full flow of percolating coffee – and, even if the valve is working perfectly, the filter holder may eventually overflow.

Without delay pull the plug from the socket, then switch off the machine. Drape a folded towel over the hotplate to soak up coffee spillage until the machine has cooled down and the water has stopped circulating. Empty out any water remaining in the reservoir.

Wipe coffee off the outside of the machine, then stand it on absorbent paper towels to soak up any leaks emanating from inside. Leave plenty of time for the appliance to dry out naturally.

You can test that the appliance is safe to use by plugging it into a circuit protected by an RCD. If in doubt, have the machine checked by a service centre before using it again.

Drape an old tea towel over the hotplate to soak up spilled coffee

SAFETY FIRST

Before putting it back into service, test a coffee maker by plugging it into a circuit protected by an RCD – see page 11. Then switch on, and if the RCD trips have the appliance tested by a qualified service engineer.

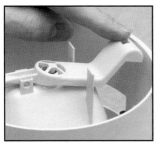

1 Check valve arm works smoothly

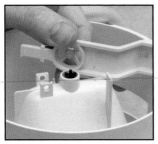

2 Remove the arm to see if the small valve is present

Jug not seated properly

Brewed coffee drips directly though a hole in the centre of the jug's lid. If the jug is not placed squarely on the hotplate, the coffee can run off the lid onto the hotplate. Follow the procedure described opposite.

Leaking non-drip valve

A faulty valve may allow a residue of coffee to drip onto the hotplate after you have removed the jug. Provided the brewing is complete, this isn't a serious problem – but it can create the smell of burnt coffee.

1 Make sure the valve arm at the base of the filter holder is operating smoothly.

2 Detach the arm to make sure the valve is still in place.

APPLIANCE IS LEAKING WATER

Split or detached hose

To gain access to the hoses that allow water to circulate, first unplug the coffee maker and remove the screws that hold the cover to the base of the machine. The base on some coffee makers may be held in place with plastic spring clips that can be detached with the tip of a screwdriver. Take care not to break these clips.

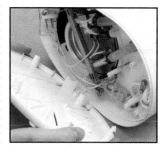

Remove the base to see hoses

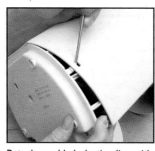

Detach moulded-plastic clips with the tip of a screwdriver

Check the flexible hoses for splits, and make sure they are pushed securely onto the ends of the boiler tube.

Some hoses are held in place with spring clips. If one of these joints appears to be leaking, reposition the clip slightly to provide a firmer grip.

If a hose has split, buy a replacement and reassemble the machine in the reverse order.

Before you plug in, fill the reservoir with water and stand the machine on newspaper or absorbent paper towels to check that there are no other leaks. If leaks persist, have the appliance checked by a service engineer.

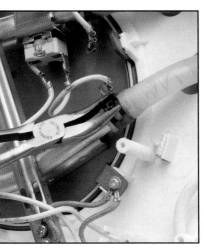

Repositioning a metal clip may provide a firmer grip on the hose

SLOW BREWING AND SPLUTTERING

Hard-water scaling
Lime scale building up inside the machine prevents the water from heating quickly and reduces circulation. Flush out the machine with a proprietary descaler – see page 33.

WATER DOESN'T CIRCULATE

Empty reservoir
Check that you remembered to put water in the reservoir before switching on.

Hard-water scaling
Severe scaling could prevent circulation altogether. Flush out with a descaler – see page 33.

APPLIANCE DOESN'T WORK AT ALL

Faulty plug or fuse
Check that the plug is wired correctly and replace a faulty fuse – see pages 17 and 19. If the fuse blows again as soon as you plug in and switch on, have the appliance checked at a service centre.

Power failure
If other appliances on the circuit have stopped working, inspect your consumer unit for a blown fuse or tripped MCB or RCD – see pages 11 and 12.

Broken flex conductor
On most coffee makers the incoming flex is connected to accessible screw terminals, so you will be able to test the flex for continuity (see page 20) and, if need be, replace it (see page 20). If the flex is suspect but you can't see how it is connected to the terminals, have it replaced at a service centre.

Loose connections
Check internal wiring for snugly fitting connectors.

Faulty thermostat
The thermostat is clamped firmly against the boiler tube/hotplate assembly. To check whether it needs to be replaced, see opposite.

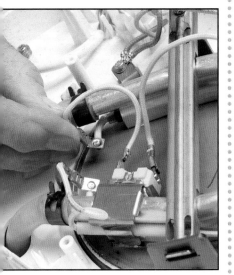

Check carefully for loose slip-on spade connectors

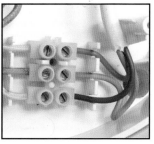

You can replace flex that is connected to screw terminals

SAFETY FIRST

When an appliance is earthed, you should always use a continuity tester to verify there is a continuous earth path – see page 22. In the case of the coffee makers described here, the earth path was tested by placing one probe of a continuity tester on the earth pin of the plug, and the other probe on the metal boiler tube and then the underside of the hotplate.

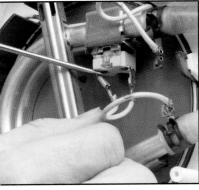
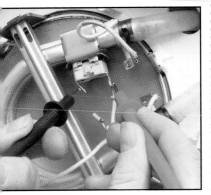

1 Ease off one connector

2 Then put a tester probe on each terminal of the thermostat

Check a thermal fuse with a continuity tester

1 Ease off one of the thermostat's connectors, using the tip of a screwdriver. Take care, since waggling a connector excessively in order to detach a wire may damage the connector.

2 With a probe of a continuity tester on each of the thermostat's terminals, the tester should give a positive indication (closed circuit). If there is no indication (open circuit), the thermostat should be replaced.

3 Make a note of how the thermostat is attached. In the appliance described here, it was held in place with a spring clip. Check that a replacement thermostat comes complete with the necessary clips and connectors. Also, you might need to apply a smear of special white heat-conductive paste to the contact surfaces if it was present originally. If it is not perfectly obvious how the thermostat is attached and fitted, have it replaced at a service centre. See also thermal fuse below.

Thermal fuse operated due to overheating

It is usually possible to take the thermal fuse out of a coffee maker by detaching the connectors at each end.

Lay the thermal fuse on a bench and test it for continuity – see page 20. If the tester is not activated, the thermal fuse has failed. This usually means the thermostat has failed, too. Have both components replaced or buy a new coffee maker.

Faulty heating element

Check whether the element is faulty by taking the connector from one end and checking the element with a continuity tester. A combined heater and hotplate is likely to prove uneconomical to replace.

Faulty switch

A switch that is combined with an on/off indicator may be difficult to test. However, if you have eliminated all the other possible faults listed above and opposite, the switch is probably suspect.

One simple option is to buy a replacement, provided the switch can be detached and then reconnected easily; make a note of the wiring by labelling the connectors before detaching them. Alternatively, have the suspect switch tested by a service engineer.

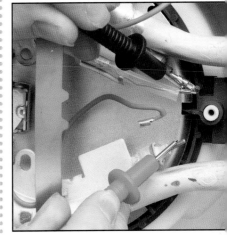

Test a suspect heating element

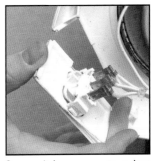

Some switches are easy to replace

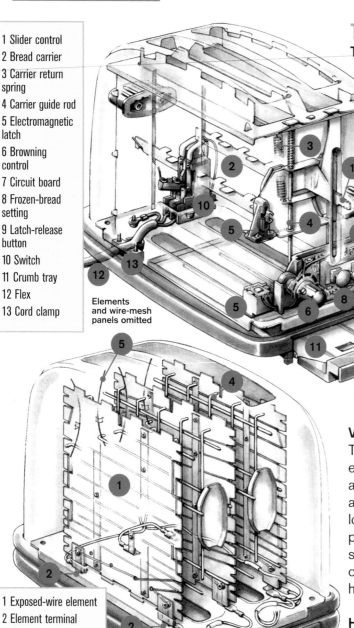

1 Slider control
2 Bread carrier
3 Carrier return spring
4 Carrier guide rod
5 Electromagnetic latch
6 Browning control
7 Circuit board
8 Frozen-bread setting
9 Latch-release button
10 Switch
11 Crumb tray
12 Flex
13 Cord clamp

Elements and wire-mesh panels omitted

1 Exposed-wire element
2 Element terminal
3 Spade connector
4 Wire-mesh panels (variable-width slot)
5 Hairsprings

Elements and wire-mesh panels only

TOASTERS

The electric toaster has been around for a long time and, however sophisticated the latest models have become, they still work on the same principles. Whatever else it provides, we need an appliance that will deliver consistently browned toast on demand.

How it works

Pressing down on the slider control lowers the bread carriers, operating a latch that holds the carriers in the lowered position. The same action simultaneously switches on the heating elements that toast the bread. With some toasters, sliding or turning the browning control adjusts a thermostat, which automatically releases the latch so that the spring-loaded bread carriers pop up. With fully electronic toasters, this process is controlled by a circuit board (see left), which releases an electromagnetic latch.

Variable-width slots

The wire-mesh panels on each side of the bread slot are moved inward by springs as the bread carrier is lowered. This maintains light pressure on both sides of a slice of bread, preventing it curling as it toasts, and so helps achieve even browning on both sides.

High-lift facility

Raising the slider control lifts the bread carriers high enough for the toast to project above the top of the toaster for easy removal.

FROZEN

MIN   MAX

Browning controls

Basic thermostats are made with a bimetallic strip that bends when heated until it manually trips the latch. Adjusting the browning control determines how far the bimetallic strip has to bend before the latch is released – the further it has to bend, the longer the bread is exposed to the heating elements. A fully electronic browning control, which is often incorporated in the latest toasters, is more accurate. After a preset period of time, a release coil controlled by a circuit board either trips a mechanical latch or cuts the power to an electromagnetic one. An electromagnetic latch will only engage when the toaster is turned on.

Reheat facility
This allows you to warm up toast that has cooled. Pressing the reheat button automatically reduces the time that the toaster will operate, preventing it burning the toast.

Frozen-bread setting
This control is in effect the opposite of the reheat facility. When it is set, the toaster allows extra time for the frozen bread to thaw.

Cool-wall toaster
Internal insulation prevents the sides of the toaster getting hot, which makes it ideal for families who like to have their toaster on the breakfast table. However, the top of the toaster still gets hot – so you need to take care when removing toast.

Cleaning your toaster
To remove fingermarks, unplug your toaster and wipe the outer case with a damp cloth – but don't allow water to seep inside. Never wash a toaster or immerse it in water.

Removing crumbs
Most people fail to clean out their toaster often enough. An accumulation of crumbs on the inside of your toaster may seem harmless, but can jam moving parts – and is also unhygienic and a fire risk. Unplug your toaster before cleaning out crumbs.

All toasters have some sort of removable tray at the base of the appliance, where the majority of crumbs collect. However, trays that swing down are invariably held in place by a screw fixing, some of which can only be loosened by a special screwdriver. A slide-out tray that covers most of the underside of the toaster is ideal. Once a week, brush the tray clean with a dry pastry brush.

Occasionally, it is worth taking the base off a toaster to remove crumbs that have lodged inside. Turn the toaster on its side and brush it out carefully. Don't be tempted to shake your toaster or bang it on the worktop to dislodge crumbs. Some heating elements are fragile and may break if they are subjected to rough treatment.

When you have replaced the base and crumb tray, plug the toaster into a circuit protected by an RCD before you start using the appliance again. If the RCD trips, have the appliance checked by a service engineer

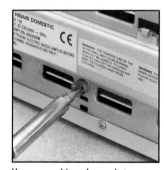
Unscrew a hinged crumb tray

Remove crumbs with pastry brush

Even with a high-lift facility and variable-width slots, a slice of toast can break up as you try to remove it, leaving a sizeable piece inside the toaster. If you try to remove the bread by turning the toaster upside down, it will tip crumbs all over the elements and may also jam the moving parts.

Never insert a knife or other metal implement into the slot, even when the toaster has been unplugged. It is a dangerous practice that can damage heating elements. Instead, unplug the appliance and use a wooden spoon, a chopstick or small wooden tongs to carefully lift the bread out of the slot. Make sure that these wooden utensil are dry. Take care not to press against the heating elements – especially infrared glass elements, which can be particularly vulnerable to sideways pressure.

A slide-out tray is easier to clean

Brush crumbs from inside a toaster

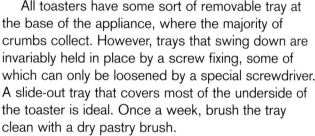

First things first

Check for the obvious before attempting to diagnose what's wrong with your toaster.

- If your toast is burnt or underdone, you may simply need to reset the browning control.

- If there is a smell of burning even when your toast is browning perfectly, it's probably time to brush crumbs from the inside.

- If the sliding mechanism won't latch, check that the toaster is plugged in.

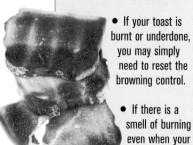

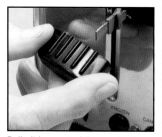

Pull slider control from spigot

Spread slot to free hooked control

Moulded clips on browning knob

TOAST BURNS

Sliding mechanism jammed

Check first that you have not tried to toast bread that is too thick. Thinly sliced bread can also jam the mechanism if it has curled while toasting. Variable-width slots are designed to counter this problem.

The most likely causes are either an accumulation of crumbs sticking to the bread-carrier guide rods or large crumbs jammed into the sliding mechanism itself.

You will have to remove at least part of the casing to gain access to the sliding mechanism. Check for visible screw fixings to see whether you need to take off a side panel, or an end panel, or both. A one-piece shell will lift off completely once you have removed the base and the slider control and possibly the browning-control knob.

The slider control is usually designed to pull straight off its spigot, but it may need easing off with a strong screwdriver. Take great care not to break the plastic knob, and if necessary protect the casing with a pad of paper towels. Some slider-control knobs may latch behind the casing – try spreading the slot with your fingers.

The browning-control knob will probably come away with the shell or panel. On many models it is held in place with moulded-plastic spring clips, which can be unclipped easily from inside once the panel or shell is free. If not, it is probably a snug fit on a D-shaped shaft.

Carefully brush large crumbs from the bread-carrier guide rods and from other parts of the mechanism. Wipe the rods clean either with a cotton bud or with paper towel wrapped around a finger. Don't spray the mechanism with a lubricant.

Check that the mechanism moves freely, then reassemble the toaster, making sure that all the components and wiring are returned to their correct locations. Before you push the browning-control knob back onto its spigot, turn the control to zero so that you can align the plastic knob accurately. Test the toaster before putting it back into use – see Safety first, pages 42 and 43.

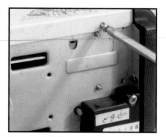

Unscrew fixings to release panels

Detach side and end panels

Brush crumbs from guide rods

Clean the sliding mechanism

Bread leaning to one side

If the bread is getting burnt on one side only, inspect the springs that move the wire-mesh support panels in a variable-width slot. These springs may be misplaced or broken.

Remove the casing or end panels to reveal the hairsprings that are located on tabs pushed out of the internal metal chassis. Look for broken springs and relocate any that have slipped out of their tabs.

Faulty release coil

The coil that releases the latch in an electronic toaster acts like a magnet. On some models, you may have to have the circuit board replaced along with a faulty coil. This is certain to be costly, and it may be cheaper to buy a new toaster.

Faulty bimetallic thermostat

If the thermostat does not measure the temperature accurately, it will delay the release of the latch. A service engineer may be able to adjust this type of thermostat.

TOAST UNDERDONE

Incorrect setting

The most usual cause is incorrect setting of the browning control.

Inconsistent thermostat reading

With a basic thermostat, the length of time the bread is exposed to the heating elements can vary, depending on whether the bimetallic strip has cooled completely between making batches of toast. Try turning up the browning control for a second batch of toast.

Using the wrong slot

With some appliances it is important to use a specific slot when toasting a single slice of bread. If you use the wrong slot, the latch may trip prematurely. Check your user's manual.

Mechanical latch disengaging early

Look for signs of wear on a mechanical latch. A badly worn latch may be disengaging prematurely and needs replacing, but that is probably too expensive to be worthwhile.

Look for broken or detached hairsprings

SAFETY FIRST

Make sure the plug is wired correctly and that the appropriate fuse is fitted.

Always unplug the appliance before cleaning or servicing it.

Check the flex regularly for signs of damage. Don't allow it to trail across a cooker or hob plates, nor through water on a kitchen worktop.

If the toaster has a flex-storage compartment, keep the exposed length of flex as short as practicable.

SAFETY FIRST

Don't place a toaster directly under cupboards or shelves.

Don't place a toaster near the edge of a kitchen worktop, where it could be reached by small children.

Don't allow young children to use a toaster unsupervised.

Don't place plastic bread wrappers next to a toaster. If the plastic melts onto the casing, it can be almost impossible to remove.

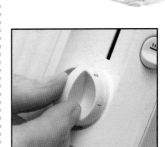

Always check your setting before looking for serious faults

Faulty circuit board

Once you have removed the shell or end panels, you may be able to spot components on the circuit board that are damaged or burnt out – but testing the circuit board for faults is a job for an expert. Take the appliance to a service centre or buy a new toaster.

CARRIERS WON'T STAY DOWN

Toaster not switched on

If it's an electronic toaster, the latch may not engage until the toaster is plugged in and the socket is switched on.

Faulty mechanical latch

See page 41.

TOASTER WON'T SWITCH ON

Faulty plug or fuse

Check that the plug is wired correctly and replace a faulty fuse – see pages 17 and 19. If the fuse blows again as soon as you plug in and switch on, have the appliance checked at a service centre.

Power failure

If other appliances on the circuit have stopped working, inspect your consumer unit for a blown fuse or tripped MCB or RCD – see pages 11 and 12.

Faulty flex

Test the flex for a broken conductor – see page 20. You can replace a damaged flex, provided it is connected to accessible screw terminals – see page 20.

Loose connections

Having removed the shell or panels, check all the internal wiring for obvious loose connections. Broken soldered joints are best left to an expert.

Faulty switch

Check the switch's strip-metal contacts for cracks and signs of burning. It may be possible to clean dirty or pitted contacts and improve their performance.

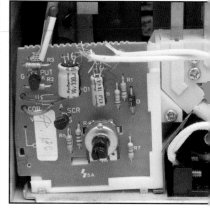

A faulty circuit board is usually too expensive to replace

The switch's strip-metal contacts should be clean

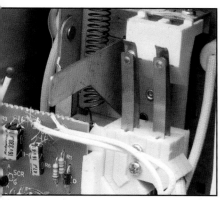

With latch mechanism engaged, switch contacts should touch

SAFETY FIRST

When reassembling a toaster, make sure the components and wiring are returned to their original locations.

Before putting it back into service, test the toaster by plugging it into a circuit protected by an RCD – see page 11. Then switch on, and if the RCD trips have the appliance tested by a qualified service engineer.

These same switch contacts should be touching when the latch is engaged. However, don't attempt to bend the strips in order to make a better contact – this could result in the toaster overheating because the switch is unable to disengage.

A faulty or broken switch may be too costly to replace – but it's worth checking with a service centre before discarding the toaster.

Faulty circuit board
See opposite.

Broken heating element
Glass infrared heaters can only be tested by an expert, and may be too expensive to make replacement worthwhile. However, you may be able to check whether an exposed-wire element is intact. This type of element is constructed by winding a continuous strip of crimped metal around a heatproof board. It is sometimes possible to detect obvious breaks in the strips simply by looking into the bread slots – but make sure the toaster is unplugged first. Alternatively, use a continuity tester to check this type of element.

1 Having unplugged the toaster, remove the base to reveal the heater terminals protruding through the bottom of the internal metal chassis.

2 Use the tip of a screwdriver to ease the spade connectors off both terminals. Don't waggle these connectors too vigorously when removing them, as the elements are particularly vulnerable at these points.

3 Place one tester probe on each terminal. If you get a positive indication (closed circuit) for each element, you can be sure they are in working order. A service centre may be able to replace a faulty wire element at a reasonable cost.

Infrared elements can only be tested by a service engineer

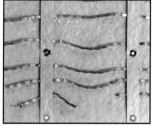
Broken wire elements can be easy to detect

SAFETY FIRST

When an appliance is earthed, you should always use a continuity tester to verify there is a continuous earth path – see page 22. In the case of the toasters described here, the earth path was tested by placing one probe of a continuity tester on the earth pin of the plug, and the other probe on an unpainted part of the metal casing and then on the top edges of the bread carriers.

Ease off the element connectors

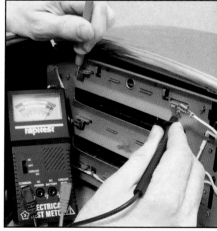
Check the element with a continuity tester

ELECTRIC KETTLES

Traditional-style electric kettles have a wide base, inherited from the old-fashioned kettles that were heated on a hob. Jug-style kettles have a base that's smaller in circumference, taking up less space on the worktop, but are proportionally taller in order to hold the required volume of water. With a jug kettle, a side-mounted handle keeps your hand away from steam venting from the lid and spout, but it puts more of a strain on your wrist when you are carrying a full kettle. Both types of kettle are made from stainless steel or lightweight heat-resistant plastic.

The vast majority of electric kettles switch off automatically when the water boils, but it may still be possible to obtain a basic model with a switch that has to be operated manually.

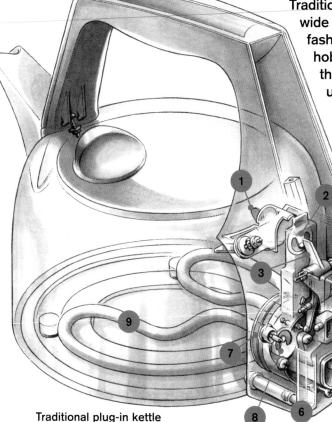

Traditional plug-in kettle

1 Steam outlet	7 Watertight seal
2 Bimetallic disc	8 Boil-dry safety cutout
3 Switch	
4 Switch rocker	9 Element
5 Power connection	10 Plug-in connector
6 Water-level indicator	11 Older-style round connector

Conditioning a new kettle

Fill a new kettle with water and let it boil, then flush out the kettle at least twice before using it. Do the same with any kettle you haven't used for a while.

Cleaning a kettle

Ensure the kettle is isolated from the power supply before cleaning it. Provided the kettle is cool, you can use a damp cloth to wipe the outside, but don't use abrasive cleaners. See page 46 for descaling a kettle.

How it works

The water is heated by an electric heating element fitted inside the kettle. Usually the element is fixed to the body of the kettle by means of a threaded collar or metal nuts or screw fixings that clamp the element against watertight seals. Depending on the model, these seals may be washers, gaskets or soft collars. These seals are the most likely source of leaks. The latest models have concealed elements built into the underside of the water vessel, which reduces the possibility of leaks and makes cleaning and descaling easier.

When the water boils, steam is directed through a small hole or tube onto a bimetallic strip or disc that is designed to bend as it heats up, moving the switch to the off position.

Nearly all kettles are fitted with a safety device that cuts power to the element should the kettle boil dry. The same device operates if someone forgets to fill the kettle before switching on. In addition, electric kettles are generally made with water-level indicators for easy reference.

The heating element is connected to the power supply by a lead – a short length of flex fitted

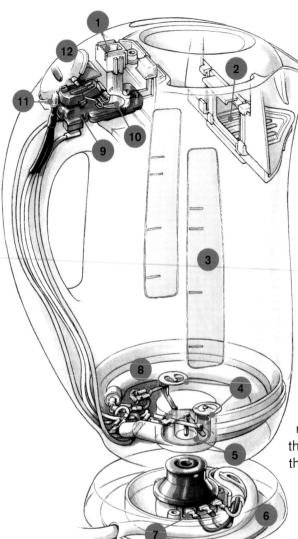

Cordless jug kettle

1 Steam outlet	7 Spade connector
2 Filter	8 Concealed element
3 Water-level indicator	9 Switch
4 Boil-dry safety cutout	10 Bimetallic disc
5 Power connection	11 Indicator light
6 Base unit	12 Switch rocker

First things first

Before attempting to diagnose faults, check for obvious omissions.

● Is the kettle plugged in and is it switched on?

● Is the lead connector pushed in completely?

● Is a cordless kettle seated properly on its base unit?

with a plug-in connector at the kettle end and a 13amp three-pin plug at the other. A lead with coiled flex saves worktop space and is less likely to be reached by small children.

Cordless kettles

The power connection on the underside of a cordless kettle plugs onto a base unit that is connected by flex to the power supply. With this arrangement, the kettle can be lifted free without having to physically detach the flex. Some cordless kettles are designed to fit onto the base unit in a fixed position, but the later models can be placed in any orientation. The base unit usually provides storage space for excess flex.

Filling a kettle

Filling a kettle is such an everyday event that there seems nothing to it – but serious faults and accidents are caused by incorrect filling. Before filling, make sure you pull the plug from the wall socket and also disconnect the lead from the appliance. Lift a cordless kettle off its base before filling it with water. As a bare minimum, water must cover the element – check your water-level indicator. Put at least a cupful of water in a kettle with a concealed element.

Underfilling may trip the boil-dry safety device and possibly damage the element. If you overfill a kettle, it may switch off prematurely and boiling water could spurt out of the spout. Make sure the lid is fitted properly, or the automatic switch may fail to respond correctly.

When using a plug-in kettle, wait until the water has stopped boiling and then disconnect the lead from both ends before pouring.

1 Steam outlet	8 Boil-dry safety cutout
2 Filter	9 Switch rocker
3 Element	10 Water-level indicator
4 Power connection	11 Switch
5 Spade connector	12 Indicator light
6 Base unit	13 Bimetallic disc
7 Watertight seal	

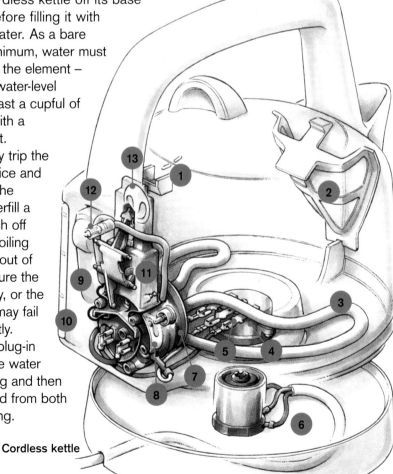

Cordless kettle

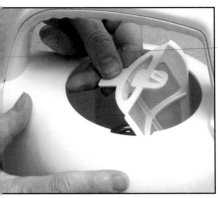

Buy a replacement filter

PARTICLES IN TEA OR COFFEE

Damaged filter

Modern kettles are fitted with fine gauze filters that prevent loose lime-scale deposits passing through the spout and into your beverage. Replacements for split filters are available from service agents. Let the water in a kettle cool before removing the filter.

Filters are designed to be detached easily for regular inspection and cleaning. If your filter is beginning to clog with lime-scale deposits, scrub it with a nylon brush under running water. Remove heavy deposits by soaking the filter in a proprietary descaler or white vinegar overnight. Rinse well before refitting.

KETTLE SLOW TO HEAT UP

Element scaled up

A heavily coated element will take considerably longer to heat the water – and if you don't rectify the problem, the element may overheat and trip the boil-dry safety device.

Use a proprietary descaler to remove lime-scale deposits from inside the kettle (make sure it won't do harm to a plastic kettle). The following procedure is typical for general-purpose descalers available from supermarkets, but always read the instructions supplied with the particular descaler you buy.

1 Half fill the kettle with water and boil it, then switch off and unplug.

2 Add the amount of descaler recommended by the manufacturer and leave it until the resulting effervescence ceases.

3 If scale remains, try plugging in and reheating the water until it fizzes – but don't allow it to boil.

4 Empty the kettle, then refill with clean water and boil again. Empty the water and rinse the kettle thoroughly. A heavily scaled element may require a second treatment.

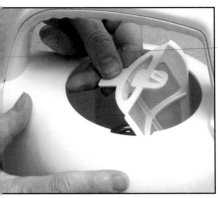

Pour in a measured dose of
proprietary descaler

SAFETY FIRST

Before putting it back into service, fill the kettle and stand it on absorbent paper towels for about 15 minutes to detect any leaks. Then plug the kettle into a circuit protected by an RCD – see page 11. Switch on, and if the RCD trips have the appliance tested by a service engineer.

Keep your hands away from the spout and steam vents when the kettle is boiling.

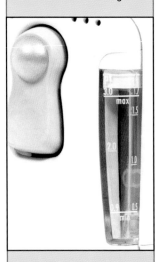

Check that the water is between the minimum and maximum levels before switching on.

Make sure the lid is positioned correctly, and don't remove it while the kettle is boiling.

KETTLE WILL NOT SWITCH OFF

Lid not fitted properly

In order for the switch to operate, steam must be directed onto the bimetallic strip or disk that operates the switch. If the lid isn't closed, the steam is diverted out of the kettle instead of through the steam hole or tube.

Switch off and allow the water to cool slightly before relocating the lid.

Steam outlet blocked

The small outlet found in older kettles can become blocked with lime scale, so steam is no longer directed onto the bimetallic strip or disc. The orifice is generally larger on modern kettles and can only be blocked by a sizeable piece of lime scale that has become detached from the heating element.

Descale the kettle (see opposite) and then check that there is nothing blocking the steam hole or tube.

Faulty switch

If the kettle is not turning off automatically, the bimetallic strip or disc is probably not able to activate the switch. This could be because the disc or strip is cracked or broken, or perhaps the small push rod that moves the switch is stuck.

The switch unit on current traditional-style kettles also forms part of the element mounting, and can be difficult to test and replace. Have a service engineer check this type of switch.

The switch on a jug kettle is likely to be a separate unit mounted in the handle and can usually be inspected and tested by removing part of the handle casing. The task may be complicated, however, by having to remove screw fixings with unconventional heads, or by having to release moulded plastic clips that could be partially concealed. If at any stage the process proves to be difficult, ask a service engineer to check the switch for you.

Typical dismantling sequence

1 Carefully detach bottom cover

2 Remove any screw fixings at base of handle

SAFETY FIRST

When an appliance is earthed, you should always use a continuity tester to verify that there is a continuous earth path – see page 22. In the case of the kettles described here, the earth path was tested by placing one probe of a continuity tester on the earth pin of the plug, and the other probe on the element inside the kettle (or onto the metal bottom inside a kettle with a concealed element). Plug a cordless kettle onto its base unit when carrying out the test.

3 And also at the top of the handle

4 Lift handle off the jug

5 Lift off plastic rocker

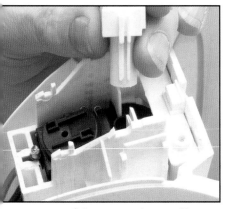

6 Remove any demountable plastic tubes and shrouds

Once you have removed the switch cover, take off the plastic rocker that covers the switch, making a note of top and bottom so that you can replace it exactly.

You may have to remove one or two plastic shrouds and possibly a screw fixing to release the switch. Turn the switch over to inspect the bimetallic disc and check that the pushrod is free to move by operating the switch mechanism manually.

If the switch proves to be mechanically sound, put one probe of a continuity tester on each switch terminal, and turn the switch on and off to see if it will pass a current. You can only perform this test if you are able to take at least one terminal connector off the switch. If the wires are crimped or soldered to the switch, you should ask a service engineer to test the switch for you.

If you detect that the switch is faulty, buy a replacement and reassemble the kettle carefully, making sure that all components and wires are put back in their original locations.

Test the kettle on a circuit protected by an RCD and check that there is a continuous path to earth – see page 22.

SWITCH CUTS OFF PREMATURELY

Oversensitive boil-dry safety device or faulty switch

If the kettle starts to heat again after it has cooled for about 15 minutes but then switches off again before the water boils, have a service agent check that the boil-dry safety device and the switch are both functioning properly.

KETTLE LEAKS

Leaks should be investigated urgently. If in doubt, either discard the kettle or take it to a service centre.

Cracked water-level indicator

Examine a plastic indicator for cracks or leaking joints. You may have to remove the switch cover to check whether an indicator is leaking from inside. Buy and fit a replacement.

7 Lift out the switch

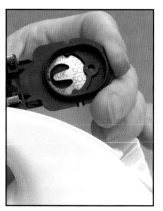

8 Inspect bimetallic disc for signs of damage

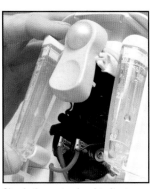

Check the water-level indicator

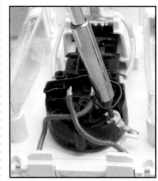

Loose heating element

Slightly tightening the clamping screws or nuts that hold a conventional element to the wall of the kettle may be enough to stem the leak. Fill the kettle and stand it on some paper towels to see if the leak persists. If it does, ask a service centre to check the appliance for you.

Tighten element clamping screws

Damaged washer or collar

Tightening up the element won't cure perished or cracked seals. Have them replaced.

Hole in base of kettle

Check a metal appliance for signs of corrosion, especially near the folded joints between the base and body of the kettle and possibly around the small feet attached to the underside of the base. There is nothing you can do to remedy this type of damage except buy a new kettle.

KETTLE NOT HEATING WATER

Faulty plug or fuse

The kettle lead probably comes with a moulded-on plug. Try replacing the fuse to see if that cures the problem – see page 17.

Power failure

If other appliances on the circuit have stopped working, inspect your consumer unit for a blown fuse or tripped MCB or RCD – see pages 11 and 12.

Broken flex conductor

If you suspect that the lead is faulty, the simplest option is to buy a replacement from a spares outlet. The flex running to the base unit of a cordless kettle may be wired with crimped connectors, which are best left to a professional to replace.

Automatic switch won't stay on

If the switch is so worn that it won't stay on, have it replaced or buy a new kettle.

Boil-dry safety device activated

If the kettle has been left to boil dry, then there is every chance that the safety device has been activated. Don't attempt to add water to the

Have a damaged seal replaced

SAFETY FIRST

Ensure the plug is wired correctly and that the appropriate fuse is fitted.

Check the flex regularly for signs of damage.

Keep the kettle and lead out of reach of children.

Don't let the lead trail across a hob unit or across a wet kitchen worktop.

Don't immerse the kettle or a cordless-kettle power base in water. Ensure that all electrical connections are kept dry.

Don't use a kettle that's leaking.

SAFETY FIRST

When reassembling an appliance, make sure the components and wiring are returned to their original locations.

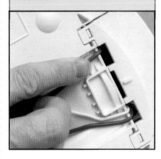

A worn switch may not stay in the 'on' position

kettle until it has been left to cool for 10 minutes or so, by which time the safety device may have reset automatically. If the kettle still does not work, the element has probably been damaged.

On some older kettles the boil-dry safety device will have to be reset manually – get advice about this from your service centre.

Heating element failed

Heavy scale deposits shorten the life of a kettle element. Most conventional elements are available as spare parts, but a concealed element is part of the hotplate and the combined unit is probably too expensive to make replacement worthwhile.

Replacing even a conventional element in a modern kettle involves stripping the appliance almost down to its constituent parts. It takes care and patience to ensure that all the components are replaced correctly and safely, and you may need specialized tools and materials. On balance it would therefore pay to have the element replaced by a service engineer, especially as it will probably extend the life of your kettle by several years.

Faulty base unit

With many cordless kettles it is not practicable to check the power connection on the underside of the kettle or the one in the base unit. However, those kettles that rotate around a cylindrical base connection are often relatively easy to inspect.

If you can remove the bottom panel of the base unit, you will be able to make a visual inspection of the wires and connectors to check for physical damage or burn marks.

It may be possible to make a similar inspection of the power connection in the kettle simply by removing a small cover panel on the underside of the appliance.

If either power connection looks suspect, provided the wires are attached with pull-off spade connectors replacing it will be relatively easy.

Having replaced either component, you must run all the wires back through their original locations and replace the cover panels with care. Check for a continuous path to earth (see page 22) and, before putting the kettle back into use, test it by plugging it into a circuit protected by an RCD.

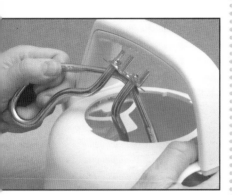

It is usually worth having the element replaced

Check connections in base unit

SAFETY FIRST

Always remove the plug from the socket before servicing an electric kettle.

Always place a cordless kettle on its base unit before switching on. And don't lift the kettle from its base unit until it has switched off.

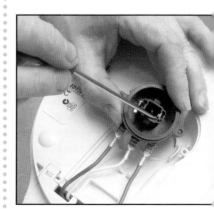

Look for burn marks around connection in kettle

FOOD BLENDERS

Blenders, also known as liquidizers, efficiently convert solid foodstuffs into fine particles or liquid in a matter of seconds. A pulse facility helps keep the solid material in suspension in order to achieve a smooth, even consistency. Good-quality blenders should give long service, provided they are used properly and cleaned thoroughly each time they are used.

How it works

The food container is a clear glass or plastic jug with a sealed lid. It will normally have a side-mounted handle and a lip designed for easy pouring. The average blender has a capacity of about 1.5 litres (3 pints) and is calibrated to help measure out ingredients accurately.

At the base of the jug are rotating stainless-steel cutters, driven by an electric motor housed in the moulded-plastic or metal body of the blender. Controls range from a simple on/off switch with a manual pulsing action to multi-speed switches and electronically controlled pulsing.

As a rule, blenders have an interlocking safety device that prevents the motor being switched on

unless the jug is latched correctly onto the body. Like the jug, accessories for grinding nuts and coffee beans are made to fit on top of the motor housing.

1 Jug
2 Latching tab
3 Cutters
4 Drive spindle
5 Drive shaft
6 Electric motor
7 Interlocking safety device
8 Switch
9 Flex

Hand-held blenders

Blenders made with compact motor units are designed to be held in one hand. This type of blender is activated by squeezing the trigger or button built into the plastic casing. The semi-shielded blade or whisk attached to one end is lowered into a plastic beaker that holds the foodstuffs to be blended. Single-speed and variable-speed models are available.

Cleaning a blender

To clean a blender, pour some hot water into the jug and add a few drops of washing-up liquid. Close the lid and pulse the appliance for a short period. Then unplug the blender and rinse the jug under running water, leaving it to drain and dry upside down.

Wash accessories, such as a coffee or nut grinder, in hot water and washing-up liquid. Use a long-handled brush to keep your fingers away from the sharp cutters.

Having unplugged the blender, wipe the body of the appliance with a damp cloth – never immerse a blender in water.

Twist and remove the jug

SAFETY FIRST

Check that the jug and lid are securely in place before switching on.

Don't remove the lid until the blade has stopped moving.

Don't run a blender with the jug empty.

Don't allow water or other liquids to spill over onto the motor housing.

Take care when washing blades – leave them to drain and dry naturally.

LEAKING JUG

If liquid leaks from beneath the jug onto the motor housing, the blade-assembly seal is probably faulty.

1 Put a thick cloth pad, such as an old tea towel, into the jug to prevent the cutters rotating. Then, by hand, unscrew the drive spindle attached to the base of the jug.

2 This will probably have a left-hand thread, so turn it clockwise (the opposite direction to normal) to remove it. The left-hand thread is to ensure the fixing nut does not come loose when the blades are rotating.
   Some blade assemblies may be bolted to the top of the shaft. To remove this type of assembly, use a small box spanner or nut driver.

3 Remove the leaking seal, and slip a new one onto the cutter drive shaft.

With some blenders, the jug (including the cutter assembly) is made in two parts joined together by a moulded screw thread. The joint is sealed with a flexible ring that can be replaced if it leaks.

TAKES TOO LONG TO BLEND

Blunt or bent blades
On some blenders, the motor will be damaged if run for longer than a specified period. If you find you're regularly overrunning, the cutters may need replacing. A bent cutter should also be replaced – as it will unbalance the assembly, causing the blender to vibrate.

Cutters or blade assemblies may be available as spare parts, in which case you can fit replacements (see above). If there is a replaceable seal, change that at the same time.
   With some blenders, it may be necessary to buy a new jug fitted with a set of cutters.

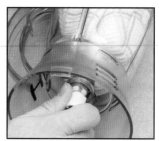

1 Turn the drive spindle clockwise

2 The fixing nut is inside

3 Replace the seal

Attachments have similar spindles

Replacement cutters may be available as spare parts

BLENDER RUNS AT ONE SPEED

Faulty speed-control switch
If your blender is fitted with a multi-speed switch, have it checked out by a service agent.

Faulty electronic circuit board
If the circuit board proves to be faulty, repairing it is likely to prove uneconomical.

BLADES NOT TURNING

Overloaded jug
Remove contents, then refill a little at a time.

Blade assembly sticking
Remove blade assembly (see opposite). Clean the cutters and lubricate the shaft with edible mineral oil.

Faulty motor
Have the electric motor checked at a service centre.

Lubricate the cutter shaft

BLENDER NOT RUNNING

Faulty plug or fuse
Check that the plug is wired correctly and change a faulty fuse – see pages 17 and 19. If the fuse blows again as soon as you plug in and switch on, have the appliance checked at a service centre.

Power failure
If other appliances on the circuit have stopped working, inspect your consumer unit to see if there is a blown fuse or tripped MCB or RCD – pages 11 and 12.

Broken flex conductor
Have a suspect flex checked by a service engineer, to avoid having to dismantle the casing.

Jug not latched securely
Rotate the jug to make sure the latching tabs are locating correctly.

Broken latching tab
If one of the moulded tabs has broken off a plastic jug, the interlocking safety device will not be activated and the motor will not switch on. Buy a replacement jug.

Faulty motor
Have the motor checked at a service centre. Unless it's possible to fit new brushes, the repair is bound to be uneconomical.

Faulty switch
Even a simple one-speed switch may be expensive to replace. Ask a service engineer for advice.

SAFETY FIRST

Don't place a blender on or near hot surfaces.

Keep a blender and its accessories out of reach of children.

Check the flex regularly for signs of damage. Coil excess flex into the storage compartment in the base of the blender.

Don't leave a blender unattended when it's plugged in.

Ensure the plug is wired correctly and that the appropriate fuse is fitted.

Dismantling a blender's motor housing carries with it the risk that the appliance's interlocking safety device may be made ineffective. For this reason, it is best to leave all internal servicing to an expert. Food processors have similar built-in safety devices and so should only be repaired by an engineer or service centre.

Before putting it back into service, test a blender by plugging it into a circuit protected by an RCD – see page 11. Then switch on, and if the RCD trips have the appliance tested by a service engineer.

HAND-HELD FOOD MIXERS

Food mixers have taken the drudgery out of mixing ingredients. Their electrically powered beaters and whisks turn foodstuffs into a perfectly blended mixture without effort – instead of laboriously stirring them with a wooden spoon. Lightweight hand-held models, which you move around the bowl, are ideal for folding, mixing and whisking smaller quantities. Three-speed and five-speed versions are available. Some models come with a stand attachment that holds the mixer over the bowl, in effect converting it into a tabletop mixer. The attachment includes a revolving base that rotates the bowl beneath the stationary mixer.

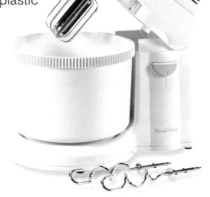

How it works

An ergonomically designed plastic body incorporating an easy-grip handle houses a 150 to 180W brush motor. The handle is fitted with a thumb-operated switch, which is used to select a range of speeds. The motor shaft is fitted with a worm drive that engages with two plastic contrarotating bevelled gearwheels. These in turn drive a pair of beaters that plug into them from below. A push button, which may double as the control switch, is used to eject the beaters. A fan is usually fitted to the end of the drive shaft to keep the motor from overheating. Airflow vents in the plastic casing aid cooling.

1 Electric motor
2 Switch
3 Worm drive
4 Gearwheel
5 Beaters
6 Cooling fan
7 Airflow vents
8 Cord clamp

SAFETY FIRST

Always remove the plug from the socket before servicing a mixer.

Ensure the plug is wired correctly and that the appropriate fuse is fitted.

Check the flex regularly for signs of damage.

When reassembling a mixer, make sure the components and wiring are returned to their original locations.

NOT RUNNING ON ALL SPEEDS

Faulty switch

On the more advanced models, speed is controlled electronically. This type of switch can only be tested and, if need be, replaced at a service centre. If your model is fitted with a relatively simple mechanical switch, you can check it visually for damaged contacts.

Operate the switch to make sure it makes contact at all points along the gradient. Remove specks of dirt and any debris stuck to the switch slide, but don't clean off the lubrication – it is essential for a smooth action and doesn't prevent positive contact.

This type of switch cannot normally be repaired or replaced economically – so you will probably have to resign yourself to a limited choice of speeds or buy a new mixer.

MIXER RUNS NOISILY

Drive mechanism in need of lubrication

Dismantle the casing (see above right) and inspect the worm drive and plastic gearwheels. The original white lubrication may have migrated to the ends of the worm drive, leaving dry surfaces.

Use a small screwdriver to redistribute the lubrication along the worm drive and to the gearwheel bearings.

If the drive and bearings are completely dry, you can buy the special white lubricant from a service centre. Apply it sparingly.

Worn motor bearings

If lubricating the drive mechanism does not cure the problem, the noise may be due to worn motor bearings. Motors for inexpensive mixers are unlikely to be available as spare parts, but it may be worth asking at a service centre before buying a new mixer.

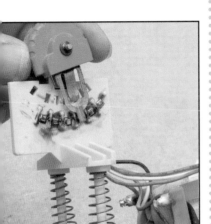

Clean switch contacts but don't remove the lubrication

SAFETY FIRST

Before putting it back into service, test any mixer by plugging it into a circuit protected by an RCD – see page 11. Then switch on, and if the RCD trips have the appliance tested by a qualified service engineer.

THE CASING USUALLY DIVIDES lengthways once a number of screw fixings have been removed. These fixings may have unconventional heads, one or more of which may be concealed. Take the trouble to label screws of different lengths to make reassembly easier.

Before separating the two halves of the casing, place the appliance flat on a bench so that you can detach the top part without disturbing internal components and wiring. Make a note of their locations, so you can put them back in their original positions.

Spread lubrication along worm drive

Lubricate gearwheel bearings

TABLETOP FOOD MIXERS

Purpose-made tabletop models are heavy-duty mixers. The arm containing the drive mechanism is cantilevered from the motor-housing base unit. This arm is hinged at the rear to facilitate removal of the bowl and mixing tools. The bowl remains stationary, and the mixing tools rotate with a planetary motion. Some mixers have additional drive points for a variety of attachments, such as blenders and mincers. The latest models have automatic electronic variable-speed control to maintain the optimum speed whatever the load.

How it works

These robust multi-purpose appliances have a powerful 700 to 800W electric motor fitted into the base unit. The shaft from the vertically mounted motor drives a toothed wheel made from hard-wearing plastic. This wheel is connected by a flexible toothed belt to a larger wheel mounted on top of a metal-cased gearbox, which turns the beaters and drives a slow-speed mincing attachment that can be mounted on the end of the arm when a coverplate has been removed.

The top end of the motor shaft serves as a drive point for a blender attachment; and on some models a coverplate at the far end of the arm shields a drive point for a juicer.

1 Toothed wheel on tip of drive shaft
2 Drive belt
3 Toothed wheel drives gearbox
4 Gearbox casing
5 Beater
6 Mincer drive
7 Juicer drive
8 Blender drive
9 Arm-latch button
10 Reset button
11 Control switch

SAFETY FIRST

Do not place a mixer on or near hot surfaces.

Don't allow water or other liquids to spill over the appliance.

Cleaning mixers

Switch off and unplug the appliance from the power socket. Remove the bowl and mixing tools from the mixer, and wash them in a solution of washing-up liquid and warm water. Wipe the casing of the machine with a damp cloth and make sure the switches are not contaminated with food particles.

MIXER IS EXCESSIVELY NOISY

Because they have metal gears and a powerful electric motor, tabletop mixers are generally relatively noisy when running. If your mixer seems nosier than usual, you may be able to narrow down the possible causes before asking a service engineer to investigate and repair any faults. To carry out any of these tests, you will need to remove the various plastic coverplates. Unplug the appliance before proceeding.

Removing coverplates

Lift off the cover that shields the high-speed drive for a blender attachment. Then operate the latch on the end of the arm to slide out the plate that covers the drive for a mincer, and remove the small plate that covers the juicer drive point.

1 Take off the blending-attachment locator by removing its screw fixings, then remove the stainless steel plate beneath it and the small thrust washer placed around the toothed drive wheel.

2 Lift up the arm cover and slide it forward until it detaches, revealing the drive belt and gearbox.

Damaged or worn gearbox

Remove the drive belt (see page 58), so that the gearbox is no longer connected to the motor.

By hand, spin the planet-hub assembly to turn the gearwheels. If the gears sound excessively noisy, your gearbox may need servicing – but inspect your planet-hub assembly (see page 58), too, before taking the appliance to a service centre.

Worn motor bearings

Having eliminated the gearbox as a source of excessive noise, leave the drive belt disconnected and replace all the covers temporarily. Turn the mixer on, so that you can detect whether worn motor bearings are making the appliance extra noisy. Have a suspect motor checked by a service engineer.

Remove small plastic cover to expose juicer drive

Lift off blender-drive coverplate

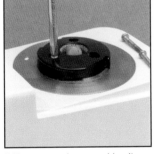

1 Unscrew and remove blending-attachment locator

2 Then remove arm cover

SAFETY FIRST

Always keep work surfaces around electrical equipment clean and dry.

Don't run a mixer with the bowl empty.

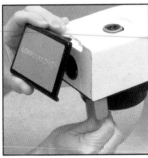

Operate latch in order to remove mincer-drive coverplate

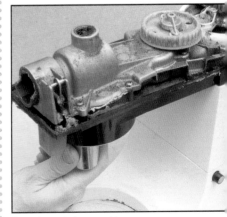

Spin planet-hub assembly

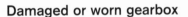

1 Undo nut and remove cover

Planet-hub assembly needs lubricating

Inspect the planet-hub mechanism mounted beneath the arm to see if it needs lubricating. This could be contributing to excessive noise.

1 Lift up the arm and undo the domed nut that holds the chromed cover in place. Ease the cover off.

2 Inspect the small gearwheel and the toothed rim inside the housing to make sure no teeth are missing. If they are all intact, clean the parts and lightly lubricate the gear teeth, using a multipurpose high-viscosity grease. Available from car-spares outlets and some hardware stores, this type of grease is coded EPL1 or NLGI1.

3 Ease the cover back into place, making sure that it is located on its shaft and that the teeth mesh snugly. Replace the domed nut.

BEATER NOT REVOLVING

Broken pin on shaft of beater

Generally, the beaters and whisks supplied with a good-quality tabletop mixer are extremely strong. However, before investigating further, check to see if the small locating pin on the beater shaft is intact. If it is broken, buy a replacement.

Broken or damaged drive belt

A loose drive belt or one with missing teeth may slip or judder, but once the belt breaks no movement can be transferred to the gearbox and the beater stops revolving altogether. To inspect the drive belt, remove the arm cover – see page 57.

1 If the belt is intact, check the tension by pinching the belt, close to the small drive wheel. If it is tensioned correctly, the two sides of the belt should be parallel just in front of the wheel. An excessively slack belt can be adjusted, but it needs an expert to do it properly.

2 To remove the belt, pull it upward while sliding it towards the larger toothed wheel.

2 Clean and lubricate parts

Check locating pin is intact

1 Check drive-belt tension

2 Slide belt towards large wheel

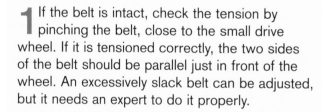

3 Inspect belt for cracks

4 Clean mixer, then replace belt

3 Turn the belt inside out to check for cracks or missing teeth. Replace a suspect belt before it breaks.

4 Before you replace the drive belt, clean accumulated food debris from the top of the gearbox and around the drive mechanism.

5 Place the new belt around the smaller wheel, then rotate the larger wheel as you ease the belt onto it.

Damaged planet-hub assembly

Serious damage to the planet-hub assembly will be obvious. The beater will probably stop revolving and there is likely to be a grinding noise from the mechanism. Switch off immediately to avoid further damage, and have the mechanism serviced.

Faulty gearbox

Perform the test described for a noisy gearbox. If the large toothed wheel does not spin or turns spasmodically, one or more of the gearwheels may have been stripped. Repairing a seriously damaged gearbox will be expensive, but it will probably cost less than the retail price of a good-quality mixer.

On older models a 'dogtooth' gear acts like a clutch on the gearbox. If a nylon pin on the top coverplate is worn or the dogtooth gear itself has broken, the gearbox will not be engaged. It is worth checking with a service centre, as either part should be replaceable at reasonable cost.

MIXER NOT RUNNING

Faulty plug or fuse
Check that the plug is wired correctly and replace a faulty fuse – see pages 17 and 19. If the fuse blows again as soon as you plug in and switch on, have the mixer checked by an expert.

Power failure
If other appliances on the circuit have stopped working, check the consumer unit for a blown fuse or tripped MCB or RCD – see pages 11 and 12.

Broken flex conductor
If on your mixer the flex is wired to easily accessible screw terminals, test the flex for continuity (see page 20) and replace it if necessary.

Overload cutout activated
Many tabletop mixers have a safety device that stops the appliance running if too much strain is put on the motor – for example, by mixing ingredients that are too thick.
Allow the motor to cool down, then operate the latch that lifts the arm. This reveals a reset button in the side of the appliance. Pushing in the reset button will allow you to switch the mixer on again.

Faulty control switch
Have a suspect switch tested by a service engineer – but check first that the plastic control knob is not just spinning on its shaft. The knob is usually a snug fit on a D-shaft or splined shaft. If the plastic cracks or wears, the knob may rotate without operating the appliance.

Faulty motor
A broken drive belt may give the impression that the mixer has stopped working, but you should be able to hear whether the motor is running. The most likely fault will be worn brushes, which can be replaced.

SAFETY FIRST

To prevent accidents, when blending, juicing or mincing attachments are not in use the plastic covers that shield their drive points should be kept in place. Check the covers regularly to make sure they are in good condition, and replace any that are cracked or no longer latch securely.

Don't leave a mixer unattended when it is plugged in.

If a mixer is earthed, use a continuity tester to verify there is a continuous earth path – see page 22.

STEAM IRONS

In the past, an electric iron was simply a source of heat for smoothing the wrinkles out of fabrics and it was necessary to dampen the cloth if the creases were particularly stubborn. Steam-generating irons have made the whole process much easier.

How it works

You fill the iron's reservoir with water and select the required temperature. Then, when the iron has been plugged in and switched on, an indicator light illuminates to tell you that the heating element built into the soleplate of the iron is heating up – a process that may take a minute or so. When the thermostat senses that the element has reached the required temperature, the indicator turns off and the iron is ready for use. The thermostat will continue to monitor the temperature, and will automatically switch the element on again when necessary.

Operating the steam selector opens a valve at the base of the reservoir that allows water to enter the steam chamber mounted directly above the heating element. Here the water is instantly turned to steam, which is emitted through vents in the soleplate. Standing the iron on its heel prevents water passing through the valve, so that no steam is generated until the iron is held soleplate down again. When the steam selector is turned off, the iron can be used dry for fabrics that would be harmed by excessive moisture.

On most models, pressing a button mounted on the handle expels a jet of water or steam to help take out deep wrinkles or cope with thick fabrics such as denim.

1 Temperature selector
2 Spray button
3 Spray nozzle
4 Steam selector
5 Control needle
6 Soleplate
7 Thermostat
8 Braided flex
9 Cord support
10 Cord clamp
11 Indicator light
12 Element

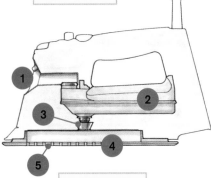

1 Water inlet
2 Water reservoir
3 Valve
4 Steam chamber
5 Vented soleplate

Variable steaming
On many irons, a steam selector allows you to regulate the amount of steam to suit different types of fabric.

Vertical steaming
Some irons are designed to generate steam even when the iron is held upright, so that you can induce wrinkles to drop from hanging clothes or curtains.

Anti-drip function
This prevents water dripping from the soleplate vents when the thermostat has been set to a temperature that is not hot enough to turn the water into steam.

Self-cleaning irons
Nowadays most steam irons can be filled with ordinary tap water. When it is heated, mineral salts dissolved in the water are deposited as lime scale (especially if the water is hard) – which eventually clogs up the vents and passageways within the iron. Self-cleaning irons are able to generate powerful jets of steam that flush out the scale. Others are fitted with silicone-coated valves that attract the mineral-salt deposits.

Some of these valves can be removed for descaling, but others are meant to be replaced when they become scaled up. Irons not similarly equipped need regular cleaning with a proprietary descaler.

STEAM SETTINGS

Adjust the steam selector to create the optimum amount of steam required for each category of fabrics. The normal ranges are:

No steam
Synthetics/silk
One-dot heat setting

Normal steam
Wool
Two-dot heat setting

Extra steam
Cotton/linen
Three-dot heat setting

Steam-ironing woollen textiles may raise a shine on the surface – so turn the garment inside out and iron the reverse side. Do the same when dry-ironing silk or synthetics.

Velvet and other fabrics that have a fine pile should be smoothed in the direction of the nap, with light pressure only. Keep the iron moving.

Don't iron over zips, buttons, rivets or press-studs. Metal items will score the soleplate, which may then snag on fabrics.

Cordless irons

Cordless irons are heated by means of a separate base unit that is plugged into a standard socket. The iron itself has no flex to get twisted or kinked. However, a cordless iron must be returned to its base unit at regular intervals in order to maintain the required temperature.

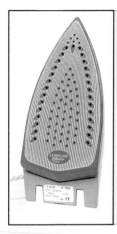

Coated soleplates

Aluminium or stainless-steel soleplates are often coated with chrome or porcelain enamel or with some other non-stick surface that allows the iron to glide effortlessly across the fabric. This not only makes the job of ironing easier and less tiring but also reduces wear on the fabric.

Auto-shutoff

This is a safety feature that cuts power to the heating element if the iron is left stationary on its soleplate for longer than 30 seconds or standing upright on its heel for a period of about 8 minutes. When buying a new iron, it's worth getting one with this invaluable safety feature.

Optimum temperatures

It's important to select the right temperature for the type of fabric you are ironing – too cool and the iron may not be able to remove the creases, too hot and the fabric could be damaged. Most fabrics and items of clothing are labelled with internationally recognized symbols denoting the recommended temperatures for ironing – see right.

Setting the temperature

Sort your ironing into three categories according to their labels, and start with synthetic garments that require the coolest setting. Gradually progress to the highest temperature setting. If a garment is a composite of different textiles, set the lowest recommended temperature.

If an item is not labelled, select a relatively low temperature and test the iron on an inconspicuous part of the garment.

One dot for cool, two for warm, three for hot

Ironing may damage the garment

When you have finished ironing

When you have finished, stand the iron upright on its heel, turn the steam selector off, and pull the plug from the socket. Allow the iron to cool down, then empty any water remaining in the reservoir into the sink. Wrap the flex carefully – a location for it is usually moulded into the casing or handle – and store the iron on its heel. Leaving an iron resting on its soleplate for long periods may result in serious corrosion.

Treating tap water

Even though your iron may be designed to be filled with tap water, most manufacturers recommend using some form of demineralized water if you live in a hard-water area. If need be, ask your local water authority for advice about the hardness of the water. You can buy special crystals for dissolving in tap water in order to reduce its mineral content.

Distilled water sold for topping up car batteries is not suitable, because it may contain acids that would harm your iron. However, it is possible to buy from supermarkets scented demineralized water produced specifically for use in steam irons.

1 Rub a dirty iron across a towel

2 Or clean the soleplate with diluted white vinegar

SAFETY FIRST

Take care when using steam – it can scald just as easily as hot water.

Don't leave a heated iron unattended, even while it is cooling down.

Make sure the plug is wired correctly and that the appropriate fuse is fitted.

Remove the plug from the socket before you refill the reservoir, or take a detachable reservoir to the tap.

STAINS ON IRONING

Dirty soleplate

Dirt, grease or traces of fabric dressing adhering to the soleplate of your iron will be transferred to the garments you are smoothing. Before cleaning the soleplate, check your owner's handbook to ensure you don't use materials that could harm a non-stick coating.

1 Select a hot setting and try rubbing the soleplate across an old towel.

2 If that doesn't work, unplug the iron and leave it to cool down. Dampen a paper towel with a solution of 1 part white vinegar to 2 parts water and use it to wipe the soleplate clean. Alternatively, use a proprietary soleplate cleaner – see below.

Melted fabric

If you have smoothed synthetic materials with a hot iron, melted fibres may be adhering to the soleplate.

1 Remove the worst of the deposits by selecting the maximum temperature setting and carefully wiping the soleplate with a thick pad of paper towels.

2 Allow the iron to cool down to a warm setting, then lightly rub a proprietary cleaning stick across the soleplate. Wipe it clean immediately with fresh paper towels.

CHALKY MARKS ON IRONING

Hard-water scaling

If your iron has not been descaled recently, it may spit out lime scale when you use the steam or water jet. How you descale an iron depends on whether it is self-cleaning.

Some irons are designed to be self-cleaning every time you finish ironing. This is achieved by resting the iron on its heel and selecting the maximum temperature. As soon as the indicator light goes out, unplug the iron and, holding it soleplate down over a sink, press the steam-jet button about 10 times in quick succession.

1 Rub off the worst of the deposits

2 Then use a cleaning stick

Most manufacturers recommend that their self-cleaning irons are descaled once a month. The exact procedure may vary from model to model, but in principle the reservoir should be a quarter full, with ordinary tap water, and then the maximum temperature selected. When the indicator light goes out, unplug the iron and hold it over the sink.

1 Turn the steam selector to the descaling position – at which point you will be able to pull the steam selector upward, causing hot water and steam to flush out the vents in the soleplate. Taking care to keep the soleplate about 150mm (6in) above the base of the sink, shake the iron gently back and forth.

2 When the reservoir is empty, pull the steam selector out of the iron. Soak the control needle at the base of the selector in white vinegar to remove any lime-scale deposits.

3 Replace the selector in the iron, taking care not to bend the needle. Heat the iron to maximum, then rub it across an old towel to clean the soleplate and vaporize any water remaining in the steam chamber.

Any iron not equipped with self-cleaning features should be flushed out regularly with a proprietary descaler, diluted according to the manufacturer's recommendations. A typical descaling procedure is described below, but always check the instructions supplied with the descaler – with some descalers, for example, it may be necessary to heat the iron.

1 Unplug the iron and pour descaler into the iron's reservoir and then adjust the iron to the 'steam' setting in order to open the valve to the steam chamber.

2 Shake the iron gently from side to side and briefly pump the solution through the iron's water-spray assembly.

3 Rest the iron, soleplate down, on a couple of wooden spoons laid in your sink. Leave the descaler to drain through the vents in the soleplate for about 30 minutes, then empty the reservoir and rinse it out two or three times with fresh water.

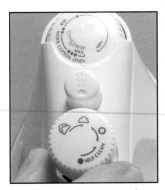
1 Pull steam selector upward to flush vents with steam

2 Soak needle in white vinegar

Pour descaler into the reservoir

3 Replace the selector in the iron

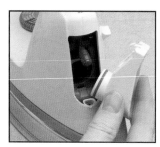

Turn steam selector off

The O-ring may need replacing

Ask a service engineer to check for leaking water-spray unit

WATER LEAKING FROM THE IRON

Temperature too low

If you are using the iron on a cool setting, the element is not hot enough to turn water into steam. Unless you have turned off the steam selector (or your iron has an anti-drip function), water will run through the steam chamber and out through the vents in the soleplate. Either turn up the temperature or switch the steam selector to 'off'.

Overfilled reservoir

Unplug the iron and empty some of the water. Turn off the steam, then rub the iron across an old towel until moisture in the steam chamber has evaporated.

Filler inlet leaking

Some steam irons have a detachable cover over the inlet through which water is poured into the iron. This cover is fitted with an O-ring seal, which may need replacing.

Water-spray unit leaking

The tube connecting the reservoir to the spray unit may be cracked, or the seals may be leaking. You will need a service engineer to replace these items.

Cracked or corroded reservoir

If the water reservoir is demountable, remove it and hold it over a sink so you can check it for leaks. Buy a replacement if necessary.

It can be difficult to detect leaks from an integral reservoir. The only way to make a thorough inspection would be to dismantle the iron down to the steam-chamber and soleplate assembly, so ask a service engineer to check the underside of the reservoir for leaking joints and corrosion. This is a straightforward procedure on many irons – but replacing major components may be uneconomical, so ask the service engineer for advice before proceeding.

Faulty thermostat

If the temperature isn't rising sufficiently to create steam even at a medium to high setting, have the thermostat tested by a service engineer.

A service engineer can check your reservoir for corrosion

POOR WATER SPRAY

Reservoir empty
When you press the spray button, if no water comes out, or it merely splutters from the nozzle, check that there's water in the reservoir. If it's empty, unplug the iron before refilling it.

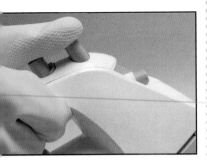
Pump descaler through the nozzle

Nozzle blocked
The tiny hole in the nozzle can become partially blocked with lime scale. Use a proprietary descaler, as described previously. Be sure to press the spray button several times to pump the descaler up into the nozzle, and leave it for the prescribed time to dissolve the scale. Descale your iron regularly to prevent this type of blockage.

IRON OVERHEATS
If the iron gets too hot at lower settings, check the following:

Broken temperature selector
Make sure the selector knob isn't broken and merely spinning on its shaft. This type of control knob is attached in various ways. The fittings described below are fairly typical – but if you cannot detach the selector easily, take your iron to a service centre for repair.

1 Some selector knobs have integrally moulded clips

1 Many selector knobs are made with a D-shaped hole that pushes onto a matching metal shaft. Some of these knobs have integrally moulded spring clips. To remove this type of selector, grip the rim on each side and ease the knob off its shaft, if necessary levering gently with the tip of a small screwdriver. Never apply too much force, or you may cause more damage.

Detach metal clips to remove knob

2 When you replace the selector knob, make sure it comes to a stop in the right places when you turn it.

2 Replace the knob and make sure it stops in the correct places

Other selector knobs are held in place with small wire clips that grip a collar moulded into the neck of the selector. Insert the tip of a small screwdriver under the selector in order to detach the spring clips from the collar. Leave the springs in place on the iron. When you push the new knob onto its shaft, the spring clips grip the neck automatically.

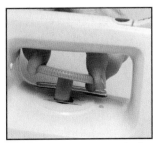
New knob engages automatically

SAFETY FIRST

When reassembling an iron, make sure the components and wiring are returned to their original locations.

Faulty thermostat
Have the iron checked by a service engineer to ensure the thermostat is working properly.

NO STEAM

If the soleplate heats up but there is no steam, check the following:

Reservoir empty
Refill with water.

Incorrect temperature setting
If the temperature is set too low, the water will not vaporize.

Incorrect steam setting
Check that the steam selector is not turned off.

Water valve or steam chamber scaled up
Use the iron's self-cleaning facility, or flush out the iron with a proprietary descaler – see pages 62 and 63.

IRON DOES NOT WORK

Faulty plug or fuse
Check that the plug is wired correctly and replace a faulty fuse – see pages 17 and 19. If the fuse blows again as soon as you plug in and switch on, have the appliance checked at a service centre.

Power failure
If other appliances on the circuit have stopped working, inspect your consumer unit for a blown fuse or tripped MCB or RCD – see page 11.

Broken flex conductor
This is a very common fault with electric irons. To subject the flex to a continuity test (see page 20), unplug the iron and remove the screws that hold the rear coverplate in position.

If the test reveals a broken conductor, you can replace the damaged flex with a length of matching braided flex (see page 18). However, you should ask a service engineer to replace crimped connectors.

Fill a detachable reservoir at the kitchen tap

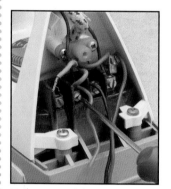
Make a note of the connections before undoing the screws

And then loosen the cord clamp

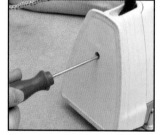
Unscrew the iron's coverplate

Removing the cover plate reveals the terminal block

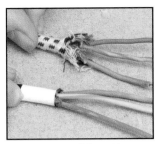

Bind new braided flex with tape
to prevent fraying

Slip on a new cord support

Before you strip off the sheathing to make the connections, bind insulating tape around the flex to prevent the cotton braid fraying.

Inspect the cord support at the flex entry point for splits. If in doubt, replace the support.

Having made the connections (see pages 19 and 20) and tightened the cord clamp, test the new flex for continuity. Make sure that all the wires are in their original locations before replacing the coverplate, then check for a continuous path to earth (see page 22). Before putting the appliance back into service, plug the iron into a circuit protected by an RCD – see below.

Faulty thermostat
If you suspect that the thermostat is faulty, have it checked by a service engineer.

Faulty heating element
On most irons the heating element is built into the soleplate, so replacing the element tends to be prohibitively expensive. If your service centre advises that replacement would be economical, ask them to test the element for continuity.

Have a faulty thermostat checked

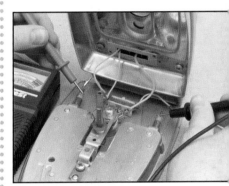

Have the heating element tested
at a service centre

SAFETY FIRST

Don't wrap the flex around an iron until the iron has been left to cool thoroughly.

Check the flex regularly for signs of wear and tear. Replace a damaged flex immediately.

Never clean an iron by immersing it in water.

Before servicing or maintaining an iron, always pull the plug out of the socket.

Before putting it back into service, test an iron by plugging it into a circuit protected by an RCD – see page 11. If the RCD trips have the appliance tested by a service engineer.

When an appliance is earthed, you should always use a continuity tester to verify there is a continuous earth path – see page 22. In the case of the irons described here, the earth path was tested by placing one probe of a continuity tester on the earth pin of the plug, and the other probe on the exposed metal edge of the soleplate. If the iron has a coated soleplate, insert the probe into a steam vent or into the gap between the soleplate and the shell of the iron to make sure the probe is in contact with uncoated metal.

TOOTHBRUSHES

Rechargeable electric toothbrushes are clinically proven to remove more plaque than manual toothbrushes do. Although relatively expensive, if properly maintained these appliances provide good service for at least five years. Brush heads can be swapped easily, enabling various members of the family to share a single powered handle but have their own individual brush.

How it works

The cleaning action is provided by an oscillating cylindrical bristle brush located at the end of the brush-head stem. The hollow stem incorporates a miniature gearbox, and is plugged onto the drive spindle of the handle. The handle, which is made as a non-serviceable sealed unit, incorporates a small low-voltage electric motor, a circuit board and a rechargeable battery cell. Some handles are made with an external sliding switch. Others have the switch concealed behind a flexible rubberized cover.

Each toothbrush comes with a charging unit on which the handle is parked for recharging. The charger is also a sealed unit – because the power is transmitted by induction to the battery in the brush handle, there are no metal-to-metal contacts between the charger and handle. The charger can be used safely in a bathroom and is fitted with a two-pin moulded plug for use with a shaver socket. If a shaver socket is not available, the charger can be plugged into a conventional socket elsewhere in the house, using a suitable adapter. A compartment may be provided in the casing of the charger for storing brush heads.

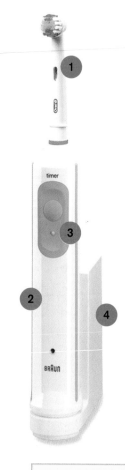

1 Brush-head stem
2 Handle
3 Concealed switch
4 Charger

Charging the battery

When charging a new unit, first place the handle on the charger – a green light will illuminate to indicate that the battery is now on charge. Leave it for the period specified by the manufacturer (typically about 16 hours), then remove the handle from the charger and leave the toothbrush running until the power is drained completely. Replace the handle on the charger and recharge for a further 16 hours or so, depending on the manufacturer's recommendations. It pays to carry out this procedure once every six months or so to keep the battery cell in good condition.

For optimum performance, it's best to leave the unit on permanent charge – it is impossible to overcharge the battery.

Pulsing action

To enhance the cleaning action, the latest models have a pulsing motion, which makes the brush move back and forth while oscillating.

Two-minute warning

Toothbrushes fitted with a built-in timer stutter for a few seconds to indicate that two minutes has elapsed since you switched on – the minimum time recommended for brushing your teeth. After this, the motor will run normally again so that you can clean your teeth for longer. With some models you can select a speed that is more comfortable for sensitive teeth and gums.

CLEANING A RECHARGEABLE TOOTHBRUSH

After brushing your teeth, rinse the brush head under running water with the motor running. Flush the bristle head and stem with water and dry the toothbrush with a paper tissue.

About once a week, remove the brush head and flush it through from the tail end to clean the inside. Wipe the drive shaft and handle with a damp cloth. Do this more frequently if you live in a hard-water area to prevent a build-up of lime scale.

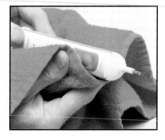

If a black sludge begins to build up on the brush, avoid using toothpaste that includes a whitening agent. Although harmless, residue from whitening agents lodge in crevices and cause this type of discoloration.

Sludge can go unnoticed behind the sliding switch that features on older models. To clean behind this type of switch, slide it backwards until it disengages, then scrub off the residue with a nailbrush under running water. When all parts are clean, press and slide the switch back into position, making sure it is the right way round.

Occasionally, unplug the charger and wipe it with a damp cloth. If your charger has a brush-head storage insert, take it out and wash it under running water. Dry the insert thoroughly before you replace it.

SAFETY FIRST

Rechargeable batteries should not be thrown away with normal domestic waste. Once a unit has failed, return it to the manufacturer's service centre for safe disposal.

BRUSH SWITCHES ITSELF ON

Water getting inside
A cracked casing or a split rubberized switch cover will allow water to penetrate. This type of damage is irreparable.

GREEN LIGHT NOT WORKING

When the toothbrush handle is plugged onto its charger, the green illuminator should light up. Make sure the charger is plugged in, then check the following:

Power failure
If other appliances on the circuit have stopped working, inspect your consumer unit for a blown fuse or tripped MCB or RCD – see pages 11 and 12.

Faulty charger
A non-contact voltage tester placed against the charging spigot will tell you whether current is present. If it looks like the unit has failed, you will almost certainly have to buy a new set, complete with brush holder.

BRUSH NOT WORKING

Water getting inside
If the handle is dropped, it could crack and water could seep into the casing.

Excessive pressure applied to the spindle while you are brushing your teeth may cause the seal to leak.

A rubberized switch cover could have split and allowed water to penetrate.

With any of these faults, an electric toothbrush brush is probably irreparable.

Battery not charging
The battery cell may have failed. First check your charger with a non-contact voltage tester (see above). If power is present, ask your service centre whether you can obtain a replacement brush handle.

Faulty charger
See above.

Time and pressure indicators
Brushes are made with coloured bristles that are designed to fade over a set period, indicating that it is time to replace the head. In any case, dentists recommend that you discard a brush head after three months, or even sooner if the bristles become bent or distorted.

Bent bristles are a sure sign that you are pressing too hard – a light guiding pressure is all that's required. The latest models have a pressure indicator to warn you. This may be a spring-loaded head that reacts to too much pressure or the pulsing action cuts out.

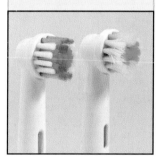

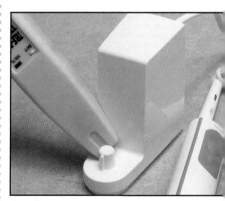

Aim a non-contact tester at the charging spigot

ELECTRIC SHAVERS

Even those who swear by wet shaving with a razor may take a portable electric shaver on business trips and holidays. The sheer convenience of being able to shave in a matter of moments almost anywhere makes these small appliances indispensable. Modern shavers are extremely reliable, provided they are cleaned regularly and the cutters are replaced as soon as renewal is indicated.

How it works

Electric shavers are either mains powered (in which case they are supplied with a coiled flex and two-pin plug) or are made to take dry-cell or rechargeable batteries.

Mains-powered shavers are plugged into special shaver sockets that are permitted in bathrooms because they contain a transformer that isolates the user side of the unit from the mains, reducing the risk of electric shock. This type of shaver usually has dual voltage, with a selector switch that can be set to 210–230V for use in Europe or to 110–130V, which is the American standard voltage. Some shavers are made to adapt automatically to the required voltage.

Foil shavers

A foil shaver (the most common type) has a straight shaving head, comprising a perforated screen that covers a multi-bladed cutter block mounted on top of a yoke that moves rapidly from side to side. This oscillation is created by a vibrating motor, which consists of a pair of magnetized coils that act like solenoids, shunting the yoke back and forth against a pair of opposing springs.

With some foil shavers, a similar action is produced by a rotary electric motor connected to the cutter block by a crank mechanism.

1 Perforated screen
2 Cutter block
3 Yoke
4 Shaving-head release button
5 On/off switch

1 Circular cutter
2 Slotted screen
3 Drive shaft
4 On/off switch
5 Lead

Rotary shavers

A rotary shaver has a group of shaving heads, each consisting of a circular cutter that rotates at speed beneath a matching slotted guard or screen. As the cutters cannot be sharpened, they need to be replaced as soon as they become blunt. These shavers are usually fitted with a rotary electric motor, which is connected to the shaving heads by means of geared drive shafts.

SAFETY FIRST

Always unplug a shaver before cleaning or changing cutters.

Don't allow an electric shaver to become wet unless it has been designed specifically for rinsing with running water – check your user's manual.

Don't dismantle the casing of a waterproof (wet-and-dry) electric shaver.

POOR SHAVE

Clogged shaving head

If you fail to clean shaving heads regularly, their efficiency drops off rapidly. Some electric shavers can be rinsed with running water, but as most shavers should never come into contact with water, it is essential to check your user's handbook.

1 After each shave, switch off and unplug a foil shaver, then press the shaving-head release buttons.

2 Tap the back of the shaving head on a flat surface to remove hair. The foil is so thin that brushing may damage it – check your user's handbook.

3 Clean the cutter block, using the soft-bristle brush supplied with your shaver.

4 Some manufacturers supply a cleaning agent for spraying onto the cutter block once a month before brushing.

5 If your skin is very dry, apply a proprietary shaving oil to your face. Alternatively, smearing the screen with a drop of the same oil may make for a smoother shave – check your user's handbook.

To clean a rotary shaver, unplug it and lightly brush across the shaving heads to remove beard particles. Then open the head assembly, so you can brush it out.

Every week, lift off the shaving-head retaining plate and lift out each cutter and screen, so you can clean them separately. For best results, don't mix up the cutters and screens.

BLUNT CUTTERS

Any shaver should give good service for a year or so before you have to change the cutters – but replace the cutter block as soon as you notice that the cutters are becoming blunt.

1 Press head release buttons

2 Tap shaving head on worktop

3 Brush cutter block

SAFETY FIRST

Don't drop used rechargeable batteries into the waste bin, and never throw them onto a fire. Dispose of batteries that are at the end of their useful life by taking them to a shaver service centre or a designated refuse tip (your local authority will tell you where the nearest one is located).

Lightly brush across shaving heads

Take off head assembly and clean

Lift out cutters and screens

Brush each one individually

Replace a blunt cutter block

The cutter block on a foil shaver detaches in one piece. Some pull straight off, others have to be turned through 90 degrees first. Check your user's handbook. Even when blunt, the edges of the individual cutters can still cut your skin – take care.

When replacing blunt rotary-shaver cutters, change all the shaving heads at the same time.

Damaged screen

A visual examination should reveal holes or cracks in a foil screen. The damage has probably taken the edge off the cutters, so you may need to replace the cutter block at the same time. When refitting the head, take care not to dent the foil.

NOISY SHAVER

Clogged shaving head

Remove the shaving head, then brush across the cutter block to clean out between the individual cutters. Replace the shaving head and lubricate the screen with a proprietary shaving oil.

Damaged screen

If the cutters are rubbing against a damaged screen or guard, replace both parts.

SLOW RUNNING

Flat battery

Recharge the battery. If it will not hold a charge, check whether it is possible to replace it.

Screen fouling the cutter

If your shaver is not running properly after you have changed the cutter block or shaving head, check that you have fitted both components properly.

SHAVER GETS HOT

Poor flex connection

If the contacts inside your shaver lead show signs of burning, buy a replacement lead before it damages the shaver irreparably.

Faulty motor or battery

Have your shaver checked out at a service centre.

Check the foil screen for damage

Check lead for poor connections

SHAVER WON'T WORK AT ALL

Incorrect voltage setting

Check that the setting hasn't accidentally been reset.

Cutter jammed

Take out the cutter block and run the shaver to see if the motor runs freely. If it does, the fault is probably a jammed cutter block. Check to see if the inside of the screen is damaged and, if necessary, replace the cutter block and screen.

Faulty flex or plug

Check the flex with a continuity tester (see page 20), putting one probe on a plug pin and the other probe into a contact at the shaver end of the lead. Trial and error will soon tell you whether the lead is faulty.

To check that there is not an intermittent fault, continue to hold both probes in place and ask someone to bend gently the flex back and forth, gradually working along the lead. Buy a replacement for a suspect lead.

Faulty on/off switch

Have the switch checked at a service centre.

Faulty charger

If you're able to borrow an identical charger, you can determine whether your shaver is capable of holding a charge. Alternatively, have the charger tested by a service centre.

Faulty motor

With both types of shaver, the motor can only be serviced thoroughly by a qualified engineer.

Washing-machine element

1 Check that connectors fit snugly

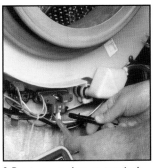

2 Put tester probes on terminals

MACHINE WON'T HEAT UP

Faulty water-level switch
A faulty pressure switch may not be able to detect that there is sufficient water in the drum to switch on the heater. Check the switch and replace it if necessary – see opposite.

Furred-up heating element
The heating element in a washing machine is similar to the ones used in electric kettles. It also suffers from similar hard-water problems, which cause lime scale to coat the element and reduce its efficiency. In most machines it is impossible to inspect the element without removing it. In principle, this ought to be a straightforward procedure; but in practice it can be difficult to dislodge an element that has been in place for a long time. On balance, it's probably worth having the element inspected by a service engineer. Installing a water softener or placing proprietary water-softening tablets in the drum may help prevent scaling in the future.

Faulty heating element
As with all electrical components, a break in the circuit will prevent the flow of current – in which case, the heating element won't work.

1 The electrical connections on the end of the element may be loose or corroded. Make sure they fit snugly and, if possible, clean the terminals with fine emery paper.

2 A break within the element can be detected by connecting the probes of a continuity tester to the terminals – but make sure at least one wire is disconnected first. If the element appears to be faulty, call out a service engineer to replace it.

Faulty thermostat
Depending on the design of the machine, the thermostat that measures the temperature of the water may be mounted on the front, rear or underside of the tub. If a faulty thermostat gives a false reading, it may switch off the heating element before the water gets hot. Once again, it is worth checking that the electrical connections are sound – but testing and replacing a thermostat is best left to a service engineer.

SAFETY FIRST
Always unplug a washing machine before you pull it away from the wall and start checking for faults. See also *Switching off the power* page 13. Before you touch any component inside a washing machine, as a final check that the power is off, remove the casing from the appliance and aim a non-contact voltage tester at the internal terminal block to which the flex is connected – see page 122. If you are not absolutely certain an appliance is disconnected safely, get a service engineer to isolate and inspect it. Never take a risk.

Have your thermostat tested

SAFETY FIRST

A capacitor is fitted in many washing machines in order to start up the electric motor. A capacitor can hold a charge for a short while after the machine is turned off. As a precaution, unplug any washing machine and wait 10 to 15 minutes to allow the capacitor to discharge before removing access panels. (Capacitors in television sets and microwave ovens retain very high voltages – which is why you should never remove a back panel or other coverplates from these appliances.)

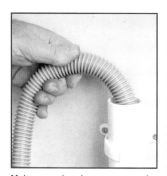

Make sure there's space around the hose, to prevent siphoning

MACHINE STOPS DURING CYCLE

Programme setting
Make sure the programmer has not been set on 'rinse-hold' or a similar 'anti-crease' setting.

Power failure
If other appliances on the circuit have stopped working, inspect your consumer unit for a blown fuse or tripped MCB or RCD – pages 11 and 12.

Plug or FCU fuse has blown
Replace the fuse in the plug – page 17. If there is a fused connection unit, check whether the fuse in the FCU needs to be replaced – see page 17.

Blocked hose
Flush blockages from inlet and outlet hoses – see pages 76–7 and 79. Dismantle a sealed anti-siphon outlet device to remove a blockage.

Blocked or faulty pump
Dismantle pump to check that the impeller can move freely – see page 84. If necessary, replace the pump.

Blocked or faulty inlet valve
Clean the valve filter – see page 79. Replace a faulty inlet valve.

Water siphoning through outlet hose
This causes the machine to continue filling, so it's unable to advance through the selected programme. Check fit of outlet hose in standpipe.

Faulty thermostat
Have it checked and replaced by a service engineer – see page 81.

Faulty heating element
Check electrical contacts before you call out a service engineer – see page 81.

Faulty timer
The timer is an integral part of the programmer. It is usually situated at the front of the machine and is set by means of buttons or a large selector knob. The timer is a sophisticated piece of equipment, which can only be tested and replaced by a qualified service engineer.

Dismantle a sealed outlet device to remove a blockage

Have a faulty motor replaced

Slip the drive belt off the pulley –
wear gloves if edges are sharp

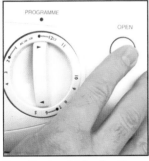

Press the door latch a few times

If you suspect the door lock is
faulty, have it tested and replaced

Faulty motor

The motor that drives the drum may be faulty. One
simple test is to remove the drive belt, set the
programme to 'spin' and then temporarily replace
the cover panels. Plug in the machine to see if the
motor runs. If nothing happens or the motor merely
hums, have it tested and replaced by an engineer.

MACHINE WON'T SPIN

Programme setting

Has the programmer been set on 'rinse-hold', or
a similar 'anti-crease' setting?

Drive belt slipping

With some machines you can adjust the tension
on the drive belt that connects the motor and
drum. To do this, slacken the bolt in the slotted
arm attached to the motor. Move the motor
downward slightly to put a little extra tension on
the belt, then tighten the bolt. Don't overdo it, or
you will strain the motor bearing. Test the
adjustment by moving the belt sideways – a
movement of about 12mm (½in) is normal.

On many machines, you can't adjust belt tension.
Replacement is your only option. If the edges of
the metal panels are sharp, wear protective gloves.

1 Pull the drive belt towards you while turning
the drum pulley clockwise. The ribbed belt
will ride out of the grooves on the pulley.

2 Install a new belt by reversing the procedure
– make sure you buy the correct size.

Faulty door lock

If the interlock safety device is faulty, it can prevent
the drum spinning. Before doing anything else,
hold the door closed and press the button a few
times in case the latch has stuck. If you suspect
the lock may be faulty, it's usually easy to replace it
with a new one. However, there are many different
types of door lock, including computer-controlled
devices. It makes economic sense to have this
type of lock tested before you have it replaced.

Faulty motor

See top of page.

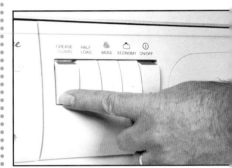

Is the programme set to pause?

MACHINE WILL NOT EMPTY

Programme delayed

Make sure the programmer has not been set on 'rinse hold' or a similar 'anti-crease' setting.

Outlet hose blocked or kinked

Flush the hose under running water, then run a marble through the hose to make sure a coin hasn't got stuck inside.

Outlet filter blocked

Some machines are fitted with a filter that prevents foreign bodies reaching the pump. These filters can usually be extracted from a small hatch near the base of the machine. Flush the filter with water.

Wash the outlet filter regularly

Pump blocked or jammed

Is the impeller within the pump free to move? Unplug the machine and turn it on its side – the pump is invariably near the base of the machine.

1 Fold up a towel to catch any water, then undo the clips holding the hoses to the pump. Check both hoses to make sure they are not blocked.

2 Using a pencil, carefully probe inside the pump and turn the impeller. Some impellers turn with a somewhat jerky motion – this is quite normal. If the impeller won't turn easily, dismantle the pump to remove a possible blockage. Ease the electrical connections from the pump, then undo the bolts that hold it in place.

3 Remove the screws or dislodge the spring clips that hold the two parts of the pump together. Make a mark on both halves of the pump before dismantling it, so you can orientate the components when you put them together again.

4 Check the impeller chamber for blockages, or threads wound around the impeller shaft. Wash the pump, then reassemble it. If there are no blockages, the easiest option is to fit a new pump.

Faulty water-level switch

A faulty water-level switch will not detect water in the tub. Look for blockages and leaks in the system (see pages 79–80); then if necessary, replace the switch.

1 Take the hoses off the pump

2 Undo the bolts that hold the pump in place

3 Dismantle the pump

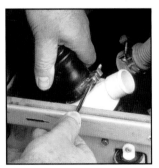

4 Reassemble the clean pump

Clean dirty terminals

Faulty wiring
Having unplugged the machine, check that there are no loose connections and clean dirty or corroded terminals with fine emery paper. If that fails, have the wiring tested by an electrician.

Faulty timer
The timer may not be allowing the programme to advance – see page 78.

WATER LEAKING FROM MACHINE

Loose hose clip
Check for signs of water staining around the hose clips. Tighten screw-type clips with a screwdriver. Loosening and moving a clip can sometimes result in a better grip on the hose.

Split hose
Turn off the valves, then disconnect the inlet hoses and drain them. Inspect these and other hoses for splits, and replace any damaged ones.

Misaligned door seal
The door seal bridges the gap between the tub and the shell of the washing machine. If the door glass doesn't fit snugly against the seal, it will leak. Manipulate the seal with your fingers to check that it is not dislodged, and make sure the clamp band or plastic flange that holds it in place is firmly fixed.

Damaged door seal
There are a number of different door seals, and some are difficult to replace. Unless your seal is one of the simple band-fixed types described here, get a service engineer to replace it for you.

1 Remove the outer clamp band or plastic flange (if fitted), then grasp the seal and pull it down to free it from the edge of the casing. Removing the seal may reveal sharp edges – so take care.

2 If on your machine the seal is connected to the detergent dispenser, undo that connection next.

3 Then loosen the metal or nylon clamp band holding the seal to the tub. Remove the band and pull the seal free.

SAFETY FIRST

Carefully brush away dust created by cleaning terminals with emery paper.

Tighten the hose clips

Check the door seal fits properly

1 Remove the outer clamp band

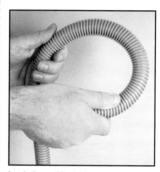

Look for splits in hoses

2 Undo dispenser connection

3 Loosen the inner clamp band

Have a noisy motor checked by a service engineer

Empty the pockets before you put clothing into the machine

4 Buy a new seal that matches the one you have just removed, then reassemble the connections in the reverse order. When positioning the new seal, make sure it fits snugly all round. Check that the clamp band or fixing clips are refitted correctly.

SERIOUS OVERFLOW

Outlet hose detached
Make sure the drain hose is correctly positioned in the standpipe – see pages 74–5.

Blocked drainpipe
Check that the standpipe and drainpipe to which the hose is connected are not blocked.

Inlet hose detached
Ensure all hose clips are in place. Check that the hoses are firmly attached to the hot and cold valves behind the machine.

Continuous filling
Unless you can detect obvious faults with the pressure-switch system (see pages 79–80) or the inlet valves (see page 79), have both systems tested and replaced by an engineer.

NOISY WHEN RUNNING

Coins in the drum
Rattling when the machine is running may be the result of metallic objects, such as coins or keys, that have fallen out of pockets. When the wash has finished, remove them from the drum. Objects that have fallen through to the tub can cause serious damage. Have them removed by an expert.

Faulty door switch
If there is a buzzing noise that stops when you hold the door closed, the safety switch is probably faulty and may need replacing. Obtain expert advice.

Drive belt slipping
A high-pitched squeal could indicate that the drive belt needs tensioning or replacing – see page 83. Or it could indicate worn motor bearings. Have the motor checked by a service engineer.

4 Reassemble with a new seal

SAFETY FIRST

To check that a washing machine is earthed, apply one probe of a continuity tester to the earth pin of the plug and touch the exposed head of a panel-fixing screw or an unpainted part of the metal casing or cover panels with the other probe. The tester's indicator will be activated if the metal components are earthed. If it is not activated, have the machine checked by a service engineer.

If your machine is connected to a fused connection unit (see page 14), to check that the appliance is earthed perform the same test but, instead of placing the one probe on the earth pin of the plug, apply it to one of the two fixing screws that hold the FCU's faceplate in place. These fixing screws are connected to earth inside the fused connection unit, and the tester's indicator will be activated if the earth in the appliance is connected to earth in the FCU.

Drum bearing

Grating or rumbling indicates that the drum bearing may need replacing.

MACHINE VIBRATES EXCESSIVELY

Overloaded machine

If possible, remove some of the load to reduce weight. See optimum loads, page 75.

Load not distributed evenly

If you can, redistribute and untangle the load or remove especially heavy items.

Adjust feet to level a machine

Machine not level

A washing machine should rest squarely on all four feet. Level a machine that is rocking, by adjusting the feet at the front. If there's no means of adjustment, chock up one wheel with corrugated cardboard.

Loose suspension springs

Check that none of the tub's suspension springs have broken or come adrift.

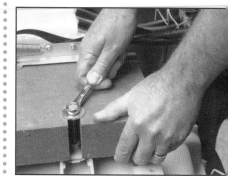
Tighten bolts holding the weights

Loose counterweights

Heavy weights, usually made from cast concrete, are bolted to the tub to stabilize the machine. Make sure the bolts have not worked loose. A cracked weight will have to be replaced.

DOOR WON'T OPEN

Safety-lock delay

The safety lock is designed to prevent the door being opened until the drum has stopped moving. It's quite usual to wait for as much as 2 minutes.

Faulty door switch

If you have to wait longer than that, the switch may need replacing.

Water still in the tub

If all the water has not pumped out, the door switch may not activate. Drain the machine, then check for wrong programme setting, blocked pipes and jammed pump.

Make sure springs are attached

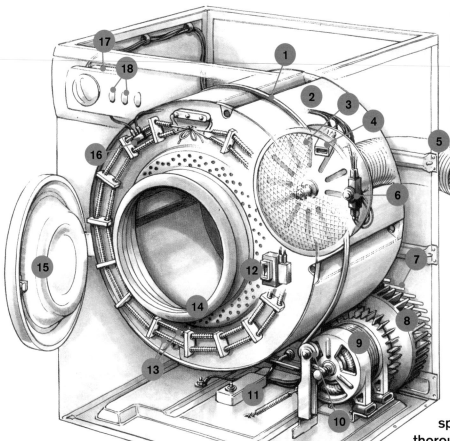

Pressurized system

1 Drive belt	11 Terminal block
2 Drum	12 Door latch
3 Filter	13 Heating element
4 Thermal fuse	14 Door seal
5 Vent hose	15 Door
6 Thermostat	16 Thermal-overload cutout
7 Air-inlet grille	17 Timer
8 Fan	18 Temperature controls
9 Electric motor	
10 Jockey pulley	

Vented tumble dryer

TUMBLE DRYERS

Nowadays most people regard electric clothes dryers as indispensable – especially in areas where the weather is too unreliable to dry clothes outdoors.

Tumble dryers are primarily designed to be used in combination with an automatic washing machine that spin-dries the clothing to remove most of the moisture. There are also washer dryers, which combine both functions in one machine. These are convenient where kitchen or laundry space is limited, but they can usually only tumble-dry half the full load of washing at a time. Also, with these machines, it is impossible to wash one load while another is drying.

Hand-washed items have to be spin-dried separately or wrung dry thoroughly by hand before they are put into a tumble dryer.

The dryers described here are electrically heated. Except for cleaning filters and other routine maintenance recommended by the manufacturers, gas-heated tumble dryers must be serviced by a qualified technician.

How it works

Although the arrangement of components may vary from model to model, most tumble dryers work on similar principles.

Fresh air is warmed and passed through the washing as it is turned over and over in a slowly rotating drum. As the washing dries, the moisture-laden air is usually extracted through the back of the machine.

An electrically driven fan draws air through an inlet grille into the cabinet, where it is warmed by heating elements. The warm air then passes through perforations in the drum, which is kept in motion by a drive belt connected to the same electric motor that turns the fan. A removable filter within the airflow traps fluff (lint) given off by the drying fabrics, preventing it being extracted along with the hot moist air that leaves the appliance via the outlet vent.

A thermostat that senses the temperature of the air being extracted automatically switches the heaters off and on, as necessary, to maintain the optimum temperature in the drum. A separate thermal-overload cutout (TOC) will switch off the heaters if there is a risk of overheating. With some machines the TOC resets automatically after

1 Drive belt	13 Timer
2 Jockey pulley	14 Temperature controls
3 Air-inlet grille	
4 Electric motor	15 Terminal block
5 Capacitor	16 Drum
6 Fan	17 Thermal fuse
7 Door latch	18 Heating element
8 Filter	19 Thermal-overload cutout
9 Door seal	
10 Door	20 Thermostat
11 Door safety-switch peg	21 Rear drum bearing
	22 Vent hose
12 Door switch	

the elements have cooled; with others you have to press a reset button before the dryer will switch on again.

Nearly all dryers have at least two heat settings, to suit different fabrics, and a timer that switches off the appliance after a period of time selected by the user. In order to reduce creasing, most machines will turn off the heating elements about 10 to 15 minutes before the appliance is finally switched off, allowing the washing to continue tumbling through a stream of cool air. Depending on the combination of settings, you can dry the load completely or leave the washing slightly damp for easier ironing.

Features to look for

If you are thinking of buying a new tumble dryer, you may want to look for the following features.

Reverse tumble action

Basic tumble dryers have a drum that rotates in one direction only. A machine that can reverse the direction of rotation at regular intervals dries the washing more efficiently and reduces tangling.

Crease guard

After the cooling-down period at the end of the cycle, some dryers rotate the drum periodically for a few seconds in order to reduce creasing. This 'crease-guard action' takes place for about an hour, during which time some form of audible warning reminds you it's time to empty the machine.

Auto sensing of temperature

With most models you can select a high or low temperature, depending on what kind of fabrics you are drying, and the selected temperature is regulated throughout the tumbling period set on the timer. More sophisticated dryers can measure the moisture content of the extracted air and will switch off the settings as soon as they detect the washing is dry, regardless of the timer setting. This not only saves electricity but helps preserve the fabrics.

Suction system

Rear-mounted fans

In some dryers, the fan is mounted just behind the filter in the back of the drum. With this type of dryer, the drum and fan are driven by two separate belts connected to the same electric motor. On some models, removing a separate coverplate exposes the fan belt without having to remove the appliance's back panel.

A kit can be adapted for venting through masonry or glass

Venting the moist air

At one time, tumble-dryer users allowed their machines to vent directly into the utility room or kitchen. Today we are more aware of the problems caused by condensation, so tend to dispose of the moisture-laden air outside. To this end, most appliance manufacturers now supply a corrugated vent hose and the necessary attachments with their dryers. If your machine is not equipped with adequate means of extraction, you can buy tumble-dryer venting kits by mail order, which come with a length of hose and plastic ducting for installing in a wall or window close to your machine. At the same time, you can order the necessary connector for attaching the hose to your particular model.

Cut a hole through the wall, using a power drill and cold chisel. Then insert the ducting and, following the instructions supplied with the kit, screw the ducting fixing plates to both sides of the wall. With the hose attached to the tumble dryer's air vent, plug the other end onto the ducting; then slide the dryer into position, making sure the hose is not crushed or kinked.

Alternatively, have a glazier cut a circular hole in a windowpane and clamp the fixing plates on both sides of the glass, using the screws and gasket provided.

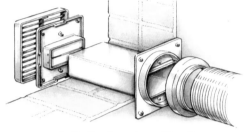

Venting through a solid wall

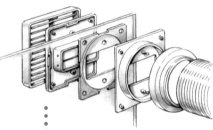

Venting through a window

Stacking machines

To save floor space, it is possible to stand a tumble dryer on top of a washing machine. This is perfectly safe if the manufacturer is able to supply a kit that holds the two machines together securely. Don't stack a machine that cannot be secured with a purpose-made connecting kit.

Condensing dryers

A radically different system is employed in tumble dryers that are designed for locations where it is difficult or impossible to vent the moist air to the outside. The hot air extracted from the rotating drum passes over a condensing plate or duct that turns the moisture vapour into liquid water, which collects in a reservoir at the base of the machine. After the moisture has been extracted, the air is passed over the heaters and back into the drum.

Condensing tumble dryer

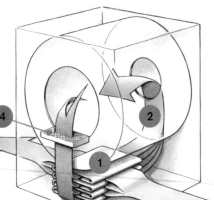

Airflow through a condensing dryer

1 Condenser
2 Circulating air
3 Cooling airflow
4 Filter

The water is either pumped directly to a waste outlet or the reservoir has to be emptied periodically.

The condenser is usually cooled by a separate flow of air that is vented into the room through grilles in the front or side of the dryer. Alternatively, cooling is achieved by circulating cold water through the condenser – this system, which relies on plumbing to supply and drain the water, is relatively expensive.

Although condensing dryers may exhibit some of the symptoms associated with vented dryers, it is best to leave internal servicing to an expert. However, it is important to clean the condenser in your machine at regular intervals to prevent a thick accumulation of fluff, which may be difficult to remove.

Condensing kit

Turn an ordinary vented dryer into a condensing dryer with a simple plastic box filled with ice cubes. The kit comes complete with a length of flexible hose to connect the box to your dryer's outlet vent. The condensing kit is an ideal stopgap if you move to a flat that has no means of venting your old machine to the outside.

What can you tumble-dry?

You can dry most cotton and man-made fibres in a heated tumble dryer. If you are in any doubt, look for International Care Labelling Codes printed or sewn onto your clothing. They come in the form of symbols that indicate the most suitable method of drying for a particular garment.

A circle within a square means it can be tumble-dried safely. A single dot indicates that a low heat setting should be selected. Select a high temperature if the symbol contains two dots. If the same symbol is crossed through, leave the garment to dry naturally.

Unless specified otherwise by the manufacturer, it is unwise to tumble-dry woollen clothing and blankets.

Don't put items made from or containing foamed rubber or plastic into a dryer. Check the labels carefully before drying garments with PVC or leather trimmings.

Never put items that have been dry-cleaned into a tumble dryer. The chemicals used in the dry-

CLEANING THE CONDENSER

The condenser is located behind a small latched and sealed door on the front of the dryer. The condenser unit, consisting of a series of rectangular aluminium tubes, must be handled with care to avoid damaging the extremely thin metal components. Aluminium tends to tarnish with use, but this does not affect the operation of the condenser.

1 Switch off and unplug the dryer, then remove the condenser unit, following the manufacturer's instructions. With most models, this is achieved by opening the access door and unclipping the unit before pulling it out of the dryer.

2 Rinse the tubing thoroughly under running water – a shower sprayhead is ideal for the purpose. Don't use a brush or other implements to remove fluff from the condenser. Gently shake off excess water and put the condenser aside to drain naturally.

3 Before you refit the condenser, clean out the recess in which the unit is housed, and wipe the seals around the access door, using a damp cloth.

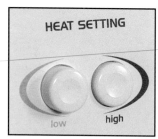

Temperature controls

Timer control

Temperature settings and timing
Although manufacturers' advice varies from model to model, generally a high heat setting is recommended for items made from cotton and a low setting for synthetics. However, you may need to experiment with the timing to ascertain what works best for your washing, and also decide whether you want the items bone dry or slightly damp for ironing. Use the settings recommended in your user's handbook as a guide, but also check the International Care Labelling Codes on each garment – see page 91.

cleaning process may produce harmful fumes when heated. Similarly, you should never tumble-dry any items that have been impregnated with flammable substances such as petrol, oil or lighter fluid.

Clothing with metal studs, buttons or zips should be turned inside out, to prevent damage to the inside of the dryer's drum and also to prevent these metal fixings snagging other clothing.

Capacity
The maximum dry-weight capacity of tumble dryers ranges from 3 to 6kg (6.6 to 13.2lb). Avoid overloading your tumble dryer – the garments will not dry efficiently and the appliance will suffer unnecessary wear and tear. With experience, you should be able to estimate a safe load for your dryer, as recommended in the user's handbook.

Even though they may not exceed the maximum capacity of your machine, it is best to reduce the load when drying bulky items, such as sheets, so they benefit from a better tumbling action.

Anti-static tissues
To freshen up your washing as it dries, place a proprietary anti-static tissue on top of the load before switching on your dryer. Impregnated with fragrant fabric conditioner, these tissues help to keep fabrics soft and prevent static electricity, which causes textiles to cling together. If synthetic fibres are subjected to a high temperature, anti-static tissues may leave small oily spots on the fabric. Should this occur, rub the stains with wet soap and then rewash the item.

Cleaning tumble dryers
If the filter is allowed to become clogged, airflow and drying efficiency may be drastically reduced and the TOC may trip. As a preventative measure, always clean the filter after using the dryer.

Unclogging the filter
All filters are designed for easy removal. Depending on the design of the appliance, the filter may be positioned at the back of the drum or it may be located at the front of the machine, just below the

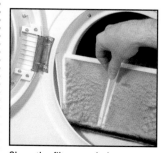

Clean the filter regularly

door. Look at your user's handbook to see how to remove and replace the filter.

Having removed the filter, peel away the layers of fluff clinging to it.

Cleaning the door seal
Heat can cause the soft door seal to perish or become sticky. Prevent this by wiping the seal occasionally with a damp cloth.

Keeping the dryer clean
Keep the cabinet and the inside of the drum free from dust by wiping them with a damp cloth – having unplugged the appliance first.

Clean the door seal, using a damp cloth

Gaining access to your dryer

It is necessary to remove at least one back panel to clean out the accumulation of fluff that collects inside any clothes dryer. As a rule, lay the dryer face down on an old blanket when unscrewing back panels; and wear strong gloves to protect your hands from sharp edges.

A one-piece back panel can usually be unscrewed without damaging internal components, but when there is a pair of panels covering the back of a dryer, it is best to remove only the smaller bottom panel. This is usually sufficient to reach the vent-hose connection and motor, for example. The heating elements or other components may be fixed to the larger of the two panels, so it is safer to leave that one for an engineer to remove when servicing the machine.

If the back panel on your dryer doesn't have easily removable fixings, call in an engineer to clean or service the machine.

Take care to replace all the screw fixings and strip seals, to ensure that air does not leak from the cabinet. With some models, this could result in poor circulation of air and overheating.

Remove a one-piece back panel

If there is a pair of back panels, unscrew the small bottom panel

Replace loose back-panel seals

Look out for missing screws

First things first

Before you call out a service engineer or start looking for more serious faults, run through the checklist below. It is surprising how often simple forgetfulness or carelessness can be the cause of a problem.

- Is the dryer plugged in? And is the socket switched on?

- Is the door closed properly?

- Has the timer been set correctly? And has the appliance been switched on?

- Is the vent hose kinked or trapped behind the machine?

- Is the filter clogged? With some dryers, you have to press a reset button if a clogged filter has caused the TOC to trip.

Check for a slack drive belt

WARM DAMP AIR IN ROOM

Provided your machine has a vent hose connected to the outside, drying your washing should not raise the humidity in your kitchen or laundry room.

Vent hose leaking or disconnected

Having unplugged the dryer, pull it away from the wall and make sure the vent hose has not become detached from the machine's outlet vent or the wall ducting.

If the hose appears to be attached properly at both ends, disconnect it from the machine and from the wall ducting or window vent. Examine the hose closely for splits that may be allowing moist air to escape into the room.

TANGLED LOAD

The reason may simply be that the load got tangled while being transferred from the washing machine to the dryer. Get into the habit of loading garments individually. However, tangled washing can also be caused by:

Static electricity

Try putting an anti-static tissue on top of the load next time you use the appliance.

Drum not rotating properly

When you look through the glass-fronted door, you should be able to see the load tumbling freely as the drum rotates. If it isn't, stop the machine and let it cool down, then reduce the load and try again.

If the problem persists, it may be that the drum's drive belt is slipping. On many machines, a spring-loaded jockey wheel automatically adjusts the tension on the drive belt. On others, the belt is simply stretched tight over the end of the motor drive shaft. Once either belt gets too slack to keep the drum in motion, it's time to have the belt replaced. You can usually gain access to the belt to see if it feels slack, but changing it is a job for an expert.

Old belts invariably show signs of cracking and should be changed before they break.

Some hoses unclip from inside

Others are screwed to the back

Load garments individually

Cracked belts should be replaced

LOAD STILL DAMP

Insufficient time set
If your washing is still damp when you remove it from the dryer, check that you have set the timer correctly. Remember, cool air only is passed through the drum for the last 10 to 15 minutes of any setting. Allow for this when resetting the timer.

Incorrect heat setting for type of load
Make sure you have set the correct temperature for the items you are drying – see page 92.

Dryer overloaded
If you have overloaded the dryer (see page 92), remove some of the items and try again.

Washing too wet when loaded
A tumble dryer is not designed to cope with washing that is dripping wet. If you don't have an automatic washing machine, buy a small spin dryer (see page 102) to extract most of the water from the washing before you put it into the tumble dryer.

Air not circulating
The warmed air must be circulating efficiently in order to remove moisture. Make sure there is sufficient space around your dryer to promote efficient circulation, then check all of the following:

1 Check whether something has fallen behind the dryer and is covering the air inlets.

2 Clean the accumulation of fluff from the filter – see page 92.

3 Disconnect the vent hose and check that it is not blocked. If the hose forms a U-bend, moisture may condense in the lower part of the hose and restrict the passage of air.

4 Having removed and cleaned the hose, check that there is nothing blocking the outlet vent on the back of the machine or the plastic wall ducting.

5 Also, check that the grille on the outside of the house is intact and that the wall duct has not been blocked by a bird's nest.

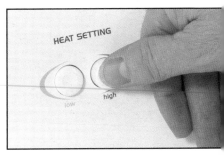
Check the temperature setting

Clean out the vent hose

Then make sure there's nothing blocking the outlet

SAFETY FIRST

Always unplug a dryer before pulling it away from the wall and checking for faults.

See also *Switching off the power*, page 13. Before you touch any component inside a dryer connected to a fused connection unit, as a final check that the power is off remove the casing from the appliance and aim a non-contact voltage tester at the internal terminal block to which the flex is connected (see page 122). If you are not absolutely certain an appliance is disconnected safely, get a service engineer to isolate and inspect it. Never take a risk.

Before putting an appliance back into service, plug it into a circuit protected by an RCD (see page 11). Then switch on, and if the RCD trips have the appliance tested by a qualified service engineer.

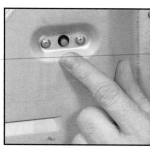

Look for a manual reset button

SAFETY FIRST

To check that a tumble dryer is earthed, apply one probe of a continuity tester to the earth pin of the plug and touch the exposed head of a back-panel fixing screw or an unpainted part of the metal casing or cover panels with the other probe. The tester's indicator will be activated if the metal components are earthed. If the indicator is not activated, have the machine checked by a service engineer.

If your dryer is connected to a fused connection unit (see page 14), perform the same test to check that the appliance is earthed – but, instead of placing one of the tester's probes on the earth pin of the plug, apply it to one of the two fixing screws that hold the FCU's faceplate in place. These fixing screws are connected to earth inside the fused connection unit, and the tester's indicator will be activated if the earth in the appliance is connected to earth in the FCU.

Recycling moist air

Check that the vent hose has not become detached from the wall ducting – in which case, it may be dumping moist air near the air-inlets.

TOC tripped to prevent overheating

If poor air circulation has gone unnoticed, the thermal-overload cutout may have switched off the heaters – see page 88.

Some TOCs reset automatically as soon as the dryer cools down. However, you still need to ascertain what caused the machine to overheat. Look for anything restricting airflow through the appliance. As a safety feature, on some machines you have to press a button in order to reset the TOC – so you are aware there's a problem that must be rectified.

Some sophisticated dryers are fitted with a warning light that alerts you to a blockage or clogged filter.

Loose fan

The fan may be spinning on its mounting and not producing sufficient airflow. If the fan is accessible on your machine, move if by hand to see if the drum turns with it – which indicates that the fan is firmly fixed in place. If the fan appears to be loose on its mounting, tighten the fixing bolt in the centre. See also Fan drive belt broken, page 98.

Faulty thermostat

See opposite.

Faulty heating element

See opposite.

NO TUMBLE ACTION

If the fan is drawing warm air into the drum but the drum remains stationary, check the following possibilities. Also, be aware that eventually the TOC may switch off the heaters in order to prevent overheating.

Drive belt slipping

If the problem is intermittent, the drum's drive belt may be slipping – see page 94.

Broken drive belt

If there is no rotation, the drive belt may have

Check that moving the fan also turns the drum

broken. This will be evident as soon as the dryer's back panel is removed. Though a simple and relatively economical procedure, changing a drive belt involves having to strip down much of the machine – a task best left to a service engineer.

DRUM TUMBLES BUT NO HEAT

Insufficient time set
Remember that cool air is circulated for the last 10 to 15 minutes of every cycle. Allow for this when setting the timer.

TOC tripped
If the TOC detects a dangerously high temperature, it will switch off the heaters. Check for poor circulation of air (see page 95) and a loose fan (see opposite).

A separate thermal fuse is sometimes fitted to disconnect the heaters when a faulty TOC fails to turn them off. On some models, the thermal fuse will turn off the dryer completely in the event of a fault. Thermal fuses can be tested and replaced by an engineer at relatively little cost.

Faulty thermostat
A faulty thermostat may have turned off the heaters unnecessarily. Have it checked and replaced by a service engineer.

Faulty heating element
A broken wire element, similar to the elements fitted in some electric room heaters, may be easy to spot. A service engineer can also check a suspect heater with a continuity tester and replace the element if necessary.

Solid heating elements, similar in principle to those found in electric kettles, should be checked and replaced by an expert, too.

TUMBLES/HEATS BUT NO AIRFLOW
This symptom will occur only until the TOC switches off the heaters.

Clogged filter and blocked vent hose
A clogged filter can prevent the circulation of air (see page 92). Airflow could also stop if there is a blockage in the vent hose or duct (see page 95).

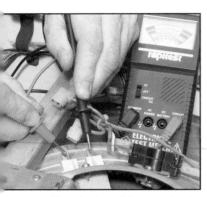
Have the thermal fuse tested and replaced by an engineer

Replacing a faulty thermostat should not be too costly

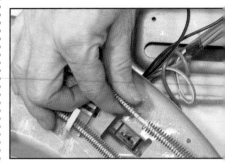
A wire element may be broken

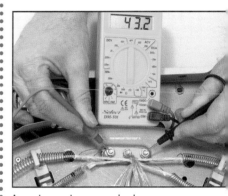
A service engineer can check a heater with a continuity tester

Clean a blocked filter

Blocked air inlet

An air vent near the base of the machine could be blocked completely if something like a thick towel has fallen behind the machine. Having unplugged the dryer, pull it away from the wall and see if there's an obstruction of this kind.

Also, make sure curtains hanging nearby are not being sucked against the air inlet when the machine is switched on; and check that there's sufficient space around the machine to promote adequate circulation of air.

Fan drive belt broken

On some models, a fan mounted behind the lint filter is driven by a flexible belt connected to the electric motor – see page 89. If this belt snaps, air ceases to circulate. This type of belt-driven fan is now a rarity, but if you can buy a replacement belt it should be easy to fit. Remember to unplug the machine first.

To expose the belt, either remove its coverplate or take off the dryer's back panel. Place the new belt around the lower pulley, then rotate the upper pulley as you ease the belt onto it.

NOISES WHEN DRUM IS ROTATING

Objects in the drum

If you hear rattling when the drum is in motion, switch off the dryer and allow it to cool. Then remove the load and check for metallic objects such as coins and keys left in pockets.

Zips or studs scratching drum

Similar sounds are caused by metal zips, studs or buttons. Make sure you turn garments inside out before putting them into the dryer.

Drum bearings worn

A grating noise from inside the machine could indicate worn drum bearings. Dust generated by worn bearings may leave dirty marks on the washing in the drum. Have a service engineer check the dryer if you suspect worn bearings.

Worn jockey pulley

The pulley that applies tension to the drive belt on some models can wear and create a high-pitched squealing. Eventually, a worn pulley may

Turn clothes inside out to prevent studs scratching the drum

Have worn drum bearings replaced by an engineer

SAFETY FIRST

If you switch off your dryer in mid cycle, allow the contents and drum to cool before opening the door.

Removing cover panels may expose sharp metal edges – so be extra careful. If necessary, wear strong protective gloves.

Check the pockets before putting clothing into a tumble dryer

A worn pulley may create a high-pitched squeal

throw the drum's belt off the motor drive shaft. In either case, you will need a service engineer to replace the pulley.

Loose fan

A low rumbling may be the sign of a fan working loose – see page 96. If your fan is accessible, check for broken blades that could throw it out of balance. It may be possible to replace the fan simply by removing a single fixing bolt in the centre.

DRYER WON'T SWITCH OFF

Faulty timer

If the dryer continues working for longer than the set time, the timer itself may be faulty. The timer is a complex component that can only be tested and replaced by an expert. However, before you call out a service engineer, try the following:

The timer control knob may have been pushed hard up against the dryer's cabinet, preventing the timer turning smoothly. Protect the knob with a cloth pad and use a pair of pliers or a wrench to ease the knob, very slightly, away from the cabinet.

Some machines are fitted with clockwork timers – which can be heard ticking even when the dryer is unplugged. Unless the spring is wound up fully each time you use the dryer, it may not have enough stored energy to switch off the machine. Check your user's manual for the correct winding procedure.

STOPS IN MID CYCLE

Door has opened

If the door opens during the tumble cycle, the machine will be switched off automatically by the door safety switch. If this should happen, the latch is probably worn and needs replacing.

Check the sprung catch on the door for signs of wear or a weak spring. You may be able to replace the catch by unscrewing a fixing plate on the inside of the door.

Also, check the latching plate screwed to the dryer's fascia. Remove the fixing screws to replace it.

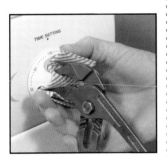
Ease a sticking timer control knob

Check the door catch for wear

SAFETY FIRST

Don't install a tumble dryer near curtains, which could block air-inlet grilles.

Ensure that matches, lighters and other objects are not left in the pockets of garments about to be put in a dryer.

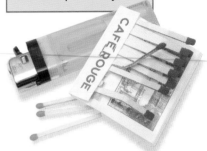

Replace a worn latching plate

A service engineer can install a new timer

Power failure
If other appliances on the circuit have stopped working, inspect your consumer unit for a blown fuse or tripped MCB or RCD – pages 11 and 12.

Plug or FCU fuse has blown
Replace the fuse in the plug – see page 17. If the fuse blows again as soon as you turn the dryer on, have the dryer checked by a service engineer. If there's a fused connection unit, check whether the fuse in the FCU needs replacing – see page 17.

Faulty timer
Have the timer checked and, if need be, replaced by a service engineer.

TOC operated
Depending on the model, the thermal-overload cutout may disconnect the heaters and electric motor in the event of overheating. Having checked for restricted air circulation (see page 95), reset a manual TOC or have an automatic device tested and replaced by a service engineer.

DRYER WON'T SWITCH ON

Timer control not activated
With some dryers it is necessary to set the timer and then activate it (switch it on) in some way.

Power failure
If other appliances on the circuit have stopped working, inspect your consumer unit for a blown fuse or tripped MCB or RCD – pages 11 and 12.

Machine not plugged in
Make sure the plug is inserted in the socket, and that the socket is switched on. Some dryers are also connected to a fused connection unit – see page 14. Make sure this is switched on, too.

Faulty wiring in plug
Take the back off the plug to check whether it is wired correctly – see page 19.

Plug or FCU fuse has blown
Replace the fuse in the plug – see page 17. If there's a fused connection unit, check whether the fuse in the FCU needs replacing – page 17.

SAFETY FIRST

If you switch off your dryer in mid cycle, allow the contents and drum to cool before opening the door.

Removing cover panels may expose sharp metal edges – so be extra careful. If necessary, wear strong protective gloves.

If fluff and dust are allowed to build up inside the dryer cabinet, especially on and around the heaters, they constitute a serious fire risk. Whenever you have cause to remove cover panels, take the opportunity to clean components with a vacuum cleaner and attachment. Always ask a service engineer to do the same.

Vacuum the heating elements

Always clean dusty components

Make sure the latch is secured

Screw a replacement peg to the back of the door

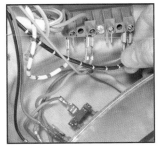
Check for loose spade connectors

Undo the fan in order to clean the motor

Door not closed

Your dryer is fitted with a safety lock to prevent the drum turning when the door's open. Push the door to make sure the latch is secured.

If that doesn't work, try holding the door closed while you operate the door-release button or handle a few times to free the latch.

On some models, there is a plastic protrusion or peg on the back of the door. This peg has to engage with a recessed safety switch before the dryer will turn on. If the peg has been damaged or broken off, screw a new peg to the door.

Faulty door switch

If the door and latch appear to be operating normally, have the door's safety switch tested and, if necessary, replaced by a service engineer.

Loose connections

Having unplugged the dryer, remove the necessary cover panels so you can check that all wires and connectors are attached securely. Don't be misled into thinking there is a fault when you discover that some terminals have no wires running to them. Certain components may also be used in other models where these spare terminals perform a function not required in your machine.

If the connections appear to be sound, the only way to be sure your circuit wiring is working properly is to have it tested by a service engineer.

Thermal fuse tripped

See page 97. This will probably entail an engineer replacing both the fuse and the TOC.

Faulty timer

Try various settings to see if you can initiate the tumbling action. You need to call out an engineer to test a timer properly and replace it if necessary. Unless the dryer is very old, putting in a new timer is usually worth the cost.

Faulty motor

As a last resort, have the electric motor tested by an engineer. If the motor has burnt out, the cost of replacement may be uneconomical.

As a preventative measure, remove an accessible fan and clean any accumulated fluff from the motor. This will improve airflow over the motor and so may prevent it burning out.

SAFETY FIRST

A capacitor is fitted in many dryers in order to start up the electric motor. A capacitor can hold a charge for a short while after the machine is turned off. As a precaution, unplug any dryer and wait 10 to 15 minutes to allow the capacitor to discharge before removing a back panel. (Capacitors in television sets and microwave ovens retain very high voltages – which is why you should never remove a back panel or other coverplates from these appliances.)

If your dryer has been running, don't remove a back panel until the machine has been left to cool down completely. With some models, this may take up to 30 minutes.

SPIN DRYERS

Before automatic washing machines became affordable, spin dryers were commonplace items in every home. Currently, there's revived interest in these simple but efficient appliances because they spin faster than even the most modern washing machines. This superior spin speed extracts more water from the washing in the drum, resulting in cost savings when the garments are transferred to an electrically heated tumble dryer.

How it works

Spin dryers use centrifugal force to extract water from the laundry. The damp clothing is placed in a perforated metal drum that rotates at high speed. The faster the rotational speed, the more moisture is extracted. Spin speeds vary, but are normally between 2500 and 3000rpm.

Drain the dryer into a sink

The drum is housed within a watertight container in which the extracted water collects. With the more basic appliances, this water is drained through a spout into a bucket or similar receptacle, which has then to be emptied by hand. The more expensive spin dryers are fitted with a pump that discharges the water via a drain hose into a convenient sink. Depending on the type of electric motor used in the dryer, the drum itself may be either belt-driven or fitted directly to the motor shaft. With some dryers, the drain pump is operated by a flexible drive belt attached to the electric motor that powers the drum. Alternatively, the drain pump may have its own dedicated electric motor.

An important safety feature of every modern spin dryer is a latching system that prevents anyone opening the lid while the drum is moving. With some models, simply closing the lid operates the latch and turns on the dryer simultaneously – the latch will not be released again until the drum stops moving. With other dryers, moving a latch lever switches off the appliance and a cable-operated brake stops the drum rotating. Only then is it possible to open the lid of the dryer.

What can you spin-dry?

Most (but not all) fabrics can be put in a spin dryer. Check the care label on delicate items and woollen garments. Some man-made fibres may be heavily creased and more difficult to iron.

1 Lid	11 Flex
2 Drain hose	12 Brake adjuster
3 Drum	13 Brake cable
4 Motor-cooling fan	14 Brake drum
5 Motor mounting	15 Bottom panel
6 Electric motor	16 Switch
7 Brake band	17 Safety latch assembly
8 Reservoir	
9 Drain pump	18 Drain to reservoir
10 Drain pump motor	19 Manual latch

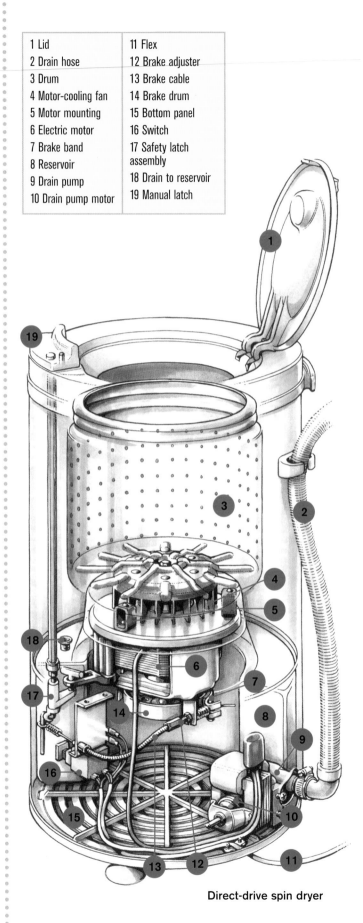

Direct-drive spin dryer

1 Lid	9 Drum pulley
2 Safety-latch mechanism	10 Drum drive belt
3 Switch	11 Suppressor
4 Manual latch release	12 Pump drive belt
5 Drum	13 Flex
6 Power cables to switch	14 Drain pump
7 Drum shaft	15 Electric motor
8 Internal drain hose	16 Outer tub
	17 Drain hose

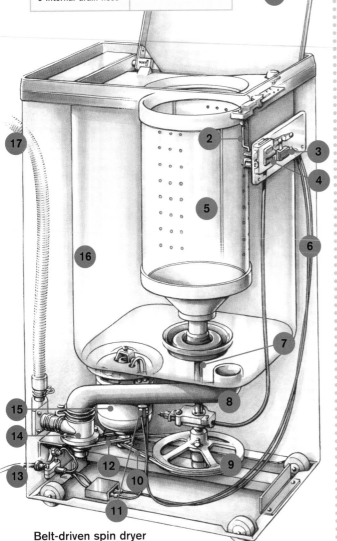

Belt-driven spin dryer

How much will it hold?

Depending on the make and model, domestic spin dryers may accommodate anything from 2.5 to 3.7kg (5.5 to 8lbs) of dry clothing. Check the user's handbook, and don't overload your machine.

Cleaning spin dryers

Unplug the spin dryer, then wipe the outside with a damp cloth. Never use abrasive cleaners. Dry the inside of the drum after use.

Unless your dryer is specifically designed to rinse clothing, never pour water into the appliance.

Getting the best from your dryer

To get the best results from your dryer it is essential to load it carefully, according to the manufacturer's instructions. This normally entails placing items into the drum one by one, starting with the lightweight articles, which should placed against the wall of the drum.

If a safety mat is supplied with your dryer, place it on top of the load before closing the lid. Otherwise, put a large piece of cloth or a towel on top and tuck it in all round the load – see your user's handbook.

If the dryer starts to vibrate excessively, turn off the appliance, then remove the garments and rearrange them to balance the load. A drum filled to capacity is less likely to spin out of balance, so it pays to top up a small load with some dry clothing or towels.

Gaining access to your dryer
Removing the bottom panel will allow you to service most components in a spin dryer. Unscrewing the rims at the top and bottom of the appliance may expose very sharp metal edges.

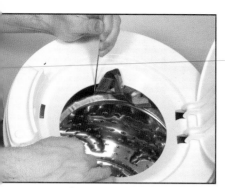

Retrieve trapped clothing

Lubricate the brake cable

DRUM REVOLVES NOISILY

Item trapped between drum and casing

If the washing wasn't loaded properly (see page 103), one or more items of clothing may have ridden up over the drum lip and found their way into the space between the drum and the outer casing.

Unplug the appliance and pull the drum to one side, so you can retrieve the item using a length of wire with one end bent into a hook.

Brake binding

When a dryer fitted with a braking system is running, you may hear a high-pitched sound similar to a wet finger being rubbed round the rim of a wineglass. This sound is caused by the brake lining rubbing against the drum, and indicates that the brake cable is seizing up.

Squeeze two or three drops of oil onto the cable, just where it emerges from its outer casing. Operate the latching system a few times to encourage the oil to flow, checking that the brake assembly is moving freely. Make sure that oil does not get onto the brake lining.

If lubrication fails to solve the problem, try adjusting the brake assembly – see page 106.

EXCESSIVE VIBRATION

Laundry distributed unevenly

Take out the clothing and rearrange the items to balance the load. Make sure the load is held down, either with a safety mat or a large piece of fabric, such as a towel, and that the drum is loaded to capacity – see page 103.

Slack drive belt

With a slack drive belt, the drum is not driven up to full speed and tends to wobble on its mountings, like a spinning top slowing down. Having unplugged the dryer, turn the large pulley to help you ease off the drive belt.

1 Slacken the nuts that secure the motor mountings to the frame, then slide the motor away from the drum pulley – only a slight adjustment will be required.

SAFETY FIRST

Make sure your hands are dry before plugging in a spin dryer.

Don't pour water into a dryer unless it has been specifically designed to rinse and spin.

Don't use a spin dryer that is leaking water.

Always unplug a spin dryer before cleaning it or checking for faults.

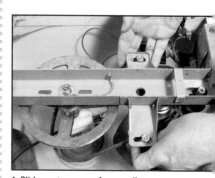

1 Slide motor away from pulley

Plug fuse has blown
Replace the fuse in the plug – see page 17. If the fuse blows again as soon as you turn the appliance on, have the appliance checked by a service engineer.

Faulty wiring in plug
If possible, take the back off the plug and check that it is wired correctly – see page 19.

Broken flex conductor
On some spin dryers, the incoming flex is connected to accessible screw terminals. In which case, you will be able to test the flex for continuity (see page 20) and replace it if necessary.

 If your appliance has a flex attached with spade connectors, either have it repaired at a service centre or order a replacement flex complete with connectors and moulded-on plug. Be sure to make a note of the wiring and terminal connections before you detach the old flex.

Faulty wiring inside dryer
Vibrations can cause connectors to work loose. If checking the accessible connectors doesn't lead you to the source of the fault, have the wiring tested by a service engineer.

Faulty motor
As a last resort, have a professional check the electric motor for possible faults.

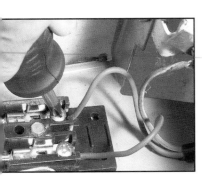
You can replace a damaged flex that has screw terminals

SAFETY FIRST

Don't let the flex trail across a wet surface.

When reassembling a spin dryer, make sure the components and wiring are returned to their original locations. Electrical components inside a dryer are often protected from leaking water by plastic shields or covers. Make sure these are replaced.

Before putting a spin dryer back into service, plug it into a circuit protected by an RCD. If the RCD trips, have the appliance tested by a service engineer.

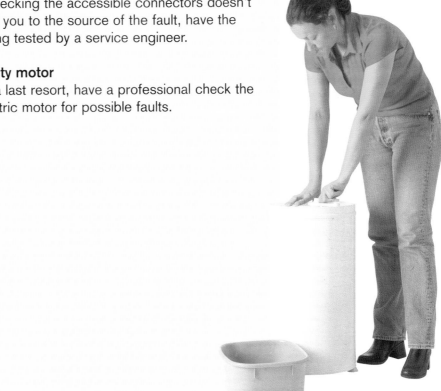

DISHWASHERS

A device designed to reduce washing-up to the minimum was bound to become one of the most popular labour-saving appliances on the market. Modern dishwashers wash and dry a full load in just over an hour – far more hygienically than washing tableware and kitchen utensils by hand. Nevertheless, an automatic dishwasher is a complex machine that has to be used with care and maintained regularly to avoid poor results and possible breakdowns.

How it works

Although some of the more sophisticated appliances have additional features, the type of dishwasher described here is typical of many of the models currently on the market, as well as the majority of machines installed in kitchens around the country.

All dishwashers offer at least three programmes: a prewash cycle, an economy wash cycle, and an intensive wash cycle for heavily soiled items. To conserve energy, some machines also offer a rapid wash cycle of relatively short duration for dishes loaded immediately after use. The prewash cycle can be selected to remove food remains from dishes that are to be left in the machine until it is full. The dirty dishes are arranged in plastic-coated wire baskets suspended from rollers that run in sliding tracks mounted on each side of the machine's inner cabinet.

At the start of each wash cycle, the dishwasher begins to fill with cold water via a hose and inlet valve. The incoming water passes through a water softener into a sump at the bottom of the cabinet. When the water reaches the optimum level, a pressure-sensitive switch (sometimes a float switch) closes the inlet valve and turns on an element, which heats the water to the required temperature.

At that point, the programmer activates a powerful circulation pump, which directs the hot water to a pair of perforated spray arms, one mounted below each wire basket. The pressurized water emerges from holes on opposite sides of the spray arms, causing them to rotate and fling water in all directions. Before the pump recycles the same water to both spray arms, food particles are trapped by filters built into the base of the cabinet. At some point in the cycle the detergent dispenser opens, depositing its contents into the water.

1 Basket	12 Circulation pump
2 Door counterbalance spring	13 Capacitor
3 Spray arm	14 Rinse-aid dispenser
4 Thermostat	15 Door-latch safety switch
5 Filters	16 Detergent dispenser
6 Outlet hose	17 Inlet valve
7 Pressure switch	18 Door seal
8 Drain pump	19 Salt-container cap
9 Sump	20 Heating element
10 Anti-flood device	21 Inlet hose
11 Programmer	22 Roller

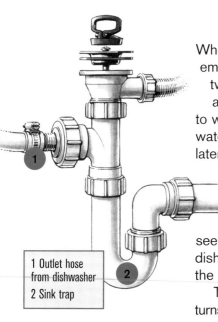

When the first phase is complete, the drain pump empties the dirty water and the machine is filled twice more with fresh water, first for a cold rinse and then for a second rinsing with heated water, to which rinse aid is added. After the last of the water has been pumped from the machine, the latent heat from the dishes causes the remaining moisture to evaporate.

The outlet hose is sometimes connected to a vertical standpipe that takes the dirty water to a drain outside – see Washing machines, page 74. However, when a dishwasher is plumbed in next to the kitchen sink, the outlet hose is often connected to the sink trap.

The door latch is connected to a microswitch that turns off the machine if the door is opened in mid cycle.

1 Outlet hose from dishwasher
2 Sink trap

Hot-water fill
The majority of dishwashers are connected to the cold-water supply only. A few models are designed to take hot water, but there's little saving unless you are using excess heat from a solid-fuel stove to heat your water.

Hot-air drying
Drying with residual heat from washed dishes is economical and efficient. However, if you want to speed up the cycle, look for a model that engages the element to help dry the contents.

Condenser drying
In some dishwashers, incoming cold water fills a reservoir built directly behind the cabinet. During the cycle, heat from inside the cabinet prewarms the water in the reservoir before it is drained into the cabinet at the appropriate time. This reduces the cost of heating water.

During the final drying stage, the hot moist air left in the cabinet condenses against the relatively cool back panel between the cabinet and reservoir. Taking moisture out of the air in this way reduces the time required for the dishes to dry.

The condensed moisture runs to the sump below the cabinet, ready to be used during the next wash cycle.

Good sound insulation
There is quite a variation in noise levels from model to model. When selecting a new dishwasher, it is well worth investigating the level of sound insulation built into the machine.

Anti-flood devices
Many models incorporate a device that turns off the water supply to prevent a flood. Various systems are employed, including ones that are in effect double inlet hoses – one inside the other. If the inner hose springs a leak, the resulting water pressure in the outer layer activates a valve, shutting off the water.

On other machines, leaking water collects on a base panel where it operates a float switch that either turns off the dishwasher or turns on the drainage pump to empty the appliance before it floods.

Adjustable baskets
A minor but useful feature is a double set of rollers that allow you to raise or lower the upper basket to make room for larger pans or dishes.

Anti-flood float switch

Size and capacity

Full-size dishwashers are invariably 600mm (2ft) wide. There are also slimline models, 150mm (6in) narrower; and compact dishwashers, about the size of a microwave oven, designed to stand on a kitchen worktop.

Full-size and slimline dishwashers

Place settings

A more important statistic is the number of place settings that can be loaded into the dishwasher. As a rough guide, a single setting consists of a full-size dinner plate, a side plate, soup bowl, cup and saucer and drinking glass, plus a set of cutlery. The average full-size dishwasher will accommodate 12 place settings. A slimline model will probably take no more than eight.

What can you put in a dishwasher?

Most modern tableware and kitchen utensils can be washed safely in a dishwasher – but check that they are labelled 'dishwasher safe'.

- Never put lead crystal in a dishwasher – it may become cloudy in appearance and the heat could cause cracking.
- Don't attempt to machine-wash antique or handpainted china, especially items with patterns painted or printed over the glaze.
- Putting any form of decorative glassware in a dishwasher is risky.
- Bone or wooden handles may be damaged, and the glue used to hold them in place could soften with heat.

- Anodized aluminium may discolour.
- Soft plastics, such as those used for food storage, may become distorted, especially if they are placed in the lower basket directly above the heating element.
- You can wash silverware safely, provided it is not left too long in the machine before washing – but don't put silver in the same basket as cutlery made from other metals.

Loading a dishwasher

Loading a dishwasher is so simple that it would seem impossible to get it wrong – but unless you follow certain guidelines the results will be unsatisfactory.

Load the baskets carefully

- Don't overfill either basket, or some items are likely to be shielded from the water spray and will not be washed or rinsed properly.
- Remove large particles of food waste from crockery and pans before putting them into the dishwasher.
- Put the larger heavily soiled items in

the lower basket and delicate pieces, such as fine glassware, in the upper one. Long-stemmed glasses should rest at an angle, supported by the folding rack in the upper basket.
- Hollow containers such as cups, glasses, bowls and saucepans should be placed upside down.

- Place cutlery in the cutlery basket, handles down. The only exceptions are sharp-pointed knives and forks, which are safer if they are placed with the handles upward. There is no need to sort cutlery for washing, but make sure the items are distributed evenly to avoid bunching.

- Long cutlery, such as ladles and spatulas, can be placed horizontally on top of the cutlery basket, or laid crosswise in the front section of the either basket.
- Before you close the door, make sure both spray arms can revolve freely without obstruction.

Unloading a dishwasher

Dishes should be left in the machine for at least 15 minutes after the wash cycle has ended, to allow them to dry and cool down. Unload the lower basket first, to prevent drops of water falling onto the contents when the upper basket is moved.

Before putting cutlery and glassware away, check them for smears – most of which can be removed immediately by polishing with a clean, dry tea towel.

Programme controller

Choosing the best programme

If there isn't enough dirty crockery to make a full load, select the prewash programme to prevent food deposits drying on dishes and cutlery; select a wash programme later, when you can fill the machine.

Both the economy wash and the intensive wash cycle will cope with a full load of mixed crockery and cutlery. If you've put heavily soiled pans in the dishwasher, select the slightly longer intensive wash cycle, which usually circulates hotter water.

If you have a lot of drinking glasses to wash (after a party, for example), it pays to machine-wash them separately, using an economy or rapid wash cycle.

Getting the best from your machine

To maintain peak performance, you must keep your dishwasher supplied with the necessary detergent, rinse aid and regenerating salt.

Pour rinse aid into the dispenser

Topping up with rinse aid

Rinse aid ensures that water drains from dishes and glasses quickly, minimizing lime-scale deposits that leave them with a streaky appearance or covered with white spots. Pour rinse aid into the dispenser reservoir, located on the inside of the dishwasher door. An indicator tells you when the reservoir is full.

During each wash cycle the correct amount of rinse aid will be dispensed automatically, but it is usually possible to adjust a regulator within the dispenser if your glassware is not drying perfectly (for instructions, see your user's handbook).

REPLENISHING WITH SALT

Regenerating salt helps prevent lime-scale deposits on the contents of your dishwasher. It also reduces the accumulation of scale, which could affect the machine's efficiency. Dishwasher salt is available in granular form for topping up the water softener built into the base or side of the machine. Don't use other types of salt, which may contain impurities such as iron and carbonates that could damage the water softener.

The screw cap of the salt container is usually made with a float that indicates when salt should be added. The average water softener takes about 2kg (4 1/2 lb) of salt. Spilt salt left in the dishwasher may corrode the metal cabinet, so use a plastic scoop or jug to load the granules and wait until you are about to switch on the machine before you refill the salt container. The container will be full of water, which is displaced as you add salt. This is quite normal and doesn't mean there is already sufficient salt in the container.

When you have filled the salt container, make sure its screw cap is replaced properly to prevent detergent or rinse aid getting into the water softener – they will damage the unit.

Adding detergent

Dishwasher detergent in powder or liquid form is poured into the detergent dispenser, which is also built into the door. You need to check the instructions printed on the detergent packaging, and fill the dispenser as appropriate.

Alternatively, drop a detergent tablet into the same dispenser. Some tablets also contain a measured dose of rinse aid, and possibly regenerating salt, too. However, when using these combined tablets, continue to fill the water softener with salt granules if you live in a hard-water area.

Detergent tablets help keep the dispenser clean

Remove the filters for cleaning

Cleaning the filters

After each wash, take out the coarse and fine filters and flush them under running water to remove food particles. When replacing the filters, make sure they are properly located in the recess in the base of the cabinet. If the filters become clogged, scrub them clean in hot water.

Take the opportunity to retrieve small items such as cocktail sticks or coffee spoons from the cabinet. If foreign bodies get past the filters, one of the pumps may get blocked or damaged.

If glass or china is broken inside the cabinet, remove all the fragments carefully before using the machine again.

Using dishwasher cleaners and fresheners

Proprietary dishwasher cleaners remove grease and lime-scale deposits from inside the machine. They also leave the dishwasher smelling fresh.

Some cleaners are supplied in a dispenser that is placed upside down in the cutlery basket. With the dishwasher empty, select a normal wash cycle to flush a measured dose of cleaner through the machine.

Load a dispenser upside down in the cutlery basket

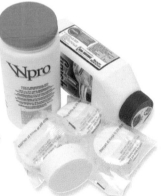

You can also buy a cleaner in tablet form. Place one of these tablets in the cutlery basket, then run the machine with a normal wash cycle selected.

Some dishwasher fresheners come in a dispenser designed to hang from the top basket. This type of dispenser can be left in the machine for up to 45 washes.

You can buy dishwasher cleaners as tablets or in dispensers

Gaining access to the machine

When servicing a dishwasher, tip it onto its back to prevent water leaking out onto electrical connections. With a condenser-drying dishwasher (see page 111), you may have to drain the reservoir before tipping the dishwasher onto its back. A drain tube is usually fitted for the purpose.

Wear gloves when removing panels

Unless the machine is fitted with an anti-flood float switch, there's usually no bottom panel to remove. However, you may have to take off a top panel (and possibly a bottom panel) before you can unscrew the side panels to get to the door springs and gain better access to some components.

The front panel, just under the door, can usually be detached once you have removed one or two screw fixings and possibly a couple of plastic catches. This may improve access to certain internal components.

Detach the outer door panel by removing the screws around its inner edges. You need to support the panel as you remove the last screws. Also, place a weight on the inside of the door to prevent it closing as the front panel comes free.

Removing cover panels invariably exposes sharp metal edges – so take care and wear protective gloves when handling these panels.

You will need to slide a fitted dishwasher out of the kitchen cabinet before you can access most of the internal components (see the manufacturer's fitting instructions).

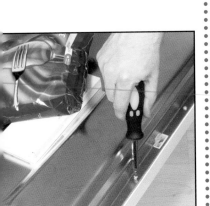

Place a weight on the door when removing the outer panel

Draining your dishwasher

If you need to drain water from your dishwasher cabinet, first make sure the machine is switched off, then pull the plug from the socket. Alternatively, switch off the power at the consumer unit (see page 13). Shut off the water by closing the supply valve (see page 123). Wearing protective gloves, disconnect the outlet hose from the standpipe or sink trap.

1 Put the end of the hose in a washing-up bowl placed on the floor. The water will begin to drain out of the machine.

2 When you want to empty the bowl, raise the hose and the water will cease to flow.

3 When no more water comes out, reconnect the outlet hose, then leave the dishwasher to cool down before opening the door.

Never overload your dishwasher

1 Drain the machine into a bowl

2 Raising the hose stops the flow

First things first

Many a service engineer has been called out to fix a dishwasher only to discover the fault has been caused by simple neglect or forgetfulness. Always run through the checklist below before you start looking for more serious defects.

- Is the dishwasher plugged in? And is the socket switched on?

- Has the water been turned off?

- Is the door closed properly?

- Has the programmer been set correctly? And has the dishwasher been switched on?

- Are the filters clogged?

- Have the holes in the spray arms been blocked by food particles?

- Are you using sufficient detergent, and keeping the salt and rinse-aid levels topped up?

- Are you loading your dishwasher correctly?

Check that the spray arms are not obstructed

UNSATISFACTORY RESULTS

There are all sorts of possible causes, but most of the problems are easily rectified. See also Glassware streaked or cloudy after washing, opposite.

Food remains left to dry

Remove large food particles from the dishes before loading them into the dishwasher. Sand-like gritty deposits are caused by starchy food left on dishes.

Food burnt onto pans or dishes

Dishwashers may find it difficult to cope with food deposits burnt onto pans and casserole dishes. Before you put the pan or dish into your dishwasher, soak it overnight in water to soften the deposits, then scrape it as clean as possible.

Wrong programme selected

Make sure you haven't inadvertently selected the prewash cycle, instead of a full wash cycle. The economy wash cycle may not be able to cope with heavily soiled dishes. Select the more vigorous intensive wash cycle to see if that gives better results.

Load not arranged properly

If you have overloaded one or both baskets, some of the larger items may shield others from the water spray. Get into the habit of putting fewer pieces into your machine, and make sure hollow items are placed upside down.

Before you close the door, always check that the spray arms are not obstructed by crockery or utensils.

No detergent

Perhaps you forgot to fill the dispenser with detergent. Or you may have turned the programme dial through 360 degrees after loading the detergent – with some models this has the effect of opening the dispenser and ejecting the detergent prematurely.

Holes in spray arms blocked

The small holes or slots in the hollow spray arms can become blocked with food particles. A few rice grains or fruit pips may be enough to stop the arm rotating.

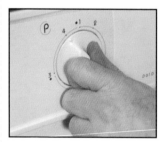

Make sure you have selected the required programme

SAFETY FIRST

Unless you are wearing protective gloves, don't put your hands in water containing dishwasher detergent. Keep detergents, rinse aids and dishwasher cleaners out of the reach of children.

Don't allow solvents of any kind to enter your dishwasher.

Don't stand on the door when it is open.

Don't touch the heating element during or immediately after a wash cycle.

1 Loosen the knurled nut to detach the lower spray arm

2 Take out the basket to detach the upper arm

3 Wash spray arms in hot water

1 The lower arm is sometimes held in place by a knurled plastic hand nut, often with a left-hand thread, that has to be unscrewed before you can lift out the arm (check this in your user's handbook). On some models, this arm is removed by holding it at the centre and pulling upwards – don't lift it by either end.

2 The upper arm may also be attached with a knurled hand nut; or it could be latched to the basket and removed by simply twisting it anticlockwise.

3 Wash both arms in warm soapy water, clearing blocked holes with a toothpick.

Filters clogged or misplaced
The flow of water to the spray arms will be restricted if the filters are clogged. Remember to flush them regularly under running water. Make sure you replace the filters properly, or debris may get through to block sprays arms and pumps.

TOO MUCH FOAM
If you notice excessive foam in your dishwasher, try reducing the amount of rinse aid (see right). If that doesn't help, use a little more detergent next time you use the machine – dishwasher detergents contain foam-suppressing agents.

CONTENTS NOT DRY
Provided the dishwasher has progressed through an entire wash cycle, the contents of your machine should be perfectly dry.

Wrong programme selected
The prewash cycle may have been selected.

No rinse aid
Refill the rinse-aid dispenser, or adjust the regulator (see right) to increase the dose during the final hot rinse.

Door opened too soon
The door may have been opened before the latent heat from the wash cycle had time to dry the dishes. If the contents are still warm, close the door and wait another 10 minutes or so.

GLASSWARE STREAKED OR CLOUDY AFTER WASHING

This is caused by lime-scale deposits. All the items in your dishwasher are affected, but the symptoms are more apparent with glassware.

It is possible that the glass itself is not dishwasher safe. Old glass (soda glass), in particular, is relatively soft and may be etched permanently by washing in a machine.

Salt needs replenishing
Streaked or dull glassware is usually the result of too little salt in the machine. Remember to top up the unit regularly.

Cap not secured on salt container
The water softener may be damaged because of failure to replace the cap properly after refilling with regenerating salt. Have the unit checked by a service engineer.

Rinse aid needs regulating
Streaked or smeared glassware can be caused by too much rinse aid being dispensed during the final hot rinse. Conversely, white spots can be the result of too little. Try slight adjustments to the regulator in the rinse-aid dispenser until you achieve optimum results.

Adjust the rinse-aid regulator

NOISES WHEN MACHINE IS RUNNING

Some machines are noisier than others. A well-insulated machine should be quiet enough to allow you to hold a conversation nearby without distraction.

Faulty pump

If there is a high-pitched squeal from the machine, either when the wash cycle is in progress or when water is emptying, the bearings of the circulation pump or drain pump are probably worn. Have a service engineer replace the one that is faulty.

Load not arranged properly

Rattling during one of the cycles usually means that some items – such as long-stemmed glasses – are not properly supported. Alternatively, one of the spray arms may be colliding with one of the larger items being washed. See also below.

Worn spray-arm bearings

If spray-arm bearings are worn, there could be sufficient play to allow the affected arm to strike the bottom of the basket above. Check this by tying each spray arm in turn to the basket above it and running a wash programme. If the noise ceases, you will know which arm needs replacing. Order a new arm complete with bearing.

MACHINE WON'T SWITCH ON

Machine not plugged in

Make sure the plug is inserted in the socket, and that the socket is switched on. Some machines are also connected to a fused connection unit – see page 14. Make sure this is switched on, too.

Machine not switched on

You may have selected the right cycle, but have you turned on the machine?

Power failure

If other appliances on the circuit have stopped working, inspect your consumer unit for a blown fuse or tripped MCB or RCD – pages 11 and 12.

Faulty wiring in plug

Take the back off the plug to see if it is wired correctly – see page 19.

Plug or FCU fuse has blown

Replace the fuse in the plug – see page 17. If there is a fused connection unit, check whether the fuse in the FCU needs to be replaced – see page 17.

Water turned off

Make sure the supply valve to the dishwasher is turned on. Also, check to see whether the inlet filter or hose is blocked – see opposite.

Faulty wiring inside machine

Having unplugged the dishwasher, check that there are no obvious loose or corroded connections inside the machine. If you discover a dirty or corroded terminal, clean the metal with fine emery paper, then carefully brush away any emery dust. If all the connections appear to be sound, the only way to be sure your circuit wiring is working properly is to have it tested by a service engineer.

Door not closed

Every dishwasher is fitted with a safety switch that prevents the machine working with the door open. Make sure you have closed the door properly – you should hear a click as the door latch is engaged.

SAFETY FIRST

Never open the door while the dishwasher is running. Turn off the appliance and wait 5 or 6 seconds to allow the spray arms to come to rest.

If you switch off the dishwasher in mid cycle, allow the contents to cool before opening the door.

Unplug the dishwasher before you start checking for faults.

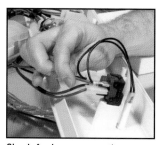

Check for loose connections

Make sure the door is closed

An engineer will operate the latch

And check the switch is working

Flush the hose with running water

Faulty door switch

If the door appears to be closed, try opening and closing the door a few times to make sure the latch mechanism and safety switch are free to move. If this doesn't solve the problem, ask an engineer to test the switch for you.

Faulty programmer

Call out an engineer to test the device. Although expensive, replacing the programmer may be a worthwhile repair.

MACHINE WON'T FILL

Water turned off

Make sure the supply valve for the dishwasher is turned on.

Inlet hose kinked or blocked

Turn off the supply valve and have a bucket or bowl ready to catch water trapped in the hose.

1 Disconnect the hose from the dishwasher's inlet valve and empty the hose into the bucket.

2 Turn on the supply valve momentarily to flush the hose into the bucket.

3 If necessary, disconnect the hose completely and flush it thoroughly in the sink. When you put the hose back, make sure it isn't kinked and check that the seals are fitted correctly.

Inlet filter blocked

Specks of grit and other debris can block the filter in the inlet valve.

1 Having turned off the supply valve, drain the hose and disconnect it from the inlet valve.

2 Using pliers, carefully pull the plastic filter from the valve, and then wash the filter under running water.

3 Slide the filter back into the inlet valve, making sure specks of dirt don't get pushed into the valve in the process. Reconnect the hose.

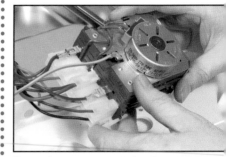

Having the programmer replaced may be cost-effective

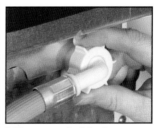

1 Disconnect the inlet hose

2 Carefully extract the inlet filter

1 Detach the inlet valve

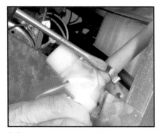

2 Remove the hose clip

3 Ease the hose off the spigot

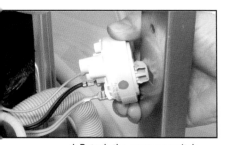

1 Detach the pressure switch

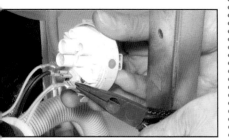

2 Ease off the connections

Faulty inlet valve

The complicated mechanism inside an inlet valve can be damaged by dirt particles getting past the filter. However, replacing an inlet valve is relatively simple, provided the valve is accessible. Remember to unplug the machine first.

1 Disconnect the supply hose (see page 119), then detach the inlet valve from the dishwasher frame.

2 Remove the internal-hose clip. Some manufacturers fit clips that cannot be reused. If this is the case, buy a screw-adjusted hose clip made from stainless steel to replace it.

3 Ease the hose off its spigot, using the tip of a flat-bladed screwdriver (pulling on the hose may simply make it grip tighter).

4 Make a careful note of the electrical connections before you detach them, using the tip of a screwdriver to ease off any stubborn connectors. If there are soldered connections, don't try to disconnect them — have the valve replaced by a service engineer.

5 Reverse the procedure to install the new valve, ensuring you return the valve and wires to their original locations. If your valve is fitted with a plastic shield to protect the wiring from leaking water, make sure you replace it, too.

Faulty pressure switch

The pressure switch is designed to turn off the water once the dishwasher is full. A faulty switch may prevent water from entering the machine.

1 Having unplugged the dishwasher, remove the switch from the machine's metal frame.

2 Make a note of the electrical connections to the switch, then use a pair of nose pliers to gently ease the connections off the terminals.

3 Ease the plastic hose off the spigot and gently blow into the spigot to test the switch – you should hear the switch click if it is working properly. Don't blow too hard, or you will damage the internal mechanism.

SAFETY FIRST

A capacitor is fitted in many dishwashers in order to start up the electric motor. A capacitor can hold a charge for a short while after the machine is turned off. As a precaution, unplug any dishwasher and wait 10 to 15 minutes to allow the capacitor to discharge before servicing the machine. (Capacitors in television sets and microwave ovens retain very high voltages – which is why you should never remove a back panel or other coverplates from these appliances.)

Removing cover panels may expose sharp metal edges – so be extra careful. If necessary, wear strong protective gloves.

3 Remove the plastic hose

4 If the switch appears to be faulty, buy a replacement and refit the hose and connections, making sure all the components are returned to their original locations.

Faulty programmer

A programmer that isn't working properly may not allow the inlet valve to open. Have the programmer tested by a service engineer.

MACHINE STOPS DURING CYCLE

Wrong programme setting

The prewash cycle may have been selected in error.

Power failure

If other appliances on the circuit have stopped working, inspect your consumer unit for a blown fuse or tripped MCB – see pages 11 and 12.

Plug or FCU fuse has blown

Replace the fuse in the plug – see page 17. If there is a fused connection unit, check whether the fuse in the FCU needs to be replaced – see page 17.

Circulation pump blocked/faulty

The circulation pump that delivers water to the spray arms may be difficult to service or replace, but it is worth checking to see whether there is anything blocking the outlet to this pump. Lift out the filter in the base of the cabinet and check there is nothing wedged in one of the outlets beneath. If there is no obvious blockage, have the pump checked by a service engineer.

Blocked or faulty inlet valve

See page 119 and opposite.

Faulty thermostat

See right.

Faulty heating element

See right.

Faulty programmer

See page 119.

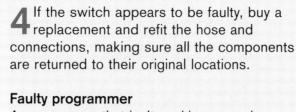

You may have selected the prewash cycle in error

Have your circulation pump checked by a service engineer

MACHINE FILLS SLOWLY

It should take no more than 4 minutes or so for the average dishwasher to fill with water.

Inlet hose kinked or blocked
Flush the hose with water to remove a partial blockage – see page 119.

Inlet filter blocked
Remove the filter and wash it under running water – see page 119.

Low water pressure
First make sure your stopcock is fully open, then contact your water authority to see whether the pressure has been temporarily reduced. If not, have a plumber check the water pressure in your home.

MACHINE WON'T HEAT UP

Faulty pressure switch
The pressure switch may not be able to detect that there is sufficient water in the cabinet to cover the heating element, and so won't allow the programme to proceed. Check the switch and replace it if necessary – see opposite.

Faulty thermostat
Checking and replacing a failed thermostat is another job best left to an expert. It is, however, almost certainly worth the cost.

Faulty heating element
Provided you top up the salt regularly, the heating element in your dishwasher should never get 'furred up' by lime scale. However, the element can fail for a number of reasons, and a replacement should be fairly economical. Ask a service engineer for advice.

Faulty motor
Have a service engineer check to see if the electric motor has failed, possibly as a result of a leak from the circulation pump.

MACHINE WON'T EMPTY

Filters blocked
Check there's nothing blocking the filters in the base of the dishwasher cabinet.

Outlet hose blocked
Remove the outlet hose and flush it out with running water.

Drain pump blocked
Provided it is accessible, the relatively small drain pump can be checked fairly easily.

1 Remove any fixing screws holding the pump in place.

2 Then detach the pump, possibly by rotating it to release the catches.

3 Carefully remove anything blocking the pump. It is quite common to find a cocktail stick jamming the pump's impeller, inside the pump body.

4 Use a pencil or plastic pen to check that the impeller is free to move. Don't put your fingers inside the pump, in case broken glass is causing or contributing to the blockage.

Faulty wiring
Having unplugged the dishwasher, check that there are no loose connections. Clean any dirty or corroded terminals with fine emery paper, then carefully brush away any emery dust. If that doesn't work, have the internal wiring tested by a service engineer.

Faulty programmer
If you suspect that a faulty programmer may not be allowing the cycle to continue, call out an engineer to test it.

1 Remove any fixing screws

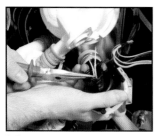
2 Detach the drain pump

3 Remove the blockage

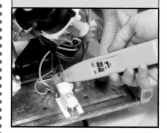
4 Check the impeller moves freely

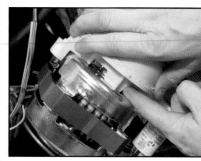
An engineer can check whether a leak has damaged your motor

SAFETY FIRST

Always unplug a dishwasher before you start checking for faults. See also *Switching off the power*, page 13. Before you touch any component inside a dishwasher connected to a fused connection unit, as a final check that the power is off remove the casing from the appliance and aim a non-contact voltage tester at the internal terminal block to which the flex is connected. If you are not absolutely certain an appliance is disconnected safely, get a service engineer to isolate and inspect it. Never take a risk.

WATER LEAKING FROM MACHINE

Dirty door seal

Flexible seals prevent water escaping from the dishwasher when the door is closed. There is usually one seal positioned around the outer edge of the cabinet, and another straight strip secured to the lower edge of the door. These seals should be compressed slightly when the door is closed, but an accumulation of grease or food particles can prevent good surface contact.

Using a soft plastic spatula, scrape off any visible debris from both seals, then wash the seals with a cloth or sponge dampened with a proprietary dishwasher cleaner.

Loose hose clip

Check for signs of water staining around the hose clips. Tighten screw-adjusted clips with a screwdriver. Sometimes loosening and moving a clip will increase the pressure on the hose and create a better seal.

Leaking hoses

Check the hose connections aren't leaking. Turn off the supply valve, then disconnect the inlet hose and drain it. Check it carefully for splits. If the hose is sound, check the hoses within the dishwasher to make sure they haven't sprung a leak. You can buy replacements for most hoses.

Blocked pressure system

If the pressure system becomes partially blocked with fatty deposits, it can prevent the pressure-sensitive switch (see page 120) turning off the water at the correct level. Have an engineer flush out the system for you.

Worn door seal

The required water level in a dishwasher is relatively low. If too much water is introduced for any reason, or the machine is not level, water invariably leaks out past the door seals. So it pays to check that your machine is standing level before going to the trouble of changing the door seals.

Check next for signs of wear or hardening of the seals. All door seals can be replaced, but it is vital to get an exact match for your model. Some

Wash the door seals

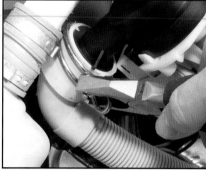
Try adjusting the hose clips

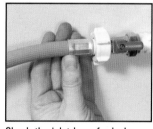
Check the inlet hose for leaks

SAFETY FIRST

Before putting an appliance back into service, plug it into a circuit protected by an RCD (see page 11). Then switch on, and if the RCD trips have the appliance tested by a qualified service engineer.

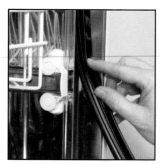

1 Push the door seal into position

2 Then press it firmly in place

seals are held in place by screw-fixed plastic or metal strips. Others are a tight push-fit in a recess. The latter can usually be removed by peeling them from one end.

1 When replacing push-fit seals, start in the middle of the strip and work towards each end. Push the seals into position, but take care not to stretch the rubber.

2 When the seal is in place, press firmly along the entire length to make sure it is seated properly.

When fitting a screw-fixed seal, start with the central fixings and work outwards toward each end of the strip.

If your door seals are riveted in place, have them replaced by a service engineer.

SERIOUS OVERFLOW

If water is flooding from beneath the machine, switch it off and pull the plug from the socket or turn off the power at the consumer unit – see page 13. Close the supply valve to turn off the water. If possible, drain any water remaining in the machine through the outlet hose – see page 115.

Outlet hose detached

Check whether the outlet hose is positioned properly in the standpipe – see page 74. If so, check the drainpipe for a blockage that could have caused the water to back up and overflow.

If the hose is connected to a sink trap (see page 111), check to see if the screw threads on the fitting are worn or a hose clip has worked loose. If necessary, replace the fitting.

Inlet hose detached

Check that the inlet hose is firmly attached both to the supply valve and to the inlet valve on the dishwasher.

If there are no obvious faults, call out a service engineer before using the dishwasher again.

SAFETY FIRST

To check that a dishwasher is earthed, apply one probe of a continuity tester to the earth pin of the plug and touch the exposed head of a panel-fixing screw or an unpainted part of the metal casing or cover panels with the other probe. The tester's indicator will be activated if the metal components are earthed. If it is not activated, have the machine checked by a service engineer.

If your dishwasher is connected to a fused connection unit (see page 14), perform the same test to check that the appliance is earthed – but, instead of placing one of the tester's probes on the earth pin of the plug, apply it to one of the two fixing screws that hold the FCU's faceplate in place. These fixing screws are connected to earth inside the fused connection unit, and the tester's indicator will be activated if the earth in the appliance is connected to earth in the FCU.

DOOR STAYS OPEN

Dishwasher doors are counterbalanced by springs, so that they do not fall open when the catch is released. If these springs stretch, the door has a tendency to stay open – which could cause someone to trip.

Slack return springs

Manufacturers have devised different ways to adjust the tension on these return springs. Some have screw adjustments, which will probably be described in your user's handbook. With some models it is necessary to remove the dishwasher's side panels to reveal the hinge mechanism, and then alter the position of the pin that holds each spring in place.

1 Wear gloves to protect your hands from sharp edges. Tie a length of strong string to the end of the spring so that you can stretch and detach the spring from its anchor pin.

2 Move the anchor pin up to increase the tension of the spring.

3 Then reattach the spring to the end of the pin. Once these springs become so slack that you cannot adjust them further, order replacements.

1 Stretch and detach the spring

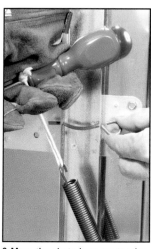

2 Move the pin to increase tension

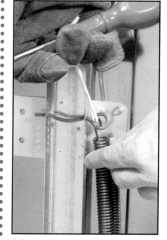

3 Reattach the spring

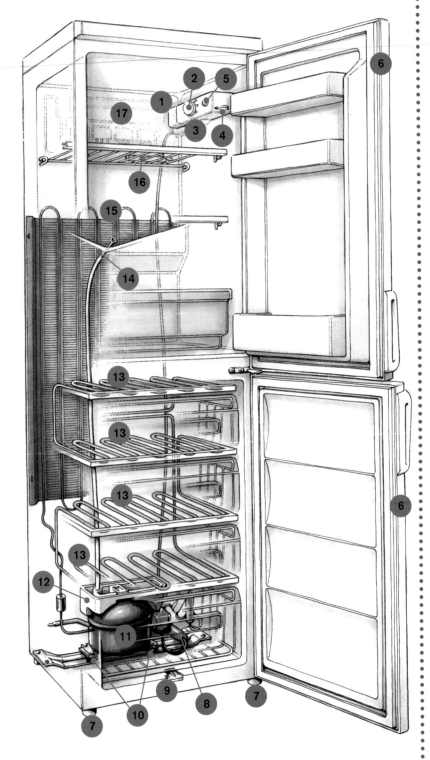

1 Internal-light screen	7 Adjustable foot	12 Reservoir
2 Temperature selector	8 Capacitor	13 Freezer cooling coils
3 Thermostat housing	9 Defrost discharge channel	14 Drain hole
4 Internal-light switch	10 Compressor mounting	15 Condenser coils
5 Fast-freeze button	11 Compressor	16 Defrost heater
6 Door seal		17 Evaporator

REFRIGERATORS AND FREEZERS

Refrigerators have been with us for a very long time – in fact, they were the first major electrical appliance that the average household could afford. The majority of fridges have a small freezer compartment for storing ice cubes and ice cream, plus a few packets of frozen food. Nowadays, the attractions of time-saving convenience foods and money-saving bulk buying have encouraged most families to own at least one capacious freezer, which needs stocking only once a month or so.

How it works

Although their operating temperatures are very different, refrigerators and freezers work on the same general principles. In the majority of cases, cooling is achieved by recirculating a gas, known as the refrigerant, through a sealed system. When the appliance is switched on, the refrigerant is drawn into an electrically operated compressor that pressurizes the gas, forcing it into the condenser tubes, usually mounted on the back of the appliance.

As the gas passes through the condenser system, it cools and liquefies. It is then filtered and travels via a small-bore capillary tube to the evaporator (cooling plate), which is mounted directly behind the back wall of the refrigerator cabinet and extends into the shelf or shelves in the freezer compartment.

On entering the evaporator, the liquid refrigerant is allowed to expand rapidly, causing a dramatic drop in temperature as it vaporizes back into a low-pressure gas. Because the system is sealed, this process continues until a thermostat registers the required temperature inside the fridge or freezer, at which point it turns off the compressor.

Autodefrost refrigerators

Moist air – which is introduced every time the fridge door is opened – turns into ice particles in the cold-storage compartment. If allowed to build into a thick layer, the ice reduces the efficiency of the evaporator. As a result, very basic refrigerators have to be

Standard refrigerator with a
small freezer compartment

defrosted manually at regular intervals to melt the
ice. However, most modern refrigerators have a
small heating element that automatically warms the
evaporator before icing reaches a critical level. The
resulting melt water runs down the back wall of the
cabinet and drains into a reservoir mounted on top
of the compressor unit, where it evaporates naturally
into the atmosphere.

Frost-free freezers
To prevent wastage and bacterial
contamination, freezers are never
defrosted automatically like fridges.
Conventional freezers have to be
defrosted manually by turning off the
appliance. A frost-free system
incorporates a dehumidifier, which
removes water vapour before it can
freeze, and a fan that distributes the
dry air throughout the storage
cabinet. As there's no accumulation
of ice, frost-free appliances are very
efficient and labour-saving.

Low-frost freezers
Low-frost freezers are designed to
prevent the normal ingress of moist
air that bypasses even the best door
seals. As moist air is only introduced
into the cabinet when the door is
opened, frost levels are reduced
considerably.

Fast-freezing
On some models, the rapid freezing of
fresh food is achieved by turning the
temperature selector to maximum or
switching on 'fast freeze' for a limited
period. Some models incorporate a
fast-freeze section of the cabinet –
usually the top shelf or a separate
partitioned area – which is in direct
contact with the evaporator.

Fridge freezer combinations
A single appliance incorporating a refrigerator and freezer will combine some
of the various features described above. For example, an autodefrost fridge
may be coupled with either a conventional freezer or one that is frost-free;
alternatively, the freezer and refrigerator cabinets may both be cooled by a
frost-free system. Whatever the combination, it is an advantage if each
compartment has its own separate compressor and temperature control.

Large-capacity chest freezer

Size and capacity
The capacity of fridges and freezers is generally given
in cubic feet or by quoting how many litres of food
they can hold. Both refrigerators and freezers, and
combined fridge freezers, vary enormously in capacity
– so much so, that it is difficult to make meaningful
comparisons. However, as a rough guide, the average
worktop-height fridge has a capacity of about 4.5 to
5.5cu ft (125 to 155 litres). Similar-size freezers
usually store slightly less food. You can expect to
more or less double the capacity if you opt for one of
the taller upright appliances. Chest freezers store
more food than upright freezers of the same size.

Fridge freezer

Upright freezer cabinets are usually furnished with a bank of sliding baskets or plastic drawers, making access to the contents particularly easy. Chest freezers are better for storing bulky items, but it is often necessary to partly empty the freezer in order to reach packages at the bottom.

Temperature settings

Some appliances, particularly freezers, have a built-in thermometer that records the interior temperature of the storage cabinet. If not, you can

buy an inexpensive fridge thermometer from a spares supplier or supermarket.

Most fridges have a simple control knob with which to regulate the temperature. You should check the storage temperatures recommended in your owner's handbook – but generally the interior of a freezer should be between -18°C and -23°C (0°F

and -10°F), and you need to keep a fridge at between 0°C and 5°C (32°F and 42°F).

The best way to regulate the average fridge is to set its temperature selector about midway and then make slight adjustments as required. With many fridge freezers, the same selector regulates the temperature of the freezer compartment, too – so remember to check that your freezer is operating at a safe temperature when making adjustments.

If possible, buy a freezer that has a visual or audible warning to indicate that the temperature inside is rising to an unacceptable level.

A single temperature selector may regulate the fridge and freezer

Choosing the best location

In adverse conditions, a fridge or freezer may have to work continuously in order to maintain the required internal temperature. The warm air that rises from the condenser coils must be allowed to circulate freely, and both appliances work best in dry, well-ventilated rooms.

Never place a fridge or freezer next to an oven, cooker or radiator, or expose either appliance to direct sunlight.

Storing food in your refrigerator

To prevent the possible spread of harmful bacteria, keep raw food at the bottom of the storage compartment and cooked food near the top.

Unwrap meat, chicken and fish and place them on a plate, with a bowl or another plate covering them, before you put them into a fridge. Some refrigerators come with a special plastic container for storing raw meat, poultry and fish.

The coldest parts of the fridge are closest to the evaporator – usually towards the back of the storage compartment.

Star ratings

Freezers are given star ratings to indicate how long you can safely store frozen food. Frozen-food packets are labelled with a similar star rating.

Up to 1 week

Up to 1 month

Up to 3 months

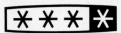

Up to 3 months and capable of freezing fresh food

Cover raw meat, chicken and fish

Storing food in a freezer

All food stored in a freezer needs to be either sealed in an airtight container or wrapped to exclude air and moisture. Wrap solid food in foil or put it into a plastic freezer bag. Squeeze out all the air, then seal the package with a twist tie or elastic band. Liquid foods should be stored in plastic containers with press-on lids.

Keep food in sealed freezer bags

Label and date any food you freeze yourself. Your owner's manual will suggest the length of time different foods can be stored safely in your freezer.

Check the star rating and use-by dates marked on packaged frozen food. Make sure this type of food is put in the freezer as soon as you get back home from shopping.

Don't refreeze food once it has thawed out. Either use it straightaway or cook it and then freeze it.

Defrosting your freezer

Unless you own a frost-free appliance, you need to defrost your freezer or freezer compartment regularly. The best time to defrost any freezer is when it is nearly empty – but don't let the ice get any thicker than about 5mm ($\frac{1}{4}$in).

Take out any food left in the freezer and wrap it in newspaper. Store the wrapped items in a cool place, preferably in a separate fridge or in a neighbour's freezer.

Unplug the appliance or switch off the fused connection unit (see page 14). In the unlikely event that your appliance is connected to an unswitched FCU, you will have to turn off the power at the consumer unit (see page 13). Leave the door open and lay newspaper or old towels on the floor in front of the cabinet.

Cover the floor with newspaper

If your freezer has a spout or channel for draining the melt water (check your user's handbook), pull it out and place a bowl under the spout or channel to catch the water. Remember to empty the bowl regularly.

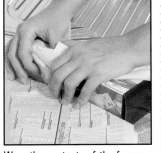
Wrap the contents of the freezer before defrosting the appliance

Catch the melt water in a shallow bowl

Using a defroster
The fastest way to remove the ice is to spray it with a proprietary freezer defroster and leave the door open. Collect the softened ice as it melts, wiping away excess water with a clean cloth.

Place bowls of hot water in the freezer compartment

Traditional method for defrosting

If you are unable to obtain a defroster, place bowls or saucepans of hot water in the compartment to encourage the ice to melt. Refill the containers regularly with hot water.

When the ice begins to melt, you can lift off softened deposits with a wooden or plastic spatula. Don't use metal utensils and don't attempt to chip off hard ice. When all the ice has melted, wash the interior with lukewarm water and dry the compartment with a clean cloth.

Switch on the freezer and allow it to cool thoroughly before you replace the frozen food.

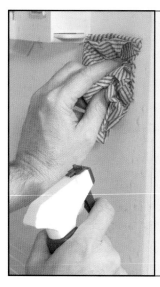

Cleaning fridges

Keep the interior of your refrigerator clean, using a proprietary antibacterial spray that you can simply wipe off the surfaces, without having to rinse them.

Alternatively, wash the inside of your fridge at least once a month with a lukewarm solution of washing-up liquid. Dry the compartment with a soft cloth or paper towels. Wipe the door seal with a cloth dampened with clean water only.

Make sure that spilt food and debris are not allowed to clog the melt-water discharge gutter and drain hole in an autodefrost fridge. Blockages can easily go unnoticed inside a well-stocked refrigerator – see opposite.

First things first

Many a service engineer has been called out to fix a fridge or freezer only to discover the fault has been caused by simple neglect or forgetfulness. Before you start looking for more serious defects, run through the checklist below.

- Has the temperature selector (thermostat) been set correctly?

- Has the temperature selector been turned off? (On some models, this will switch off the internal light.)

- Is the door closed properly?

- Does the appliance need defrosting?

- Is the appliance plugged in? And is the socket switched on?

A deodorizer will keep your fridge fresh for weeks

Preventing odours

Avoid unpleasant smells in your fridge by keeping the appliance clean and wrapping or covering strong-smelling foods.

Placing a proprietary deodorizer in the compartment will keep your fridge smelling fresh for up to 10 weeks.

Another solution is to fill an eggcup with bicarbonate of soda and place it on a shelf in the refrigerator.

Rearrange the contents

Make sure the appliance is level

SAFETY FIRST

Always unplug a fridge or freezer before you start checking for faults. Do the same before cleaning either appliance.

Don't store glass containers in a freezer – they could burst if the contents include liquids that expand when they freeze.

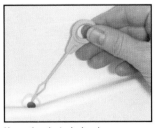

Keep the drain hole clear

APPLIANCE IS NOISY

The normal vibrations associated with a working refrigerator or freezer may get amplified in various ways.

Contents vibrating

Glass jars and bottles rattling in a fridge can be very irritating. Rearrange the contents, making sure that glass containers are not touching each other.

In contact with surroundings

If your appliance is in contact with a kitchen unit or a wall, vibrations set up by the compressor can be greatly amplified. Try moving the appliance away from the unit or wall.

Appliance not level

If the floor is uneven, either adjust the feet to level the appliance or, if there's no means of adjustment, chock up one of the feet with corrugated cardboard.

Compressor mounting rattling

Compressors are usually mounted on rubber feet or pads to prevent vibration. If you hear rattling from behind the fridge or freezer, check to see whether these mountings have worked loose.

WATER INSIDE REFRIGERATOR

You will often see water droplets or light frosting on the back wall of an autodefrost refrigerator. This is quite normal and can be ignored. However, if a pool of water collects at the bottom of the fridge, that means the melt water is unable to drain into the reservoir.

Drain hole or tube blocked

When the appliance is working normally, the melt water drains through a hole in the discharge gutter formed in the back wall of the compartment. Use the tool supplied or a pipe cleaner to clear the hole and the tube running from it to the reservoir.

FREEZER DOOR WILL NOT OPEN

When loading a freezer with frozen food, it is often necessary to open and close the door several times in quick succession. Under these conditions,

Vibration can cause compressor mountings to work loose

Wait 2 or 3 minutes when the freezer door won't open

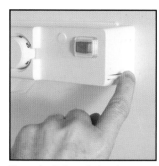

Press the light switch a few times in case it is stuck

1 Remove the translucent screen

2 Replace a faulty bulb

a partial vacuum may form inside the compartment, temporarily preventing the door from opening. Simply wait 2 or 3 minutes before retrying.

INTERNAL LIGHT DOESN'T WORK

Refrigerator doors close against a switch that turns off the light inside the compartment. With the door open, operate the switch manually a few times to make sure it is moving freely. If the light doesn't come on, check the bulb.

Bulb defective

Isolate the appliance from the electricity supply by unplugging it or by switching off the FCU – see page 14.

1 Take off the translucent plastic screen covering the bulb. This usually slides off or requires gentle squeezing to release moulded plastic catches. Old screens can be brittle, so take care.

2 Unscrew or take out the bulb and replace it with an identical one of the same wattage.

Replace the plastic screen and reconnect the appliance to the electricity supply. Before closing the door, press the switch to make sure the light goes out.

Faulty switch

If changing the bulb doesn't solve the problem, unplug the appliance and remove the thermostat housing to test the switch.

1 Look for plastic screw caps that have to be prised off with a screwdriver to reveal hidden screw fixings.

2 Remove the screw fixings that hold the thermostat housing on the fridge wall.

3 Then carefully detach the thermostat housing, taking care not to damage internal wiring or components.

4 Locate the switch mounted near the front of the housing, remove any fixings and carefully lift it out.

SAFETY FIRST

Old appliances may contain environmentally harmful chlorofluorocarbon gases (CFCs), which will be released into the atmosphere if the refrigerant is allowed to escape. Ask your local authority for advice on how you should dispose of any refrigerator or freezer.

1 Locate any hidden fixings

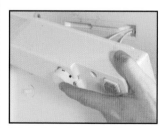

2 Remove the screws

3 Detach the thermostat housing

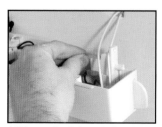

4 Lift out the light switch

5 Test the switch for continuity

5 Ease off one of the connectors and test the switch with a continuity tester, placing one probe on each terminal. If the tester is not activated, buy a new switch.

With the new switch installed, screw the thermostat housing back in place, making sure all the components and wiring are returned to their original locations.

APPLIANCE NOT COOL ENOUGH

If you can hear your appliance running normally but the storage compartment is not cooling to the required temperature (see page 128), check out the following possibilities.

Incorrect thermostat setting

The temperature selector may have been turned down accidentally. Readjust it.

Readjust the temperature selector

Faulty thermostat

Having checked that the temperature selector has been turned on and set correctly, call out an engineer to test and, if need be, replace the thermostat.

Ambient temperature too high

Is the appliance close to a source of heat such as a cooker or radiator? Move the fridge or freezer away from the source of the heat, and consider relocating the appliance to a cooler environment.

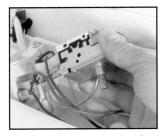

Have your thermostat replaced

Condenser coils dusty

A coating of dust on the condenser coils will prevent heat dissipating. The coils are usually fixed to the back of conventional fridges and freezers, but on some models they are mounted underneath (look for a removable grille along the front of the appliance).

Unplug the appliance and carefully clean off accumulated dust, using a vacuum cleaner and a soft brush – don't use wire brushes or other metal utensils on the coils. If it is difficult to gain access to the coils, ask a service engineer to clean them.

Freezer needs defrosting

Excessive icing will prevent the evaporator working efficiently and may damage door seals. Defrost the freezer (or the freezer compartment of a fridge) – see page 129.

Internal light stays on

If the switch is faulty, the interior light may be staying on all the time and generating enough heat to prevent the compartment cooling efficiently.

As soon as you open the fridge door, cup your hand around the light cover (don't touch the bulb or cover itself). If it feels warm, press the light switch – see opposite. If the light stays on, turn off the power, then remove the thermostat housing in order to test the switch.

Ease off one connector and test the switch with a continuity tester, placing one probe on each terminal. Have someone press the switch button while you hold the probes on the terminals. With a switch that is working properly, the tester will not be activated when the button is pressed, but will be activated when the button is released. Buy a new switch if the tester remains activated when the button is pressed.

Replace the housing, making sure all the components and wiring are returned to their original locations.

Does the light cover feel warm?

Seals that are not screw-fixed should be replaced by an engineer

Remove screws to detach old seals

1 Mark mitre joint on new seal

2 Press down with a sharp blade

3 Insert the magnetic strip

4 Glue the corner joint

Faulty doors seals

If the soft seals around the edge of the door show signs of wear or deterioration, warm moist air may be entering the compartment, preventing it from ever cooling down to the required temperature.

Not all door seals can be replaced – with some appliances a new door would have to be fitted, which may not be cost-effective. However, depending on the make and model, you may be able to renew damaged seals yourself.

Peel back the edge of the door seal to expose the fixings. If the seal is held in place with screws, order an exact replacement from a service centre. If the seal is not screw-fixed, have it replaced by a service engineer.

If you are unable to obtain an exact replacement for the seals in your appliance, buy a 'universal-seal' kit. Two profiles are available by mail order – choose the one that is closest to the seal on your fridge or freezer.

The kit consists of two right-angle seal assemblies, already joined at the corners. All you have to do is cut and join the other two corners, using the glue and plastic corner pieces that come with the kit.

1 Use your old seal as a template to mark out the kit assemblies, then mark the mitre joints, using a set square and fine-point pen.

2 Place the seal on a cutting board and use a sharp knife to cut the mitres. Press straight down with the blade – don't cut with a slicing action or you will distort the profile.

3 Measure the length of the magnetic strip inside the old seal and use electrician's side cutters to crop the strip supplied with the kit. Slide the cropped strip into the profile's outer recess.

4 Glue the plastic corner pieces into one half of each joint. Spread a little glue onto the cut edge of the profile and the other half of the corner piece, then slide the joint together.

When the glue has set, attach the assembled seal to the door.

APPLIANCE OPERATES BUT DOESN'T COOL AT ALL

When a fridge or freezer appears to be operating normally but is incapable of cooling the storage compartment, there is usually a fairly serious problem.

Loss of refrigerant
If there has been a serious leakage of gas from the sealed cooling system, you have no choice but to have the system tested by a qualified refrigeration engineer. If the source of the leak can be remedied, the same engineer can refill the system with gas.

Pipework blocked
A similar problem arises when any of the small-bore pipework gets blocked. Ask an engineer to extract the refrigerant and evacuate the system to remove any moisture that is causing the blockage. He or she will then fill the system with fresh gas.

Faulty thermostat
If the thermostat has failed, it can usually be replaced economically.

SAFETY FIRST

Before putting a fridge or freezer back into service, plug it into a circuit protected by an RCD. If the RCD trips, have the appliance tested by a service engineer.

Check your thermostat setting

APPLIANCE TOO COLD

You can expect a certain amount of icing up with conventional freezers, but place a thermometer inside the cabinet to make sure the operating temperature falls between the accepted limits – see page 128.

If foodstuffs such as butter and milk are partially freezing, then the refrigerator is getting too cold.

Incorrect thermostat setting

The temperature selector may have been accidentally turned to the wrong setting. Readjust it.

Fast-freeze switch left on

If your appliance has a fast-freeze facility (check your user's handbook), make sure it has not been left on inadvertently.

Faulty thermostat

Have the thermostat tested by an engineer.

Faulty autodefrost heater

Appliances with autodefrost may ice up if the evaporator heater has failed. Testing and replacing this heater is a job for a service engineer.

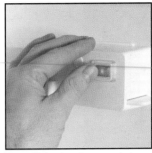
Turn off the fast-freeze switch

APPLIANCE DOESN'T SWITCH ON

Machine not plugged in

Make sure the plug is inserted in the socket and that the socket is switched on. Some appliances are also connected to a fused connection unit -- see page 14. Make sure this is switched on, too.

Power failure

If other appliances on the circuit have stopped working, inspect your consumer unit for a blown fuse or tripped MCB or RCD – pages 11 and 12.

Faulty wiring in plug

Take the back off the plug to see if it is wired correctly – see page 19.

Plug or FCU fuse has blown

Replace the fuse in the plug – see page 17. If there is a fused connection unit, check whether the fuse in the FCU needs to be replaced – page 17.

Faulty compressor
Leave the appliance door open for a few minutes. If you don't hear the compressor start up, have the unit checked by a service engineer.

Most compressors will last the lifetime of a fridge or freezer, but you can damage a compressor inadvertently by turning the appliance on again as soon as you have turned it off for any reason. Always wait a few minutes before restoring the power.

SAFETY FIRST

To check that a fridge or freezer is earthed, apply one probe of a continuity tester to the earth pin of the plug and place the other probe on one of the copper tubes running to the compressor, or on the head of one of the screws that holds the condenser coils to the back of the appliance. The tester's indicator will be activated if the metal components are earthed. If it is not activated, have the appliance checked by a service engineer.

If your fridge or freezer is connected to a fused connection unit (see page 14), perform the same test to check that the appliance is earthed – but, instead of placing one of the tester's probes on the earth pin of the plug, apply it to one of the two fixing screws that hold the FCU's faceplate in place. These fixing screws are connected to earth inside the fused connection unit, and the tester's indicator will be activated if the earth in the appliance is connected to earth in the FCU.

WASTE-DISPOSAL UNITS

Once considered to be a luxury, a waste-disposal unit able to grind and flush away vegetable waste, small bones, fruit stones, even paper napkins, has become a 'must have' appliance. The unit can be connected to a standard-size sink bowl, but it is more convenient if you have a smaller waste-disposal bowl alongside the main sink. To accommodate a waste-disposal unit, the sink outlet must be 89mm (3½in) in diameter – larger than a conventional sink outlet. The waste-disposal units described here are typical models, but may not match your unit exactly.

How it works

Waste-disposal units have a powerful vertically mounted electric motor. The motor shaft drives a shredding mechanism, which grinds waste material into pieces small enough to pass easily through the household waste-water system. The shredding mechanism is housed in a robust watertight chamber connected to a standard waste pipe and trap.

Older waste-disposal units usually have cutting blades mounted directly onto the motor shaft. When the unit is switched on, the blades rotate at high speed and shred whatever is fed into them. The modern equivalent has a rotating disc with pivoting weighted cutters attached to the upper surface. A number of stationary blades surround the disc. The weighted cutters help break up the larger scraps and then propel the waste material onto the ring of fixed cutters. Most units are fitted with a thermal-overload cutout (TOC), which switches off the unit to protect the electric motor when the cutters jam. The TOC usually has to be reset manually.

Getting the best from your waste-disposal unit

Most of the problems that arise result from neglect or from the appliance not being used correctly.

• Always ensure there's a continuous flow of cold water before and during shredding and for a minute or two afterwards. The noise level reduces as soon as the unit has finished shredding.

• Blockages and jamming are most often caused by kitchen utensils, bottle caps or bones finding their way into the shredding chamber. To reduce the chance of objects being dropped accidentally into the unit, insert the stopper when you are not using the appliance.

• Don't pour bleach or strong caustic cleaning agents into a sink fitted with a waste-disposal unit. These chemicals can shorten the life of watertight seals, including the motor's shaft seal. Failure of this seal allows water to penetrate the motor, which in turn causes the motor to run noisily, vibrate, and possibly seize up or short-circuit. Have shaft seals renewed as soon as there are signs of a leak.

• Waste-disposal units can cope with fat and grease, but it pays to put substantial amounts of fat or grease into the waste bin.

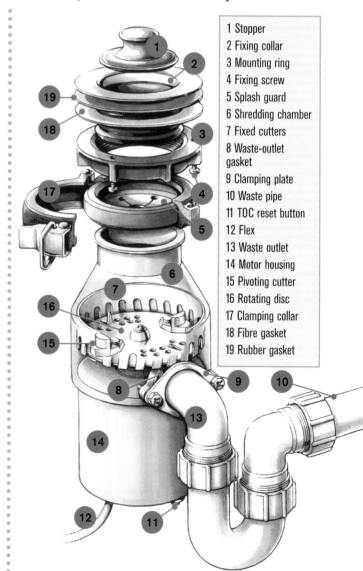

1 Stopper
2 Fixing collar
3 Mounting ring
4 Fixing screw
5 Splash guard
6 Shredding chamber
7 Fixed cutters
8 Waste-outlet gasket
9 Clamping plate
10 Waste pipe
11 TOC reset button
12 Flex
13 Waste outlet
14 Motor housing
15 Pivoting cutter
16 Rotating disc
17 Clamping collar
18 Fibre gasket
19 Rubber gasket

WATER SOFTENERS

Harmful impurities are removed from water before it is supplied to our homes, but minerals absorbed from the ground are still present. It's the concentration of these minerals – primarily calcium and magnesium – that determines whether the water is hard or soft. Hard water, which contains higher concentrations of calcium and magnesium, does not pose a threat to our health. However, problems arise when these minerals are deposited in the form of hard scale on the inside of pipes, water-storage tanks and hot-water cylinders.

The more obvious consequences of hard water are blocked shower fittings, stained bathtubs, basins and sinks, and a white film or spots deposited on dishes and cutlery left to dry. Even washing in hard water can leave your skin feeling dry, and your hair becomes dull and lifeless.

Many people resign themselves to living with these effects, but they can be reduced or even eliminated by a properly installed and maintained domestic water softener.

How it works

Water softeners work on the principle of ion exchange. The incoming water flows through a compartment containing synthetic-resin beads that absorb the scale-forming calcium and magnesium ions and release sodium ions in their place. Sodium has none of the adverse properties associated with hard-water minerals.

After a while, the resin beads become saturated with calcium and magnesium and the water softener automatically flushes the compartment with a concentrated saline solution to regenerate the resin. The mixture of brine and minerals is drained away to a standpipe (see page 74), and the softening process then starts all over again.

The water softener is connected to a complicated series of pipes and valves that allow the unit to be isolated for servicing while maintaining the supply of water to the rest of the house. A branch pipe just after the main stopcock supplies unsoftened drinking water to the kitchen sink. The same pipe may also supply a garden tap and possibly a downstairs WC cistern, simply as an economy measure. Water regulations stipulate that the plumbing must include a non-return valve to prevent the reverse flow of softened water.

Water softeners may be operated from a standard 13amp wall socket or wired to a switched fused connection unit.

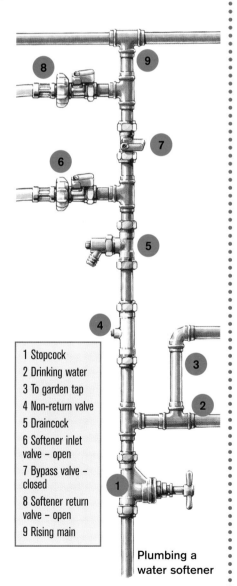

1 Stopcock
2 Drinking water
3 To garden tap
4 Non-return valve
5 Draincock
6 Softener inlet valve – open
7 Bypass valve – closed
8 Softener return valve – open
9 Rising main

Plumbing a water softener

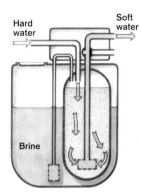

Softening cycle

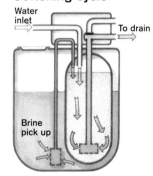

Regeneration cycle

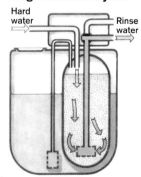

Rinse cycle

First things first

Water softeners are generally maintenance-free appliances, and many a service engineer is called out to fix a unit only to discover the fault has been caused by simple neglect or forgetfulness. Before you start looking for more serious defects, run through the checklist below.

- Is the softener plugged in? Is the socket or FCU switched on?

- Has the water been turned off?

- Has one of the isolation valves been closed?

- Has the timer been adjusted correctly, and has it been activated?

- Is there sufficient salt in the reservoir?

- Is the prefilter clogged?

SAFETY FIRST

If the unit is fitted with a 13amp plug, make sure the plug is wired correctly and that the appropriate fuse is fitted.

Don't use a water softener that is leaking water.

When reassembling the unit, make sure the components and wiring are returned to their original locations.

Before putting a water softener back into service, test it on a circuit protected by an RCD. If the RCD trips, have the appliance tested by a qualified service engineer.

NO SOFT WATER

If you suspect that your unit is not working properly, buy a test kit to check the hardness of your water. Tablets are added one at a time to a sample of the water until the colour changes from plum red to dark blue. The result is calculated from the number of tablets used.

Incorrect timer setting

Is the timer set to the right time of day? And is the am/pm setting correct? If you have had a power cut, the clock may no longer be set to the correct time. If necessary, reset the clock.

Inconvenient timer setting

Perhaps the softener is running through its regeneration sequence during the time of day when you use most hot water. As a result, your hot-water cylinder may be filling with unsoftened water.

Reset the timer to regenerate in the early hours of the morning.

Valves set to bypass softener

Have you recently had a plumber working in your house or flat? Perhaps the valves have been set to allow water to bypass the softener. Check the valves (see page 141) and adjust them if necessary.

Needs topping up with salt

The amount of salt you need will depend on how much water you and your family use, but the average household gets through about 25kg (55lb) of salt per month. If you don't keep your softener topped up with salt, the regeneration sequence will be ineffectual – simply because the concentration of brine is too low.

You can fill the reservoir with tablet salt; but only half-fill it if you are using granular salt.

Salt caked in the unit

Every softener needs topping up regularly with salt. If the reservoir in your unit seems to be full most of the time, the salt may have 'caked', so the unit is unable to regenerate itself properly. Tap the side of the salt reservoir to see if the salt settles. Don't be surprised to see your reservoir half full of water – this is quite normal.

Buy a hard-water test kit

Reset the softener's clock

Reset the timer

Regularly top up with salt

SAFETY FIRST

When an appliance is earthed, always use a continuity tester to verify that there is a continuous earth path – see page 22. In the case of the water softener described here, the earth path was tested by placing one probe of a continuity tester on the earth pin of the plug and the other probe on the metal motor housing.

If your water softener is connected to a fused connection unit (see page 14), perform the same test to check that the appliance is earthed – but, instead of placing one of the tester's probes on the earth pin of the plug, apply it to one of the two fixing screws that hold the FCU's faceplate in place. These fixing screws are connected to earth inside the fused connection unit, and the tester's indicator will be activated if the earth in the appliance is connected to earth in the FCU.

Faulty meter or timer

Softeners with metered or timer-controlled regeneration can develop faults within the control unit. If you have eliminated other possibilities, get an engineer to check your softener.

LEAKING WATER

Unplug the appliance and check whether the hose connections behind the unit are leaking. Also, make sure water is not overflowing from the standpipe. You can replace flexible pipes, but call out an engineer if the unit itself has sprung a leak.

DISCOLOURED WATER

The water in the reservoir can be discoloured by low-quality regeneration salt or by iron in your water supply. If the reservoir needs cleaning, isolate the unit and bale out as much water as possible, then scoop out any sludge remaining at the bottom. Top up with fresh salt, then turn on the water and the electricity supply to the unit.

UNIT NOT WORKING AT ALL

Socket not switched on

Make sure the plug is inserted in the socket, and that the socket is switched on. If the unit is connected to a fused connection unit (see page 14), make sure it's switched on.

Faulty wiring in plug

If your unit is connected with a 13amp plug, take the back off the plug and check that it is wired correctly – see page 19.

Plug or FCU fuse has blown

Replace the fuse in the plug – see page 17. If there is a fused connection unit, check whether the fuse in the FCU needs to be replaced – see page 17.

Power failure

If other appliances on the circuit have stopped working, inspect your consumer unit for a blown fuse or tripped MCB or RCD – see pages 11 and 12.

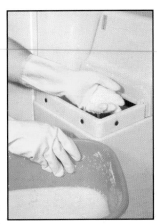

Check hose connections for leaks

Scoop out sludge and then top up with fresh salt

SAFETY FIRST

Always unplug a water softener before you start checking for faults.

If the unit is connected to a fused connection unit, see *Switching off the power* on page 13. If you are not absolutely certain that the appliance is disconnected safely, get a service engineer to isolate and inspect it. Never take a risk.

DEHUMIDIFIERS

Rising and penetrating damp are conditions that sometimes require extensive work, and possibly professional help, in order to eradicate them completely. However, many householders find that a portable dehumidifier can be effective for reducing condensation – which, if ignored, can lead to mildew and fungal growth on walls and ceilings, as well as an unpleasant musty smell. Although the cost of domestic units has come down considerably, dehumidifiers still command prices that make regular maintenance and timely repairs worthwhile.

How it works

Air carries moisture in the form of water vapour, and the temperature of the air determines how much water vapour it can hold. As air becomes warmer, it expands and can therefore absorb more moisture. When this warm moisture-laden air comes into contact with a cold surface, the air cools rapidly until it can no longer hold the water it has absorbed and it condenses, depositing the moisture onto the cold surface. You see this happening on the inside of a window pane when it's cold outside. Dehumidifiers aim to remove moisture from the air before it condenses on windows or other cold surfaces.

A dehumidifier has cooling coils where high-pressure liquefied refrigerant from a motor-driven compressor expands back into a gas – thus creating a cold surface that attracts the moisture in the air, which is drawn over it by a large fan. The water that condenses onto the cooling coils drips down into a removable reservoir.

A device called a humidistat switches off the compressor when the humidity (moisture content) of the surrounding air has dropped to the required level.

Additionally, most dehumidifiers are fitted with a simple float-operated switch that prevents overflowing and turns on a 'tank full' indicator to remind you to empty the reservoir.

The more sophisticated models may feature an autodefrost thermostat that turns off the appliance for a short time to stop the cooling coils icing up.

1 Outlet grille	7 Reservoir
2 Fan	8 Cooling coils
3 Overflow-prevention switch	9 Filter
4 Compressor	10 Inlet grille
5 Flex	11 Humidistat
6 Float	12 Selector switch

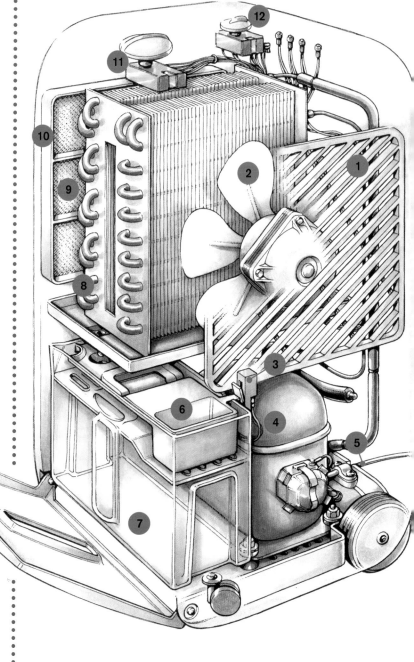

Getting the best from your dehumidifier

Provided you empty the reservoir from time to time, a dehumidifier will usually look after itself.

Optimum room temperature

Dehumidifiers work best at a room temperature of about 21°C (70°F). Ice may begin to form on the cooling surfaces in temperatures lower than 18°C (65°F). Models fitted with an autodefrost system automatically go into defrost mode when icing is detected. However, if the ambient temperature remains below 18°C (65°F), the appliance may attempt to defrost continuously and as a result fail to do its job efficiently. Don't continue to use a dehumidifier that keeps freezing up in this way, as it will ultimately damage the sealed system. Heat the room before trying again.

If your dehumidifier does not have an autodefrost facility, you will have to defrost the appliance manually This is usually as simple as turning it off and allowing the ice to melt – but consult your user's handbook.

Positioning a dehumidifier

A dehumidifier must have air circulating around it, so for peak performance position it at least 150mm (6in) from the walls and furniture. Don't tuck the unit into a corner of the room, nor place it too close to soft furnishings.

Setting the humidistat

To begin with, set the humidistat to 'high' or 'continuous' and allow the appliance to run until you feel the humidity of the room has been reduced to a comfortable level. Slowly turn down the humidistat until its indicator light goes out and the appliance will continue to monitor the humidity at that level.

A point to consider is that an overdry atmosphere is uncomfortable and may cause woodwork to warp and crack.

Gaining access to your dehumidifier

Some dehumidifiers, including the model shown here, are designed to provide easy access for routine maintenance. Being held in place by visible screw fixings or simple moulded-plastic catches, the inlet and outlet grilles are detachable. For more extensive maintenance, it is necessary to release screws or catches in order to lift off the outer casing. Removing the complete casing is the only way to gain access to the components of many dehumidifiers.

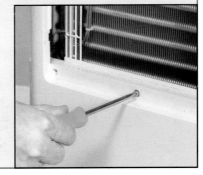

CLEANING A DEHUMIDIFIER

Unplug the dehumidifier and wipe the exterior casing with a damp cloth, then dry it thoroughly before using the appliance. Wash the reservoir at regular intervals to prevent possible contamination from mould spores.

Cleaning the filter and vents

Dehumidifiers are fitted with filters that remove dust and fluff from the air flowing through the appliance. It's good practice to clean the filter about once a week, depending on how often you use the appliance.

1 Take out the filter and remove the accumulation of fluff. With some dehumidifiers, the filter can be washed in warm (not hot) water. The filter must be left to dry thoroughly before it is returned to the dehumidifier.

2 From time to time, use a vacuum cleaner and a soft paintbrush to clean the inlet and outlet vents in the casing. If the grille is detachable, you can wash it in warm soapy water. Dry it thoroughly before you replace it.

First things first

Many a service engineer has been called out to fix a dehumidifier only to discover the fault has been caused by simple neglect or forgetfulness. Always run through the checklist below before you start looking for serious defects.

• Is the dehumidifier plugged in? And is the socket switched on?

• Is the reservoir in place? And is it empty?

• Has the humidistat been set correctly?

• Is the filter clean?

Clean the condenser coils regularly

Have an engineer check your pressurized cooling system

RESERVOIR FILLS QUICKLY

High humidity
The need to empty the reservoir regularly simply indicates that the appliance is working correctly. As the room dries out, you will find the reservoir takes longer to fill. However, check to see that the humidistat has not been set at too dry a setting.

If the situation does not improve with time, have your house or flat inspected by a building specialist to make sure there is no evidence of serious damp within the structure.

RUNS BUT RESERVOIR EMPTY

Humidistat incorrectly set
Check that the humidistat is set correctly, then try again.

Compressor turned off for de-icing
This would occur for a short period only, and only with appliances that have an autodefrost facility.

Filter clogged
Clean the filter and vents – see page 145.

Dirty condenser coils
At least once a year (perhaps more often if the appliance is used on a regular basis) carefully clean the cooling coils, using a small soft brush and a vacuum cleaner attachment. Take great care not to damage the delicate pipework of the sealed cooling system.

Faulty sealed pressurized system
Try cleaning the unit as described above. If that doesn't help, have the cooling system checked at a service centre.

RUNS BUT NO AIRFLOW

Blocked air vents
Clean out the vents, using a soft paintbrush and a vacuum cleaner. Clean the filter at the same time.

Fan is jammed
Unplug the appliance and check that the circulation fan turns freely. If the fan slows down

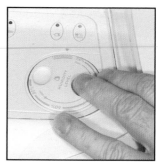

Check your humidistat setting

ICE ON THE COOLING COILS

If you turn off the dehumidifier, the ice will melt quickly and the appliance will come to no harm. However, you should try to prevent the dehumidifier icing up again.

Room too cold
The room should be heated to about 21°C (70°F). Don't use the dehumidifier until the temperature of the room reaches at least 18°C (65°F).

Dehumidifier standing on the floor
Even when the room appears to be warm, the air close to the floor is often much cooler. Try placing the dehumidifier on a suitably safe and strong table so that it can draw in warmer air.

Does the fan move freely?

An engineer can check your motor

Internal wiring is very complex

quickly when you spin it, remove any fluff build-up on the fan and motor. If that doesn't help, have the appliance serviced professionally.

Faulty fan motor
The electric motors in these appliances are extremely reliable – but if you suspect that your motor has seized or failed in some way, have the dehumidifier checked by a service engineer.

Faulty internal wiring
Since dehumidifiers are portable appliances, the connections inside them can work loose. However, the wiring is likely to be very complex and can only be tested effectively by an expert.

WILL NOT WORK AT ALL

Reservoir full
Empty the reservoir and try again.

Water reservoir not located correctly
Make sure there's nothing stopping the reservoir fitting properly, then replace it carefully and try switching on.

Defrost cycle activated
An autodefrost facility will turn off the dehumidifier if the room temperature is too low – see opposite.

Power failure
If other appliances on the circuit have stopped working, inspect your consumer unit for a blown fuse or tripped MCB or RCD – pages 11 and 12.

Dehumidifier not plugged in
Make sure the plug is inserted in the socket, and that the socket is switched on.

Plug fuse has blown
Replace the fuse in the plug – see page 17. If the fuse blows again as soon as you turn the machine on, have your dehumidifier checked by a service engineer.

Faulty wiring in plug
If possible, take the back off the plug and check that it is wired correctly – see page 19.

SAFETY FIRST

Always unplug a dehumidifier before cleaning it or checking for faults.

Ensure the plug is wired correctly and that the appropriate fuse is fitted.

When a dehumidifier has been turned off for any reason, always wait at least 10 minutes before you turn it on again. Your user's manual may recommend a longer period.

Remember to empty the reservoir before moving a dehumidifier.

Don't use a dehumidifier that is leaking.

SAFETY FIRST

Check the flexible cord regularly for signs of damage, and never move the appliance by pulling on the flex.

Don't use an extension lead to power a dehumidifier.

When reassembling the appliance, make sure the components and wiring are returned to their original locations.

SAFETY FIRST

Don't attempt to work on the sealed pressurized system. This is a job for a refrigeration specialist. When the appliance reaches the end of its working life, it must be disposed of correctly by the relevant authority. Contact your local waste-disposal department and ask how this should be done in your local area.

A dirty fan may be out of balance

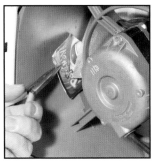

Check for an obstructed fan

Tighten motor-mounting screws

Broken flex conductor

With most dehumidifiers, the flex is connected to accessible screw terminals – you will be able to test the flex for continuity (see page 20) and replace it if necessary. If it is not obvious how the flex is connected to the terminals, have a suspect flex checked and replaced at a service centre.

Faulty humidistat

A faulty humidistat will turn off the appliance when it erroneously detects a dry atmosphere. Have this type of fault checked by a service engineer.

Faulty internal wiring

See page 147.

NOISY WHEN IN USE

Dirty fan

An accumulation of dust and fluff on the fan can cause it to run out of balance. Brush dust off the fan and clean the filter and vents.

Obstructed fan

If something has worked loose or has found its way into the dehumidifier, it may have become lodged near the fan. Unplug the appliance, then carefully remove the obstruction. Make sure the fan is undamaged and free to rotate.

Loose fan-motor mounting

Vibration can cause mounting screws to work loose. Check that these screws are tight.

LEAKS WATER

Cracked reservoir

Take out the reservoir, fill it with water and stand it on some paper towels. After a short while, check the towels for signs of moisture.

Faulty overflow-prevention switch

Check that the float moves freely, then press the switch toggle to make sure it is operating – you should hear the switch clicking when you press it.

Get professional help if there is no obvious reason for a leak, and don't use your dehumidifier until the leak has been detected and rectified.

SAFETY FIRST

When any appliance is earthed, you should always use a continuity tester to verify that there is a continuous earth path – see page 22. In the case of the dehumidifier described here, the earth path was tested by placing one probe of a continuity tester on the earth pin of the plug and, at the same time, carefully touching the metal cooling coils with the other probe.

Before putting a dehumidifier back into service, plug it into a circuit protected by an RCD – see page 11. Switch on, and if the RCD trips, have the appliance tested by a service engineer.

Older dehumidifiers may be fitted with a capacitor. A capacitor can hold a charge for a short while after the appliance is turned off. As a precaution, unplug any dehumidifier and wait 10 to 15 minutes to allow the capacitor to discharge before removing the casing.

Operate the switch toggle

HUMIDIFIERS

Most people know that too much moisture in the air can be detrimental to health and property, but it is not always appreciated that a dry atmosphere can be just as damaging. Dry air can lead to an increased risk of infections. A dry atmosphere causes natural materials such as wood to shrink and crack, and wallcoverings can peel at the edges. In a typical house with modern standards of insulation and heating, the average level of humidity in the winter months can be as low as 15 per cent, which is virtually bone dry – so it's not surprising that many householders find a humidifier essential in order to keep the humidity at a comfortable level.

1 Drive roller	8 Permeable belt
2 Control panel	9 Centrifugal fan
3 Oscillating louvres	10 Fan motor
4 Water inlet	11 Internal-flex connection
5 Water-level indicator	12 Belt-drive motor
6 Reservoir	13 Filter
7 Bracing rod	

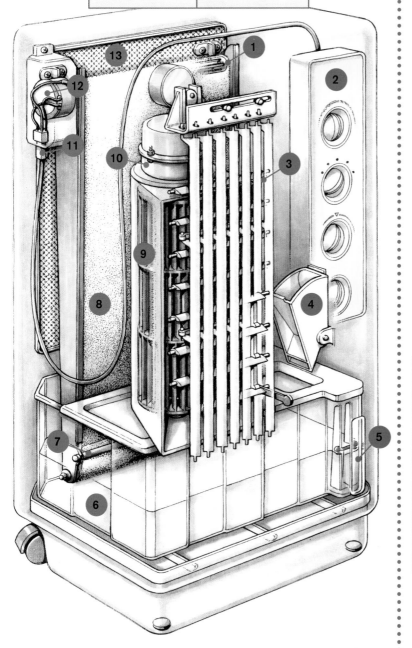

How it works

Humidifiers employ various ways of introducing moisture into the atmosphere – including ultrasonic high-frequency vibrations that create a 'cold mist'. However, most of these appliances are not suitable for DIY repairs and maintenance. A cool-air humidifier – which incorporates a fan that blows air through a wet permeable membrane – is the type of appliance you can to a certain extent service yourself.

A cool-air humidifier incorporates a reservoir for water and an electric motor that drives a fan. In addition, there's usually a speed-selector switch, a timer, an air filter and, most importantly, a broad belt of permeable material to soak up the water. A separate motor moves the moist permeable belt through the airflow from the fan.

When the appliance is working, moisture is absorbed by the air as it passes through the belt and out of the appliance. This increases the humidity of the air in the room and reduces its temperature at the same time.

Cleaning the filter

A filter membrane prevents dust entering the appliance. To gain access to the filter, unscrew or lift off the inlet grille. Wash the filter in warm soapy water, and leave it to dry flat before you reattach it to the grille.

1 Lift off the back panel

2 Detach the internal flex

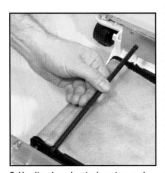

3 Unclip the plastic bracing rod

Remember to reconnect the belt-drive motor

UNPLEASANT SMELL WHEN IN USE

Dirty permeable belt

Remove and clean the permeable belt. Your back panel and belt-drive mechanism may be different in detail from the examples shown here, but the procedure for removing and cleaning the belt will be similar.

1 Having unplugged the humidifier, unscrew or lift off the back panel.

2 Detach the internal flex connected to the small belt-drive motor.

3 Remove the slim plastic rod, which braces the roller frame.

4 Slide the bottom roller from inside the permeable belt.

5 Detach the top roller from the motor drive shaft.

6 Replace the belt if it's in poor condition. Otherwise, wash it in warm soapy water and leave it to dry flat before reassembling the mechanism.

Take the opportunity to wash the water reservoir.

RUNS BUT DOES NOT USE WATER

Drive mechanism disconnected

Make sure you remembered to reconnect the belt-drive motor.

Permeable belt broken or jammed

Discard a torn permeable belt and obtain a replacement. However, if the belt is intact, remove it (see above) and inspect the ends of the roller to make sure they are turning freely in their mountings.

Faulty belt-drive motor

The belt is driven by a small dedicated electric motor, which you can usually test and replace fairly easily – see opposite.

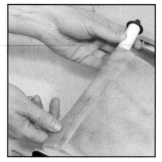

4 Slide out the bottom roller

5 Detach the drive roller

6 Wash the belt in warm water

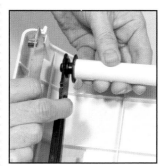

And make sure the bottom roller is able to rotate freely

1 Mark the drive roller

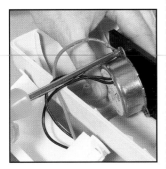

2 Replace a faulty motor

SAFETY FIRST

Never use a humidifier to dry or air clothing.

Don't direct the airflow from your humidifier onto other electrical appliances or mains-supply outlets, such as sockets.

Before you start checking for faults, always unplug a humidifier and ensure that the water reservoir is empty.

When reassembling the appliance, make sure the components and wiring are returned to their original locations.

Before putting a humidifier back into service, plug it into a circuit protected by an RCD – page 11. Switch on, and if the RCD trips, have the appliance tested by an engineer.

1 To check that the motor is operating, mark the drive roller. Assemble the appliance, switch on and let it run for 30 seconds. Turn the humidifier off again and check the marked roller to see if it has rotated.

2 If the roller hasn't moved, the drive motor should be replaced. The example shown here can be detached easily by removing simple screw fixings and disconnecting plug-in wiring. If your belt-drive motor is substantially different, have it replaced by a service engineer.

WILL NOT WORK AT ALL

Power failure
If other appliances on the circuit have stopped working, inspect your consumer unit for a blown fuse or tripped MCB or RCD – pages 11 and 12.

Humidifier not plugged in
Make sure the plug is inserted in the socket, and that the socket is switched on.

Plug fuse has blown
Replace the fuse in the plug – see page 17. If the fuse blows again as soon as you turn the appliance on, have your humidifier checked by a service engineer.

Faulty wiring in plug
If possible, take the back off the plug and check that it is wired correctly – see page 19.

Broken flex conductor
With most humidifiers, the flex is connected to accessible screw terminals – you will be able to test the flex for continuity (see page 20) and replace it if necessary. If it is not obvious how the flex is connected to the terminals, have a suspect flex checked and replaced at a service centre.

Faulty switch
With a sophisticated humidifier, there are so many switches that it pays to have them tested and repaired by a qualified service engineer.

Faulty wiring
See right.

Jammed fan
Check that the fan is free to move. If it sticks or slows down quickly when you spin it, have the humidifier serviced professionally.

Seized motor
Have the fan motor checked and replaced by a service engineer.

Faulty wiring
Since humidifiers are portable appliances, the connections inside them can work loose. If you don't find any obvious loose connections, have the wiring tested.

Blocked air vents
Replace the filter attached to the inlet grille – see page 149.

SAFETY FIRST

If your humidifier is earthed, check that it has a continuous earth path - see page 22. In the case of the humidifier described here, the earth path was checked by applying one probe of a continuity tester to the earth pin of the plug and touching the metal motor cover with the other probe. The tester's indicator will be activated if the metal components are earthed. If the indicator is not activated, have the appliance checked by a service engineer. This test does not apply to double-insulated appliances - see page 18.

ELECTRIC COOKERS

The conventional electric cooker is a freestanding appliance that combines the functions of an oven, a hob and, usually, a grill. In the modern fitted kitchen, these elements are often installed as separate units – a hob set into a worktop, for example, and perhaps a built-in oven unit that may incorporate the grill as part of a second oven. Theoretically, repair and maintenance requirements are the same, whether the units are combined into a single appliance or fitted separately. However, accessing built-in appliances can be tricky and time-consuming, and you may decide that with these it is best to leave all but simple cleaning and maintenance to a professional service engineer.

It must be emphasized that the suggestions and instructions given here relate only to electric ovens, hobs and grills. You should always get gas appliances (including combined gas and electric appliances) serviced by a qualified technician.

How hobs work

Despite all the advances and changes in style, the more basic units still make use of parts that have changed little from earlier models. Every hob consists of a number of individual heating elements, which are controlled separately.

Radiant elements

Radiant elements, similar to those used in electric kettles, are formed into flat spiral units for heating saucepans and frying pans. Single and double elements look superficially similar – a double element consists of two individual elements, one surrounding the other. Radiant elements are usually controlled by energy regulators (also known as 'simmerstats').

Solid hotplates

Made from cast iron, solid hotplates can be rectangular or circular in shape, with flat surfaces. Heat is produced by two or three individual elements fixed permanently

1 Regulators	9 Oven element
2 Terminal block	10 Lining panel
3 Radiant element	11 Door-latch post
4 Element support strip	12 Door-latch keeper
5 Oven-thermostat probe	13 Door seal
6 Hinge	14 Grill element
7 Hinge lock	15 Bezel
8 Element fixing plate	16 Power cable
	17 Earth terminal
	18 Control knobs

7 Detach the faulty element

SAFETY FIRST

Allow plenty of time for the appliance to cool down before cleaning or servicing an oven or a grill or hob.

Cookers, especially built-in models, are heavy and can be difficult to manhandle. Always get help when moving heavy appliances. If moving your cooker is likely to be problematic, call out a professional service engineer.

Before cleaning cookers – including separately installed hobs, grills and ovens – make sure the appliance is switched off at the cooker control unit (see page 15).

7 Withdraw the terminals through the holes in the support strip. Reverse the procedure to reassemble the element and its fixtures, ensuring that every component and wire is returned to its original location.

Faulty energy regulator

The following sequence is for testing a single-element regulator. For double-element regulators, you need to follow the same procedure for both single and double operations of the switch – from the off position, an anticlockwise turn switches on one element (usually the inner), while a clockwise turn from the off position will switch on both the inner and outer elements together.

Take care not to touch a hot element during the following test.

1 Turn off the cooker control unit, then rotate the regulator control knob slowly clockwise from the off position. There should be an audible click when the knob reaches the lowest mark on the dial – the thermal switch is now on.

2 Return to the off position by slowly rotating the knob anticlockwise. There should be an audible click before the knob reaches the off position – the thermal switch is now off. If you don't hear a click as you rotate the knob in either direction, the regulator is faulty.

Leaving the control knob in the off position, switch on the cooker control unit and turn the knob slowly clockwise until you hear the click again, then leave the knob in that position. If the hob is fitted with an indicator light, it should remain illuminated during the test.

You should hear another click in approximately 5 to 10 seconds, as the switch turns off automatically. If there's no second click and the heating element remains on, the regulator is faulty and should be replaced.

Even if the energy regulator is operating satisfactorily at the low end of the scale, you should now check that is working at higher temperatures – see page 158.

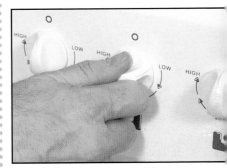

1 Turn knob until you hear a click

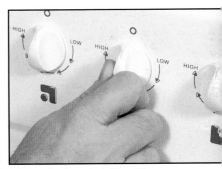

2 Return knob to the 'off' position

3 Turn the control knob to the halfway position. At this position, the thermal switch should cycle on and off automatically and you should hear a click at intervals of approximately 30 seconds.

4 Now turn the same control knob to the maximum temperature setting. The hob element should glow red-hot after a few minutes and stay on.

If the element heats up at every stage (with the cooker control unit turned on), both the regulator and element are working correctly. If the element heats at some stages but not at others, the regulator is faulty and should be replaced. If the element does not heat up at any stage, check it with a continuity tester – see page 156. If that proves the element is working satisfactorily, replace the regulator.

It is usually possible to install a regulator in a freestanding cooker yourself because you can pull the appliance away from the wall and remove an access panel to reveal the regulators. This is invariably more difficult with built-in hobs, so have these serviced by an engineer.

5 Before you start, make sure you have switched off the power at the consumer unit – see page 13. Pull off the push-fit control knobs in sequence, making a note of the particular location of each knob.

6 Unscrew and remove the back panel covering the regulators. Wear gloves to protect yourself from sharp edges.

7 Unscrew the regulator support bar attached to the back of the cooker.

8 Turn the support bar over so that you can remove the pair of screws that hold the faulty regulator in place.

9 Make a note or draw a diagram of the wiring attached to the regulator before carefully easing off each spade connector with long-nose pliers. Some replacement regulators come with self-adhesive labels for marking the wiring prior to removal.

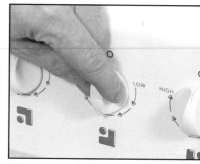
3 Rotate to the halfway position

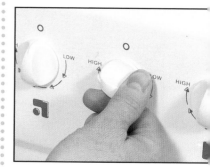
4 Turn up to maximum setting

5 Pull off the control knobs

6 Take off the small back panel

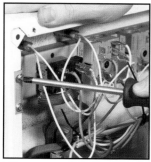
7 Unscrew regulator support bar

8 Unscrew the energy regulator

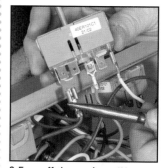
9 Ease off the spade connectors

Installing a new regulator is a straightforward reversal of the procedure described opposite.

Faulty rotary switch

Rotary switches controlling solid hotplates (see page 153) should be tested and replaced by a service engineer.

Faulty wiring to hob element

The only way to be sure that internal wiring is working perfectly is to have a service engineer test it for continuity. However, you can at least check that there are no loose connections in the wiring running to the suspect element – see page 156.

GRILL WON'T HEAT UP

Door not open

With some appliances, the element won't switch on if the grill-compartment door is closed.

Faulty grill element

With the majority of grills, it is necessary to remove various access panels in order to test and replace the element. And with built-in cookers, the appliance may have to be removed from its housing to carry out a replacement. In such cases, call out an engineer to service your grill.

However, some grill elements are simply plugged into a special socket in the back of the appliance. This makes for easy replacement if they fail.

1 There is never any need to apply excessive force when unplugging this type of element.

2 Lay the element on a bench and apply one probe of a continuity tester to each of the outer pins. The longer central pin is the earth terminal. If the pins show any signs of burning, call out an engineer to check the socket at the back of the grill compartment.

When you replace a plug-in element, make sure the pins are pushed home and that the element is supported, usually by sliding it into grooves on each side of the grill compartment.

Is your grill door closed?

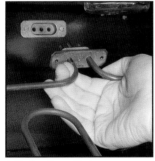
1 Unplug the grill element

2 Test the element for continuity

SAFETY FIRST

Before you start to service a cooker, it must be completely isolated from the mains power supply (see *Switching off the power*, page 13). Switching off the cooker control unit alone is not sufficient – the appliance must be isolated at the consumer unit.

Before you service any component inside an oven, hob or grill, as a final check that the power is off remove the access panel from the appliance and aim a non-contact voltage tester at the internal terminal block to which the incoming cable is connected. If you are not absolutely certain that an appliance is disconnected safely, get a service engineer to isolate and inspect it. Never take a risk.

Aim a non-contact voltage tester at the terminal block

Rotate the control knob to test the grill regulator

Faulty energy regulator

The energy regulator for a grill is very similar to a regulator for a hob unit (see page 152–3). Fault testing is essentially the same for both regulators, except that the grill control knob will probably have to be rotated further to select the low and medium temperature settings. The thermal switch may also cycle at different rates (it takes longer to switch on and off) compared with a hob-element regulator. Replace a faulty grill regulator as described on page 158. If you are in any doubt, consult an engineer.

Rotary switches (see page 153) controlling grill elements should be tested and replaced by a service engineer.

Faulty wiring to grill element

Have this checked by an expert.

OVEN WON'T HEAT UP

Faulty element

If a single element fails, the oven will be slow to heat up and heat distribution will be uneven. Removing an oven element can be tricky, particularly from built-in ovens. Even freestanding ovens often have to be stripped down and insulation removed in order to disconnect the elements. Elements in fan-assisted ovens are best left to a professional, because they too can be difficult to access.

However, some oven elements can be withdrawn from inside the cooking compartment, which makes them relatively easy to replace. An internally fitted element will have a single screw head in the centre of its fixing plate. If there's no visible fixing, call out an engineer to replace the element.

1 Switch off at the consumer unit, then lift off or unscrew the lining panels covering the elements on the inside of the oven.

2 Remove the screw in the centre of each element fixing plate. A lining-panel spacer bracket may be trapped behind this fixing plate.

3 Carefully withdraw the terminals attached to the back of the fixing plate and make a note

2 Remove element fixing screw

SAFETY FIRST

Special heat-resistant cable is used within cookers. Make sure all cable runs are routed correctly, and not trapped or allowed to come into contact with sharp edges or hot surfaces. When reassembling an appliance, ensure that all components are returned to their original locations.

1 Lift out the lining panels

3 Ease off the spade connectors

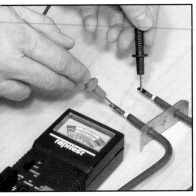
4 Test the element for continuity

SAFETY FIRST

A relatively common problem with radiant heating elements is low insulation. This can result in the appliance blowing fuses or tripping MCBs or RCDs. Try resetting the MCB or RCD or replacing a blown fuse (see pages 11–13), but if the new fuse blows or the MCB or RCD trips as soon as power is restored, the cooker must not be used until the problem has been traced and rectified by an electrician or service engineer.

of the wiring before you ease off the spade connectors. Take care to avoid stretching the wires or rubbing them against the sharp edges of the holes in the back of the oven. Wearing rubber gloves is a wise precaution, to protect your skin from stray insulation fibres.

4 Lay the element on a bench and place one probe of a continuity tester on each terminal. If the tester's indicator is not activated, buy an exact replacement for the element and reassemble it.

A new element may give off a little smoke for a few seconds when first used. This is merely a protective coating burning off.

Faulty thermostat

The only way to check whether your oven thermostat is reading temperatures correctly is to place a special oven thermometer in the oven compartment. However, the following test will help you diagnose whether the thermostat has failed completely.

1 With the power turned on, rotate the oven control knob to a low temperature setting on the dial. Within about 10 minutes the oven should have warmed up sufficiently to cause the thermostat to switch off the elements. On most models, an indicator light turns off at this point.

2 Open the oven door and allow heat to escape. After a few seconds, the indicator light should come on again, showing that the thermostat has switched the elements back on.

3 Now turn the oven control knob to the off position. The indicator light should go out, and the oven should cool down normally.

If the oven fails to operate as described above at every stage, have the thermostat checked and possibly replaced by a service engineer.

OVEN GETS TOO HOT

Faulty thermostat

The most likely cause of overheating is a faulty thermostat. Have it tested by a service engineer.

1 Select a low temperature setting

2 Allow heat to escape

Some seals are fixed with hooks

Others are held with spring clips

OVEN NOT HOT ENOUGH

If your oven is slow to heat up or cooking takes longer than expected, check out the following possibilities.

Wrong setting

Make sure you have set the control to the proper temperature.

Worn door seal

The door seal, made from flexible heat-resistant rubber or woven-fibre tubing, is designed to prevent heat escaping from the oven. If the seal is worn or out of position, the oven is unable to sustain the required temperature.

Seals are held in place in various ways, but those with metal hooks or simple spring clips are particularly easy to replace. Squeezing the spring clips with long-nose pliers detaches the seal.

Some seals are formed into a complete rectangle with fixings at each corner; others simply run across the top and down both sides of the door opening. It should be possible to buy replacements for all leading makes and models. However, if it is not obvious how your door seal is fitted, ask an engineer to supply and fit a replacement.

Faulty door latch

A worn or poorly adjusted latch may prevent the door compressing the seal.

If your oven has an adjustable latch post, slacken the lock nut with a spanner, then screw the post in or out to adjust the fit. Tighten the lock nut when the door is fitting satisfactorily.

When the keeper attached to the oven door becomes worn, no amount of adjustment will create an efficient seal.

On some ovens, all that's required to replace the keeper is to remove two fixing screws on the inside of the door. With other models, it is necessary to remove the door lining. To do so:

1 Remove the fixing screws around the edge of the oven door.

2 Take off the metal door lining and carefully peel back the layer of insulation on the inside. Wear rubber gloves to protect your skin

Slacken latch-post lock nut

Rotate the post to adjust the fit

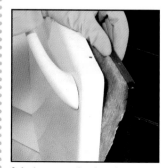

1 Take out the fixing screws

2 And remove the door lining

3 Unscrew the latch keeper

4 Fit an exact replacement

Unscrew a round bulb cover

Prise off a rectangular cover

from irritation caused by glass-fibre particles. If you suffer from breathing problems, wear a simple face mask when handling insulation.

3 Undo the fixing screws that attach the latch keeper to the inside of the lining.

4 Then detach the keeper and fit an exact replacement. When you reassemble the door, make sure the insulation's metal-foil surface faces the oven compartment.

Faulty thermostat

A faulty thermostat may be turning off the elements at too low a temperature. This is referred to as the thermostat being out of calibration. However, it may be that one of a pair of elements is faulty, resulting in only half of the oven compartment reaching the correct working temperature. If the oven elements can be removed easily (see page 160), check that they are working satisfactorily. Otherwise, have the elements and thermostat tested by an expert.

Fan not circulating hot air

It is obvious when the single element in a fan-assisted oven stops working, because the oven remains cold. Any failure to reach the required temperature is most likely to be caused by poor air circulation within the oven compartment.

Have an engineer check whether the fan motor is running slowly. This could be the result of worn bearings or a distorted fan. Both items can be replaced at a reasonable cost.

NO LIGHT IN THE OVEN

Internal bulb blown

When the light fails to come on in your oven, switch off the appliance at the cooker control unit (see page 15) and either unscrew a round glass cover to gain access to the bulb or use a stout screwdriver carefully to prise off a rectangular cover.

If replacing the bulb doesn't solve the problem, have an engineer locate and test the oven-light switch.

COOKER DOES NOT WORK AT ALL

Cooker control unit switched off
Make sure the cooker switch (see page 15) is in the 'on' position.

Power failure
A cooker is powered by its own dedicated circuit running from the consumer unit. Has the circuit fuse blown or has the MCB or RCD tripped? If so, see pages 11 and 12.

SAFETY FIRST

To check that a cooker is earthed, apply one probe of a continuity tester to the exposed head of a panel-fixing screw or an uncoated part of the metal casing or cover panel. Place the other probe on one of the two fixing screws that hold the faceplate of the cooker control unit in place – these fixing screws are connected to earth inside the control unit, and the tester's indicator will be activated if the earth in the appliance is connected to earth in the control unit. If it is not activated, have the cooker checked by a service engineer.

MICROWAVE OVENS

Nowadays, most of us have a microwave oven in the kitchen, usually to supplement a conventional electric or gas cooker. Yet despite the obvious popularity of cooking with microwaves, misunderstandings and scares abound regarding its safety. An appreciation of how microwave ovens work and the safeguards built into them should alleviate any misconceptions.

The main danger is not microwave leakage (which is extremely rare) but the very high voltages generated inside the appliance. All internal servicing must therefore be left to professional microwave engineers. Consequently, it is not the intention of this book to recommend or encourage DIY repair of microwave ovens.

Nevertheless, a great many potential problems are the result of misunderstanding, misuse or simple neglect – and general care and maintenance, coupled with safe procedures, will extend the life of your oven.

How it works

A large transformer increases the standard 230 volts tenfold before the current is passed through a high-voltage capacitor able to hold that charge even when the appliance is turned off and unplugged. The transformer and capacitor power a device called a magnetron, which converts the electrical energy into powerful radio waves. The waves produced are a form of electromagnetic energy, which is directed into the cooking chamber by an aerial on the magnetron.

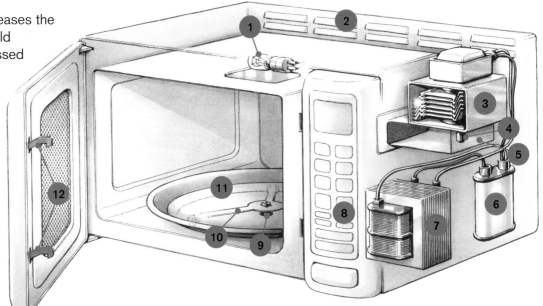

In a manner similar to the way a magnet affects the needle of a compass, microwaves within the cooking chamber realign the atoms that make up the food, changing their orientation from north to south some 2450 million times per second (2450MHz). The friction thus generated creates heat, which cooks the food to a depth of about 2.5cm (1in). With thicker foods, conduction transmits the heat deeper still. Consequently, to ensure that it is cooked right through, food must be allowed to stand for a time after the microwaves have been turned off.

To make sure the contents are cooked evenly, the microwaves must be distributed evenly throughout the interior of the oven. One of three systems can be used to achieve this:
● A rotating turntable
● A rotating antenna
● A 'stirrer' with metal fins that reflect the microwaves, causing them to bounce around the oven compartment.

1 Bulb
2 Vents
3 Magnetron
4 Aerial
5 Microwave guide
6 Capacitor
7 Transformer
8 Control panel
9 Drive piece
10 Turntable support
11 Turntable
12 Door latch

Combination ovens
A combination oven makes use of the best characteristics of conventional and microwave cooking. Defrosting and cooking to a set temperature are faster and more efficient using microwave energy, but food is generally more attractive when cooked with heating elements. Depending on the design, a combination oven may incorporate a grill, a fan-assisted oven, and even a toaster.

Leaking microwaves
Some people fear that they will be exposed to microwaves simply by standing near an oven when it is turned on. Provided all the covers panels are in place and the appliance is in good condition, there should be no possibility of microwave leakage – and it is virtually impossible for microwaves to escape from the air vents.

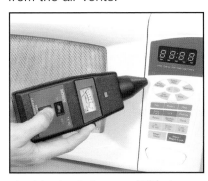

However, if you are concerned about your oven, it can be tested for leakage. And after a repair, a competent engineer will carry out a microwave-leak test, using an approved detector. These instruments are expensive, and so not usually available to the average householder. However, you can buy a reasonably priced test meter that is designed to provide an indication of dangerous leakage. These meters are usually available from electrical retailers or DIY stores.

To test for leakage, put a cup of water in the oven and switch on. With the tip of the detector touching the oven, run the instrument at a steady pace along the gaps around the door. Also run the tester across the front of the door from one corner to the other, and then across the other diagonal. Check the control panel and air vents for possible leakage, too.

If a leak is indicated or even suspected, make sure the lip and the inner face of the door are perfectly clean, then test the appliance again. If the test meter still registers a leak, turn off the oven, unplug it to prevent anyone using it, and call in a qualified microwave engineer. Don't attempt to service the appliance yourself.

Cleaning microwave ovens
Besides being more hygienic, an oven that is cleaned regularly is less likely to break down. A dirty door may not close properly – which may prevent the appliance starting up or, worse still, allow microwaves to leak. Always unplug a microwave oven before cleaning it.

Some combination ovens are self-cleaning (check your user's handbook).

COOKING TIMES
Selecting the right power output (high, medium, low or defrost) and the optimum cooking time is the key to successful microwave cookery. The exact combination of power output and timing is always specified in recipes, and is usually printed on frozen-meal packages.

Remember that food cooked with microwaves goes on cooking for a period after the oven is switched off. The recommended standing time is also normally given in cookbooks and on packaging.

The power produced by the magnetron differs from model to model. It is rated in watts and is usually specified on a rating plate and in your user's handbook. The wattage output of an oven is proportional to the supply voltage – so an oven with a nominal output of 700W will only achieve this if the mains voltage is 230 volts.

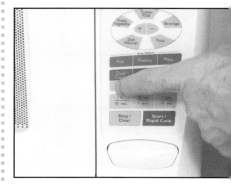

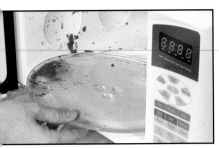

1 Take a dirty turntable to the sink

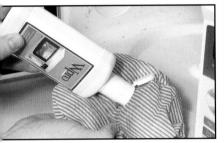

2 Wipe up spills with paper towel

3 Use a microwave-oven cleaner to sanitize the interior

Cleaning inside

Never use corrosive cleaning liquids or pads. Ensure that all surfaces are clean and dry before you use the oven again.

1 Remove the turntable and wash it in hot soapy water. Dry it thoroughly before you put it back in the oven.

2 Use a paper towel or a slightly damp cloth to wipe up spills and splashes before they solidify.

3 Then use a proprietary microwave-oven cleaner squeezed onto a cloth to wipe and remove greasy patches. This type of cleaner sanitizes and deodorizes the oven.

On some models, the bottom liner of the cooking chamber is removable and can allow liquids to seep into the cavity beneath. The appliance may be damaged if these spills go unnoticed.

Steaming the interior

To remove stubborn deposits, fill a small microwave-safe container with water and place it in the centre of the oven. Switch onto full power for a few minutes, allowing the water to boil – but not to boil dry. The steam produced should loosen the deposits, which can then be wiped off with a cloth.

Cleaning the door

Don't allow food particles or debris to build up on the lip or inner surface of the door. Wipe both of these regularly with a slightly damp cloth.

Cleaning the outside

The outer surfaces of the oven can be cleaned with a slightly damp cloth or sponge. Don't allow liquid to run into the vents or behind access panels.

Cleaning the control panel

Use a cloth that is only very slightly damp to wipe the touch-control panel of your microwave oven. You should never allow this panel to get really wet, as moisture could penetrate, rendering the appliance inoperable until it dries out – and you might even have to have a new control panel fitted.

GETTING THE BEST FROM YOUR OVEN

● Use the correct settings for the type of food being cooked.

● Make sure that the oven is cleaned regularly.

● Avoid spatters by covering dishes with their own microwave-safe lids. Alternatively, place a paper towel on top.

● If your oven doesn't have a removable glass turntable or shelf, put the food on a plate or paper towel to keep the floor of the oven clean.

First things first

Before you call out a microwave technician, run through the checklist below. It is surprising how often simple forgetfulness or carelessness can be the cause of a problem.

- Is the oven plugged in? And is the socket switched on?

- Is the door closed properly?

- Are the timer and power settings correct?

- Has the clock been set correctly?

- Is the oven clean?

Check the turntable support ring

Make sure drive piece fits snugly

UNPLEASANT ODOURS IN OVEN

Spicy foods
Odours can linger in the oven after certain foods have been cooked. If normal cleaning doesn't solve the problem, try the following.

Mix 1 part lemon juice with 3 parts water in a microwave-safe container. Place the container in the oven, set the oven to high, and let the juice and water boil for 3 to 4 minutes. Leave the container and its contents to cool, then remove them from the oven and dry the interior with a paper towel.

TURNTABLE DOES NOT REVOLVE

Turntable drive not located
Remove and refit the turntable (and the support ring, if your model has one), then try switching the oven on again.

Broken drive piece
A plastic drive piece, fitted to the shaft of the turntable motor, protrudes through the floor of the oven. Check to see if this is a tight fit on the shaft of the motor. If the drive piece is loose and can be lifted out easily, buy and fit a push-on replacement.

Faulty turntable motor
A small motor and gearbox drives the turntable. If the motor fails, the turntable will not revolve even though the drive piece is secure on its shaft. Get a qualified technician to check and replace a faulty drive motor.

NO LIGHT IN THE OVEN

Blown bulb
Provided the oven is working normally, the internal light should come on when you open the door and/or during cooking. If the bulb appears to have blown, don't attempt to change it yourself. Have it replaced by a qualified microwave engineer. It is safe to use the oven while you are waiting for a bulb replacement.

SPARKING WITHIN THE OVEN

Metal foil or utensils in the oven
Metal objects placed in the oven reflect microwave energy, causing an electrical discharge known as 'arcing'. Arcing can shorten the life of the magnetron. Avoid using metal containers (except for those specifically recommended for use in microwave ovens), wire bag ties, meat skewers, and crockery with metal-foil patterns.

To prevent burning, some recipes recommend wrapping small pieces of metal foil around vulnerable items such as fishtails or the exposed bone of a chicken drumstick. However, you should never put food wrapped completely with foil in the oven. Consult your user's handbook or a good microwave cookbook for details.

Accumulation of food particles
Clean the oven thoroughly and regularly – see opposite.

STEAM ESCAPING

Normal venting of steam
Air blown over the magnetron to keep it cool passes into the cooking chamber to be vented through apertures in the rear of the oven. This air movement carries with it the steam produced during cooking. Consequently, it is quite normal to see steam escaping from vents in the appliance, and sometimes from around the door. As the steam cools, it may condense on the inside of the glass door panel. This is also quite normal.

Increase cooking time

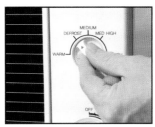

Check the power setting

1 Identify both containers

2 Place containers in the oven

3 Take temperature of the water

FOOD UNDERCOOKED

Incorrect cooking time set

Check the weight and type of food being cooked and, if necessary, adjust the time setting accordingly. Remember to allow for standing time.

Frozen food

Have you forgotten to set the extended time required to cook frozen food?

Incorrect power setting

Check which power setting should be used to cook the food.

Faulty magnetron or internal circuitry

If you find you are consistently extending cooking times to get the desired results, carry out the following test to check that the power output of your oven matches its specified wattage output – see page 165. If the test indicates that the appliance is not performing to its specification, either the magnetron or the internal circuitry could be faulty.

For this test, you will need two microwave-safe containers of at least 500ml capacity and a thermometer able to measure temperatures, in centigrade, between 10°C and 50°C.

1 Mark the containers A and B, so that they can be identified easily, and fill both of them with 500ml of water. Stir the water and then measure its temperature. This should be about 15°C; if it's above 20°C, the results will be inaccurate. Make a note of the temperature of the water in each container and record it as T1 (temperature at start).

2 Place the containers in the centre of the oven, set the oven to full power, and switch on. Allow the oven to operate for 87 seconds, then switch off.

3 Remove both containers and stir the water again before taking its temperature. Note the increase in temperature and record it as T2 (temperature after 87 seconds).

4 Subtract T1 from T2 in both cases and calculate the average rise in temperature

see page 165

SAFETY FIRST

If you wear a pacemaker, ask your doctor for advice before using a microwave oven.

Before you use an oven, make sure that all the panels are in place and that the door is closed correctly. Get a service engineer to repair a damaged door.

Never remove the panels or outer cover of a microwave oven. This will expose you to very high voltages, even when the appliance is switched off and unplugged.

Don't use a microwave oven if the inner oven compartment is cracked or corroded. Consult a qualified engineer.

Don't switch on an oven when it is empty. Operating a microwave oven when it is empty can damage the magnetron. To prevent this happening, some people keep a cup of water in the oven when it is not in use.

Check the flex regularly for signs of damage, and don't let it trail across a hob unit or across a wet surface.

SAFETY FIRST

Keep air vents clear.

Don't use a microwave oven to dry clothes.

Don't heat oil or fat in a microwave oven.

Food and liquids continue to heat up after they have been removed from the oven. Allow food and milk to stand, and then test it carefully before giving it to a baby or small child.

Air vents must not be obstructed

between the two. Then multiply the average temperature rise, in centigrade, by 50 (which represents the power-supply cycle in the UK of 50Hz). This calculation gives you the output of the magnetron in watts. Check that the output matches the manufacturer's specification given on the rating plate.

A variation of plus or minus 10 per cent is acceptable – but if the results are much lower than the specified rating, there could be a fault within the appliance. If your appliance is not performing to specification, clean and dry the oven and then double-check all readings. If the result is still low, have the microwave circuitry checked by a qualified engineer. Don't continue using the oven until an engineer has diagnosed the problem.

Low voltage supply
This is an unusual occurrence – but if you are running a number of major electrical appliances while using the microwave oven, the voltage level could be reduced, which would affect the power output of the oven. The remedy is to use fewer appliances when cooking with your microwave oven.

FOOD OVERCOOKED

Incorrect cooking time set
Check the weight and type of food being cooked and, if necessary, adjust the time setting accordingly.

Incorrect power setting
Check which power setting should be used to cook or heat the food.

Air vents blocked or covered
Check that the air vents have not been covered or blocked. Make sure there is ventilation space between the appliance casing and the walls.

WORKS INTERMITTENTLY

Condensation
Problems may arise if the appliance is too close

An example of a typical test on a 650W oven might be as follows:

Container A	
T1	T2
15°C	27°C

Container B	
T1	T2
15°C	29°C

The rise in temperature (T2 minus T1) is 12°C for container A, and 14°C for container B.

The average temperature increase is therefore:

$$\frac{12 + 14}{2} = 13°C$$

The output wattage is calculated by multiplying the average rise of 13°C by 50:

$$13 \times 50 = 650W$$

SAFETY FIRST

When any appliance is earthed, you should always use a continuity tester to verify that there is a continuous earth path – see page 22. In the case of the ovens described here, the earth path was tested by placing one probe of a continuity tester on the earth pin of the plug and then touching the exposed head of a panel-fixing screw with the other probe.

Steam can penetrate control panel

SAFETY FIRST

Ensure the plug is wired correctly, and that the appropriate fuse is fitted.

If you suspect that there is a fault, plug the microwave oven into a circuit protected by an RCD – see page 11. Switch on, and if the RCD trips, have the appliance tested by a service engineer.

Reset the clock

Check that the latch operates

to an open cooking area where steam from a kettle or saucepans can penetrate behind the touch-control panel.

If the oven works after you have left it to dry out naturally, try moving it to a part of the kitchen where it is less likely to be subjected to high humidity. If the fault persists, consult a qualified engineer.

OVEN WON'T SWITCH ON

Oven not plugged in
Make sure the plug is inserted in the socket, and that the socket is switched on.

Faulty plug
Take the back off the plug to check whether it is wired correctly – see page 19. If in doubt, fit a new plug.

Check and, if need be, replace the cartridge fuse – see page 17.

Power failure
If other appliances on the circuit have stopped working, inspect your consumer unit for a blown fuse or tripped MCB or RCD – see pages 11 and 12.

Clock needs resetting
Is the display illuminated? If it is, check the clock setting. Some ovens will not start up unless the clock is set correctly. This problem often occurs after a general mains power failure.

Door not closed properly
Open and close the door a few times to check that the latch is operating mechanically. If this does not solve the problem, the latch may need replacing. Ask a microwave engineer for advice.

Faulty internal fuse
Microwave ovens are fitted with internal protective fuses, which can fail for a number of reasons. Ask a qualified microwave engineer to check the internal fuses.

Faulty timer or on/off switch
Only a qualified microwave technician can diagnose and correct this type of fault.

FIRE IN THE OVEN

Food overheated
In the unlikely event of a fire occurring within the oven, switch off the appliance at the socket and remove the plug. Keep the door closed and let the fire burn out.

With some microwave ovens, turning off the appliance with its own switch or latch automatically opens the door – so in this type of emergency always switch off at the socket.

Have the oven checked by an engineer before you use it again.

TELEVISION OR RADIO INTERFERENCE

If there's a portable TV set or radio in your kitchen that suffers from interference when your microwave oven is in use, try moving the set further away from the oven. If the interference persists, suspect the following.

Faulty internal mains filter/suppression unit
This type of fault can be checked only by specially trained personnel.

No earth path
This is a serious fault. Unplug the appliance and check the earth path, using a continuity tester – see pages 22 and 169. Also, use a plug-in tester (see page 15) to check the earth in the socket.

If a fault is indicated with either test, don't use the appliance or the socket until the fault has been identified and rectified by a microwave technician.

EXTRACTOR FANS

Extractor fans are often installed in bathrooms and kitchens in order to remove moisture-laden air and unpleasant odours. Being little more than a bladed fan (impeller) driven by an electric motor, there is little to go wrong with this type of appliance, provided it is maintained regularly.

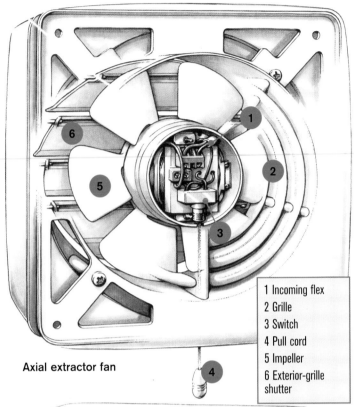

Axial extractor fan

1 Incoming flex
2 Grille
3 Switch
4 Pull cord
5 Impeller
6 Exterior-grille shutter

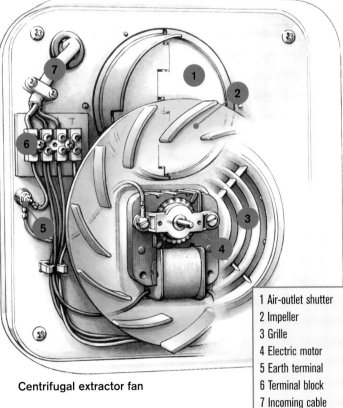

Centrifugal extractor fan

1 Air-outlet shutter
2 Impeller
3 Grille
4 Electric motor
5 Earth terminal
6 Terminal block
7 Incoming cable

How it works

The majority of extractor fans are fitted with axial impellers, mounted on the electric motor. Air is drawn through the grille on the front of the appliance and passes straight through the device to be expelled outside. In order to prevent backdraughts, the exterior grille may be fitted with shutters that close automatically when the fan switches off. Axial fans can be installed in a window; and with the addition of a short length of ducting, some models will extract air through a solid or cavity wall. To overcome the pressure created by a long run of ducting, some extractor fans are made with centrifugal impellers that direct the air sideways, at right angles to the shaft of the impeller.

Some fans are switched manually, usually by means of a pull cord. Other models switch on automatically when the humidity in the room reaches a predetermined level. Some types incorporate a timer that will switch the fan off after a certain interval.

In kitchens, the majority of fans are wired to a fused connection unit – see page 14. An extractor fan in a bathroom may be wired to a flex outlet (see page 14) that is connected to a FCU outside the room, or the fan may be connected to the lighting circuit and controlled by a ceiling-mounted switch operated by a pull cord.

Optimum performance

Your extractor fan won't work efficiently if it is incapable of removing the required volume of air from the room, and no fan will perform well if it is positioned inappropriately in relation to the source of replacement air.

Capacity

The size of the fan – or to be more accurate, its capacity – should be determined by the type of room in which it is installed and the volume of air it has to extract. A fan installed in a kitchen must be capable of changing the air 10 to 15 times an hour. Bathrooms require 6 to 8 changes per hour – 15 to 20 if there's a shower in the bathroom. A separate WC needs 6 to 10 changes per hour. To calculate the minimum capacity required, calculate the volume of the room (length x width x height) and then multiply the volume by the recommended number of air changes per hour – see example below.

CALCULATING THE CAPACITY OF A FAN FOR A KITCHEN			
Size of kitchen			
Length	**Width**	**Height**	**Volume**
3.35m (11ft)	3.05m (10ft)	2.44m (8ft)	24.93cu m (880cu ft)
Air changes	**Volume**	**Fan capacity**	
15 per hour x	24.93cu m (880cu ft)	= 374cu m per hour (13,200cu ft)	

Positioning a fan

Stale air extracted from a room must be replaced by fresh air – normally through the door leading to other parts of your house or flat. If your fan is placed too close to the source of replacement air, it will promote local circulation but have little effect on the rest of the room. The ideal position is directly opposite the source of replacement air, and high enough to remove heated air that collects near the ceiling. In a kitchen, try to locate the fan

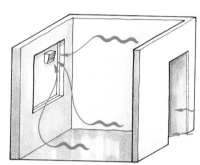

Fan opposite replacement air

adjacent to the cooker, where it can easily extract cooking odours and steam.

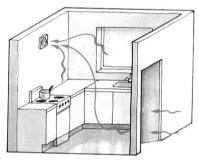

Fan adjacent to cooker

Better still, fit a cooker hood – see page 175.

If the room contains a fuel-burning appliance with a flue (a boiler, for example), you must ensure that there is sufficient ventilation to supply replacement air. This prevents fumes from the appliance being drawn down the flue when the extractor fan is switched on. The only exception is an appliance with a balanced flue, which takes its air directly from outside. If in doubt, consult a heating engineer.

Adjusting automatic controls

Extractor fans designed to operate automatically have a means of adjusting the sensitivity of the humidistat and the length of time the fan will run

before switching itself off.

Adjustment in electronic fans is invariably simple,

usually by means of turning a dial with a small screwdriver. It is usual to make slight adjustments one way or the other until the fan operates satisfactorily.

Better still, fit a cooker hood – see page 175.

REPLACING A PULL CORD

The pull cord that operates the switch on a fan may break, usually just where it enters the casing. On some models, a broken cord can be replaced simply by passing a new length of similar cord through a toggle on the switch and then tying a knot on the end.

With some fans, however, there is no easy way to connect a replacement cord and the only solution is to buy a new switch, complete with pull cord. This type of switch can usually be eased out of its housing, and the wiring disconnected from simple screw terminals.

Before removing the casing, isolate the fan from the supply of electricity – see page 13.

If your switch is more complicated, or it is not perfectly obvious how the wiring is connected, have the switch replaced by a service engineer.

Spare parts may not be available for inexpensive fans.

1 Brush dust from the grille

2 Remove casing to clean inside

SAFETY FIRST

Before cleaning or servicing a fan, you must make sure that you have completely isolated the power circuit or lighting circuit to which the fan is connected. So, while the appliance is in good working order, it's worth finding out which circuit supplies it with power. To do this, systematically remove each circuit fuse or turn off each miniature circuit breaker (MCB) in the consumer unit (see pages 11 to 13) and then, each time, switch on the fan, until you have identified the relevant circuit. Once you know which it is, label it in your consumer unit. If you cannot determine which circuit supplies power to the fan, seek the advice of a qualified electrician.

NOISY FAN

Fan needs cleaning

If there's a heavy accumulation of grease and dust on the impeller and motor assembly, a fan may get out of balance and begin to run noisily.

Most people clean the visible grille of an extractor fan, yet neglect to remove the accumulation of grease and dust from inside the appliance. This is worth doing at least once a year. Your fan may differ from the one described here, but the cleaning procedure will be similar. Before you begin, isolate the fan from the supply of electricity – see page 13.

1 Brush away dust that has accumulated on the grille of the appliance.

2 Take off the casing or grille by removing exposed fixing screws or by unlatching moulded clips. Wash the casing or grille in warm soapy water and dry it.

3 Use a soft brush and a vacuum cleaner to remove a heavy accumulation of dust and fluff from the impeller.

4 If possible, detach the impeller, so you can wash it in warm soapy water. Many impellers are a simple push-fit onto the end of the drive shaft – but before exerting any force, make sure there's not a grub screw clamping the impeller to the shaft. If your impeller won't detach easily, just clean behind it with a small paintbrush.

5 Use a dry brush to clean the electric motor. Take care not to wet any electrical components. When you reassemble the fan, make sure the impeller is free to move without touching the casing or other components.

FAN WON'T TURN ON

Not switched on

Some fans are connected to a switched fused connection unit – see page 14. Make sure the FCU is switched on, and then check that the fuse in the FCU is functioning – see page 17.

SAFETY FIRST

Before you touch any component inside a fan connected to a fused connection unit or flex outlet, as a final check that the power is off remove the casing from the appliance and aim a non-contact voltage tester at the internal terminal block to which the flex or cable is connected – see pages 13 and 177. If you are not certain an appliance is disconnected safely, get a service engineer to isolate and inspect it.

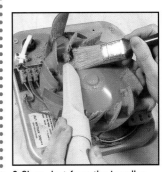

3 Clean dust from the impeller

4 Detach the impeller

5 And then clean behind it

Power failure

If other appliances on the circuit have stopped working, inspect your consumer unit for a blown fuse or tripped MCB or RCD – see pages 11 and 12.

TOC tripped

Some models are fitted with a self-setting thermal-overload cutout that will switch off the fan to prevent the motor overheating. If your fan begins to work again after it has cooled down, try cleaning the impeller and motor (see page 173) to prevent the TOC tripping again.

If the TOC trips regularly, have the appliance checked by a service engineer.

Faulty switch

If spares are available, it may be possible to replace a simple on/off switch wired with screw-type terminals. However, if the switch in your fan is substantially different from the ones described here, have it checked and replaced by a service engineer.

Remember to isolate the appliance from the supply of electricity before removing the casing.

Some switches are held in place with a spring clip, which can be eased off using a small screwdriver. Other switches have to be eased out of a saddle housing. If it is not obvious how to detach the switch in your fan, have the appliance serviced by an engineer.

Having detached at least one wire from the switch, use a continuity tester to check whether the switch is working. With one probe on each terminal, turn the switch on and off. If the tester's indicator is not activated, buy a replacement switch.

Faulty internal wiring

Having disconnected the extractor fan, check inside the appliance for obvious loose connections. If all the connections appear to be sound, the only way to be sure your circuit wiring is working properly is to have it tested by a service engineer.

Faulty motor

The electric motor could be faulty. However, even if a replacement motor is obtainable, it's likely to cost almost as much as a new fan.

Prise off the spring clip

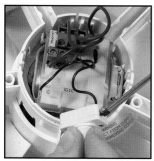
Or ease switch out of its saddle

Detach wires from their terminals

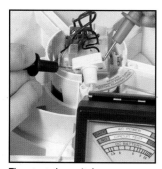
Then test the switch

SAFETY FIRST

The majority of fans are double-insulated, but those that are made with metal back plates will be earthed. To check that the latter has a continuous earth path, apply one probe of a continuity tester to the earth pin of the plug and, with the other probe, touch the metal back plate or the uncoated head of a screw that holds the casing to the back plate. The tester's indicator will be activated if the metal components are earthed.

If your fan is connected to a fused connection unit or a flex outlet, perform the same test – but instead of placing one of the tester's probes on the earth pin of the plug, apply it to one of the two fixing screws that hold the faceplate of the FCU or flex outlet in place. The tester's indicator will be activated if the earth in the fan is connected to earth in the fitting.

If your fan is connected to the lighting circuit, have the earth path checked by an electrician.

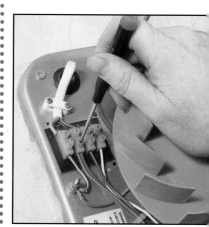
Tighten any loose connections

COOKER HOODS

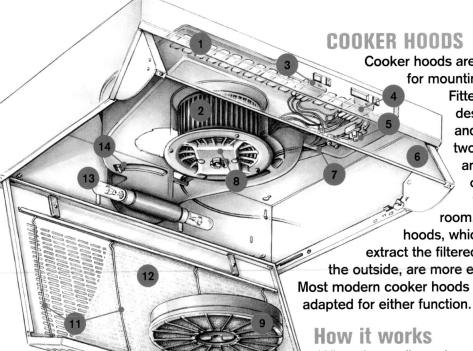

Cooker hoods are simply specialized extractor fans for mounting directly above a cooker or hob. Fitted with filters, cooker hoods are designed to rid your kitchen of steam and greasy cooking smells. There are two basic types of hood – recirculating and ducted. Recirculating hoods filter out odours, grease and water vapour, then return the air to the room. Ducted hoods, which extract the filtered air to the outside, are more efficient. Most modern cooker hoods can be adapted for either function.

Recirculating cooker hood

Top-vented cooker hood

Rear-vented cooker hood

How it works

When the appliance is switched on, an electrically driven impeller or fan draws air through a large inlet grille, behind which is mounted a grease filter made from synthetic fibre or paper. In the case of a ducted hood, the air is then extracted directly to the outside. A recirculating hood contains a secondary carbon filter, designed to trap cooking odours before the air is returned to the room.

Most hoods are fitted with a variable-speed switch, which may be activated automatically when the appliance's air-intake flap is opened. In addition, there's likely to be one or two bulbs that illuminate the cooking area directly beneath the hood.

Cooker hoods are either plugged into a wall socket or connected permanently to a fused connection unit.

1 Recirculating vents
2 Centrifugal fan
3 Light switch
4 On/off switch and speed control
5 Terminal block
6 Visor
7 Flex
8 Motor housing
9 Optional secondary carbon filter
10 Grille
11 Retaining wires
12 Grease filter
13 Bulb
14 Venting control

CLEANING A COOKER HOOD

It pays to clean your cooker hood regularly. Wipe the casing with a cloth dampened with warm soapy water, then dry the appliance with a soft cloth. Whenever you replace the grease filter, detach the grille and wash it in the kitchen sink in hot soapy water.

When to change the filters

The grease filters in most cooker hoods change colour to indicate that it's time they were replaced – the efficiency of the appliance is reduced drastically if you neglect to perform this essential task regularly. It depends on how often you use the hood, but as a general rule you will need to change your filter every 3 months or so.

It is possible to wash fibre filters in warm soapy water, but for peak performance it's best to replace them.

Carbon filters in recirculating cooker hoods are disposable, but they last for anything from 6 months to 2 years (check your user's handbook).

COOKING ODOURS IN THE KITCHEN

Get into the habit of switching on the hood a few minutes before you start cooking, and leave it running for about 15 minutes after you have finished. Both measures will help to remove lingering odours.

If you don't change the filters regularly, the cooker hood will no longer be able to extract odours and grease from the air. This is particularly noticeable with a recirculating hood.

Ineffective carbon filter

To replace a carbon filter, first remove the hood's inlet grille, then detach the filter itself by turning it anticlockwise or by removing a central screw fixing.

If you can't buy a replacement filter, look carefully to see if your old filter can be taken apart at the seams. If the filter can be dismantled, you may be able to refill the filter with carbon granules available from spares outlets.

Grease filter needs replacing

The perforated inlet grille is lined with a replaceable grease filter.

1 Detach the grille and lay it face down on the kitchen work surface.

2 Unclip the sprung filter-retaining wires and lay them aside.

3 Peel off the old filter and wash the inlet grille before inserting a clean filter.

If you can't get the hood manufacturer's filters, buy 'universal' filters that you can cut to size with scissors. Use your old filter as a template.

NO LIGHT OVER THE COOKER

Bulb has blown

If the fan is working but the hood is not illuminating the cooker or hob, try replacing the bulb. Unplug the appliance or switch off at the consumer unit – see page 13.

Depending on the model, either remove the inlet grille or detach the translucent bulb cover. Replace the bulb with one of the same size and wattage.

Can your filter be dismantled?

If so, you can replace the granules

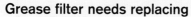
Use the old filter as a template for cutting a universal filter to size

1 Detach the air-inlet grille

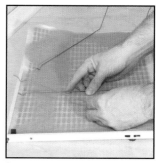
2 Unclip the retaining wires

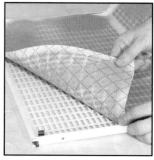
3 Peel off the old grease filter

Replace with identical bulb

SAFETY FIRST

Before cleaning or servicing a cooker hood, remove the plug from the socket or disconnect the supply of electricity at the consumer unit – see page 13. Before you touch any component inside a cooker hood, as a final check that the power is off, aim a non-contact voltage tester at the internal terminal block to which the flex is connected – see page 13. If you are not absolutely certain an appliance is disconnected safely, get a service engineer to isolate and inspect it. Never take a risk.

Before putting a cooker hood back into service, test it on a circuit protected by an RCD – see page 11. If the RCD trips, have the appliance tested by a service engineer.

A new motor may be too costly

Faulty light switch
If changing the bulb does not solve the problem, have an engineer check the light switch mounted on the cooker hood.

HOOD WON'T SWITCH ON

Hood not plugged in
Make sure the plug is inserted in the socket, and that the socket is switched on. If your hood is connected to a fused connection unit (see page 14), make sure the FCU is switched on.

Faulty switch
The on/off switch can be difficult to test because, in many models, it also controls fan speed. Leave its replacement to an engineer.

Power failure
If other appliances on the circuit have stopped working, inspect your consumer unit for a blown fuse or tripped MCB or RCD – see pages 11 and 12.

Faulty wiring in plug
Take the back off the plug to see if it is wired correctly – see page 19.

Plug or FCU fuse has blown
Replace the fuse in the plug – see page 17. If there is a fused connection unit, check whether the fuse in the FCU needs to be replaced – see page 17.

Faulty wiring inside hood
Suspect wiring within the cooker hood should be tested by a service engineer.

Faulty motor
You may want to ask an engineer to quote you a price for fitting a replacement motor and compare it with the cost of installing a new hood. However, unless your cooker hood is particularly expensive or it's integral to the style of your kitchen, replacing the motor is unlikely to be a cost-effective option.

Have the light switch checked

Get the on/off switch replaced

SAFETY FIRST

To check that a cooker hood is earthed, apply one probe of a continuity tester to the earth pin of the plug. Place the other probe on the exposed head of a fixing screw driven into the metal casing. The tester's indicator will be activated if the metal components are earthed.

If your cooker hood is wired to a fused connection unit, perform the same test – but instead of placing the probe on the plug pin, apply this probe to one of the two fixing screws that hold the FCU's faceplate in place. The tester's indicator will be activated if the earth in the appliance is connected to earth in the FCU.

This test does not apply to double-insulated cooker hoods – see page 18.

VACUUM CLEANERS

All vacuum cleaners, including those incorporating the latest technology, work on much the same principle. A powerful electric motor drives one or more fans (impellers), which create a fast-moving airflow that carries dust and grit particles along with it. At some point the dust is filtered out and collected in a receptacle, while the air is exhausted back into the room.

However, there are important differences between the various models on the market – all of which could affect the way you approach the basic servicing and maintenance of your particular vacuum cleaner.

How it works

At one time vacuum cleaners fell neatly into two categories – uprights and cylinders. Although these terms no longer provide an entirely accurate description of many of the models now available, they are still widely used by manufacturers and retailers.

In addition, besides the more traditional cleaners, there are now bagless (cyclonic or vortex), wet-and-dry and portable models.

Upright vacuum cleaners

A single fan fixed to one end of the electric-motor shaft creates the airflow, which draws dust into the appliance. The other end of the motor shaft serves to drive a flexible belt that rotates a brush roller mounted just above the floor. Bristles fixed to the roller pick up dust, pet hairs and other debris from the floor and deposit them into the airflow. The rows of bristles are usually interspersed with rigid ribs, known as beater bars, that tap the surface of the carpet in order to disturb particles embedded deep in the pile. Far from damaging the floorcovering, this vigorous brushing and beating action removes grit that would otherwise wear away the pile and woven base of the carpet.

Operating a knob or slider control mounted on the cleaner's hood adjusts the distance between the brush roller and the floor. There are probably four to six height settings to suit anything from a smooth floor surface to long-pile carpets.

Air and dust drawn into the appliance pass into the fan chamber and on through flexible or rigid ducting to a dust-collecting bag. Made from permeable paper, the bag traps the dust particles but allows the air to pass through and escape via grilles formed in the plastic casing that surrounds the bag. Very early models were equipped with a fabric dust bag, attached to the handle.

Although extremely efficient, this system has one serious drawback. All the debris drawn into the appliance comes into contact with the fan, and stones or small metal objects picked up by the cleaner can seriously damage the fan blades.

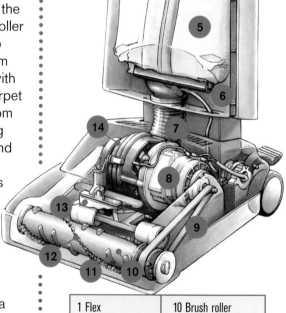

1 Flex	10 Brush roller
2 Cord clamp	11 Beater bars
3 Terminal block	12 Bristles
4 Exhaust grilles	13 Height control
5 Dust bag	14 Fan chamber
6 Rigid ducting to dust bag	15 Bag-attachment nozzle
7 Flexible ducting	16 Removable access panel
8 Motor housing	17 On/off switch
9 Flexible drive belt	

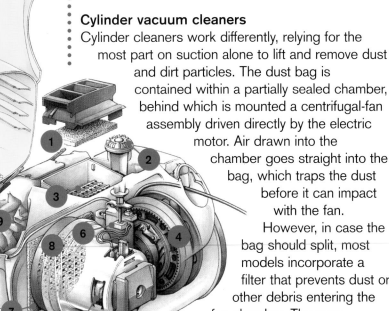

Cylinder vacuum cleaners

Cylinder cleaners work differently, relying for the most part on suction alone to lift and remove dust and dirt particles. The dust bag is contained within a partially sealed chamber, behind which is mounted a centrifugal-fan assembly driven directly by the electric motor. Air drawn into the chamber goes straight into the bag, which traps the dust before it can impact with the fan. However, in case the bag should split, most models incorporate a filter that prevents dust or other debris entering the fan chamber. The now relatively clean air continues through the fan assembly, cooling the electric motor in passing, and escapes via vents in the appliance. A flexible hose attached to the air-inlet socket is designed to take a range of extensions and tools or attachments for cleaning floorcoverings, upholstery and curtains.

Hybrid cleaners

To avoid some of the drawbacks associated with these two types of vacuum cleaner, designers gradually incorporated the better features of each to create what are in effect hybrid models.

For example, there are now many upright cleaners that incorporate the cylinder-type through-flow system. Air and dust are drawn into the brush-roller housing and taken via a flexible hose directly to a dust bag contained within a semi-sealed plastic case. The motor and fan assembly housed at the base of this case is protected by a replaceable filter.

One end of the flexible hose can usually be detached from the appliance and fitted with attachments so that the upright cleaner can be used to vacuum upholstered furniture, stairs and curtains.

The through-flow system provides better protection for the fan and motor, but the average cylinder model does not clean carpeted floors as well as an upright vacuum cleaner fitted with a brush roller. To overcome this disadvantage, some manufacturers offer an attachment head with a revolving brush roller.

1 Exhaust filter
2 Switch control/ power selector
3 Exhaust grille
4 Automatic flex rewind
5 Electric motor
6 Switch
7 Premotor filter
8 Fan housing
9 Dust bag
10 Lid seal
11 Bag carrier
12 Hose nozzle
13 Flexible hose
14 Lid
15 Bag-full indicator

1 Cord clamp
2 Flex
3 Terminal block
4 Flexible hose
5 Exhaust filter
6 Air vent
7 Fan chamber
8 Motor housing
9 Flexible drive belts
10 Brush roller
11 Beater bars
12 Bristles
13 Height control
14 Hose socket
15 Premotor filter
16 Dust bag
17 Bag-attachment nozzle
18 Access-panel seal
19 On/off switch

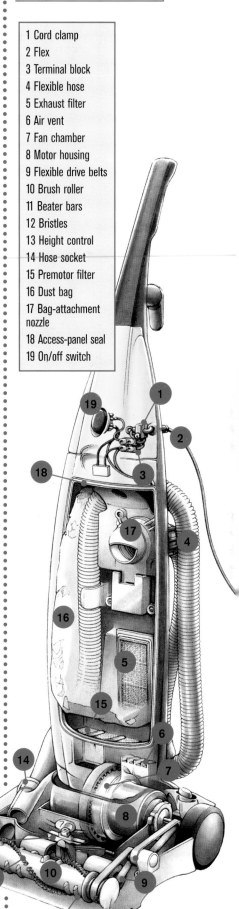

Additional features

Like all other domestic appliances, vacuum cleaners have become more and more sophisticated, with a range of features designed to improve performance.

Variable power

Many models are now fitted with variable-power controls that allow you to increase or reduce suction as required. Some cleaners monitor the volume of dust in the airflow and automatically adjust the power for optimum performance.

Infrared dust sensor

To tell you when your floorcoverings and furniture are clean, a dust-detection system switches on an indicator when the amount of dust in the airflow falls below a certain level. A brand-new carpet tends to confuse the infrared sensor, but the system starts to give accurate readings as soon as the floorcovering stops shedding loose pile.

Automatic flex (cord) rewind

Since the flexible cord on vacuum cleaners needs to be fairly long, many models are fitted with a spring-loaded drum that winds the flex back into the appliance.

You should pull out the required length of flex before plugging in, and when rewinding the flex prevent the plug striking the appliance casing.

Don't let the flex spring back

Cordless models

There are cordless models that can clean a floor area of about 140sq m (1500sq ft) before you have to recharge the batteries.

Noise reduction

Specially designed air-exhaust systems reduce operating noise to a minimum.

Filters

At one time the dust bag was the only means of filtering dust out of the air, but the modern vacuum cleaner is almost invariably fitted with secondary filters that protect the motor and fan assembly, and prevent harmful particles as small as 0.3 microns

DUST BAGS

The majority of vacuum cleaners are fitted with disposable paper bags that collect the dust and other debris.

Failure to replace or empty a full bag is the most common reason for poor cleaning performance and breakdown. As soon as airflow is restricted, suction drops and the motor begins to overheat. On many models, a thermal-overload cutout (TOC) switches off the power to prevent serious damage to the motor.

Some bags are designed to be used several times before they need replacing, but even these reusable bags will not work effectively once the paper becomes clogged with fine dust.

Double-wall dust bags are made with two layers of paper that, together, remove particles down to about 1 micron in size.

Never fit dust bags that are not designed for your vacuum cleaner, and don't attempt to use any other type of paper or plastic bag as an alternative. It pays to have one or two 'genuine' spare bags handy.

Bag-full indicators

A useful feature found on many vacuum cleaners is an indicator that tells you when the dust bag needs to be emptied or replaced.

If you suspect that the indicator is faulty, switch on and repeatedly place the palm of your hand over the end of the cleaner's hose (don't fit any attachments). The indicator should show 'bag full' when the hose is covered, then change as soon as you remove your hand.

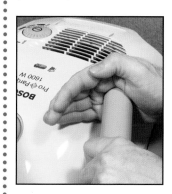

passing out into the air. These appliances, which trap pollen grains, dust mites and even tobacco-smoke particles, are ideal for allergy sufferers. It is essential to wash or replace your filters regularly. The number and types of filter vary from model to model – so consult your user's handbook.

Premotor filters
A filter just before the motor housing is an intrinsic component of a through-flow system.

Carbon filter
This type of filter, which is designed to remove odours from air passing through the appliance, is not found on all vacuum cleaners. Some models are fitted with perfumed air-freshener pads.

Exhaust filters
These filters are designed to trap the smallest of particles. Some electrostatically charged filters (S-class filters) remove sub-micro particles.
     HEPA (High Efficiency Particulate Air) filters are the most effective types used for domestic vacuum cleaners. True HEPA filtration systems conform to the stringent standards required in hospitals and health clinics.

Hand-held cleaners
Small portable vacuum cleaners are ideal for cleaning worktops or benches and inside cars. Some models have a rotating brush roller, and many hand-held cleaners are cordless.

Mains-powered hand-held cleaner

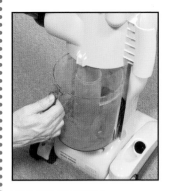

BAGLESS CLEANERS
Instead of having a bag to trap the dust, cyclonic or vortex vacuum cleaners cause the airflow to rotate at high speed, creating a centrifugal force that extracts the dust particles. The dust is collected in a rigid 'cup' or container, which is emptied when full. Bagless vacuum cleaners have highly efficient filtration systems – some washable filters are guaranteed to last the lifetime of the appliance.

Wet-and-dry cleaners
Picking up liquids would do irreparable harm to an ordinary vacuum cleaner – but specialized canister cleaners, known as wet-and-dry cleaners, have been designed to pick up spilled water as well as household dust.
     As the water level rises inside a wet-and-dry cleaner, it gradually lifts a floating ball valve that eventually seals off the airway into the fan chamber and motor housing, preventing any further ingress of water.

Adjust the power selector

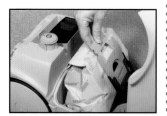

1 Remove and seal the dust bag

2 Carefully insert a new bag

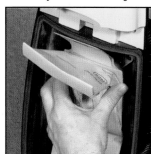

POOR SUCTION

If the motor is running but your vacuum cleaner is not generating sufficient suction, try the following:

Wrong power setting

On models with variable-power control, check that the power selector has not been turned down accidentally.

Bag full

A bag that is clogged with dust will reduce suction considerably. To change the bag:

1 Unplug the cleaner and remove the lid or access panel to reveal the dust bag. Carefully lift out the bag and seal the aperture, unless it is self-sealing, then (depending on the type) discard or empty the bag. Never operate the cleaner, even temporarily, without a bag in place.

2 Insert a new or clean bag, making sure its aperture fits perfectly onto the nozzle. The first sign that you have failed to do so will probably be when the motor overheats or you discover the bag chamber is packed with dust!

If your bag is designed to slide into a plastic carrier, make sure you orientate the bag correctly – following the instructions or arrows printed on the bag.

3 Tuck the bag in all round before replacing the lid or access panel. Check to see whether filters need replacing, too (see below).

Before you refit a replaceable bag, check for splits along folds and seams. Discard a damaged bag.

Filters clogged

Check your user's handbook to see how many filters are fitted in your vacuum cleaner and where they are located. Unplug the cleaner, then:

Carefully lift out the premotor filter, making sure loose grit and dust don't fall into the fan chamber.

On some models, this filter can be washed in warm soapy water (check your handbook) and then left to dry flat before it is put back in place. However, always fit a new filter after three or four bag changes; and around the same time, lift out the exhaust filter and fit a new one.

3 Tuck the bag in all round

Change the premotor filter

Lift out the exhaust filter

1 Check the hose for blockages

2 Run a marble through the hose

Carefully probe the hose socket

Clear the airway behind the roller

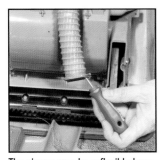
The airway may be a flexible hose

Blocked hose

Having changed the bag and filters, check the flexible hose for blockages. Take off any attachments you have been using, then stretch the hose to its full length and switch on the vacuum cleaner to see if full suction will clear the blockage. If not, unplug the vacuum cleaner and:

1 Disconnect the hose and check both ends for obvious blockages.

2 Straighten the hose and run a marble through it to check for a blockage midway. Pass a narrow broomstick or bamboo cane into the hose to dislodge dust and debris packed inside. Probe carefully, to avoid puncturing the hose.

Blocked airways

Before you reconnect the hose, check for blockages in the hose socket at the front of a cylinder machine or in the hood of an upright. Make sure the cleaner is unplugged, then carefully probe the socket with a screwdriver.

Some older-style uprights have a rigid tube running from the hood up to the dust bag. If this tube can be removed easily, take it out and dislodge any blockage. Otherwise, detach the rigid tube at both ends and probe it with a straightened wire coat hanger.

Finally, check the airway running from the brush roller towards the back of the roller housing. On some models, it is necessary to unscrew a base plate to gain access to this airway. With other cleaners, you have to unscrew and lift off the hood.

Air leaking from a semi-sealed system

The through-flow system employed in cylinder cleaners and many modern uprights relies on good seals to promote suction.

1 Check that the hose is connected properly where it enters the appliance.

2 If that doesn't improve the suction, disconnect the hose and check it for splits between the corrugations.

3 Remove the lid or access panel and see if the seals are missing or misplaced. Press these seals home firmly, and replace any that are too misshapen to fit snugly.

1 Is the hose connected properly?

2 Check the hose for splits

Replace a damaged seal

Adjust roller-height setting

Test the length of the bristles

SAFETY FIRST

Never use a vacuum cleaner to pick up smouldering cigarettes, ashes or cinders.

Never use a vacuum cleaner to pick up liquids, unless it is specifically designed for that purpose.

Don't unplug the appliance by pulling the flexible cord.

GOOD SUCTION BUT POOR PICK-UP

Sometimes an upright vacuum cleaner won't pick up threads or fluff, although the brush roller is revolving and the suction is satisfactory.

Wrong brush-roller setting

Check that you have the correct roller height set for the type of surface you are cleaning. It is usually easier to reset the control if you tip the appliance back onto its rear wheels.

Worn bristles

Unplug the cleaner, then test the length of the bristles to see if the brush roller needs replacing.

Place a straightedge, such as a ruler, across the opening in the base plate (also known as the mask plate) and turn the brush roller by hand. If the bristles don't touch the straightedge across the entire width of the appliance, replace the roller – see below.

BRUSH ROLLER STOPS REVOLVING

Broken belt

Although there are minor differences between models, the method described here for replacing a broken drive belt is fairly typical. Make sure you buy an exact replacement for the broken belt. If your cleaner is fitted with a pair of belts, change both belts at the same time. To change the belt:

1 Unplug the appliance, and either unscrew the base plate or lift the hood off the cleaner to reveal the brush roller.

2 Prise up the roller at both ends and lift it out of the cleaner.

3 Loop one end of the new belt over the motor drive shaft, and then slip the other end into the slot moulded into the roller.

4 Pull on the roller to stretch the belt and carefully fit both ends of the roller into their locations. Some rollers have a round fitting at one end and a squared or 'keyed' fitting at the other. Make sure you've got this type of roller the right way round, and insert the round fitting first.

1 Remove the base plate or hood

2 Lift out the brush roller

3 Slip a new belt onto the roller

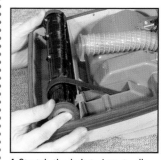

4 Stretch the belt to insert roller

carried out of the top vent. Air drawn in
through the bottom vent is heated in turn,
creating a current of warm air that circulates
throughout the room. This is a highly
efficient system that provides good overall
levels of comfort.

Convector heaters may be fitted with open
wire (spiral) elements supported by heat-
resistant mica or ceramic holders. Modern
heaters are more likely to be fitted with
'stitched-wire' elements that zigzag back and
forth through heat-resistant supports.

As well as a simple on/off switch, most
convector heaters will have heat-setting
switches that enable the user to turn on one
or more elements. A variable thermostat is included to allow the required
temperature to be maintained. A thermal-overload cutout (TOC) is usually fitted
to prevent overheating.

1 Top vent
2 Thermal-overload cutout
3 Indicator light
4 Temperature-control knob
5 Thermostat
6 Earth terminal
7 Flex
8 Terminal block
9 Heat-setting switches
10 Bottom vent
11 Stitched-wire element

Fan heaters
Fan heaters are the most popular type of portable heating appliance. Though
small in size, they are capable of warming large volumes of air relatively quickly,
making them the ideal choice for backup heating.

Air drawn into the appliance by a fan passes over
spiral or stitched heating elements similar to those
fitted in convectors. A set of switches or a single
rotary switch allows a combination of
elements to be selected, resulting in a
variable heat output. Most models
also incorporate a cold-blow
feature, which allows the fan to run
without switching on the heating
elements. The majority of fan
heaters are fitted with a thermostat and a TOC.

Some fan heaters are mounted on a stand, which
contains a mechanism that causes the entire
heater to oscillate back and forth in order to
direct the flow of heated air over a wide area.

Cleaning heaters
Before cleaning any type of room heater, unplug
the appliance and allow it to cool down completely.

Cleaning radiant heaters
Radiant heaters require little in the way of cleaning except
to keep the reflector polished. To avoid damaging the
fragile elements, it is preferable to remove them before cleaning the
reflector (see page 194); but this is not essential, provided you take care.
Unplug the heater and lift off the wire grille, which may be held in place

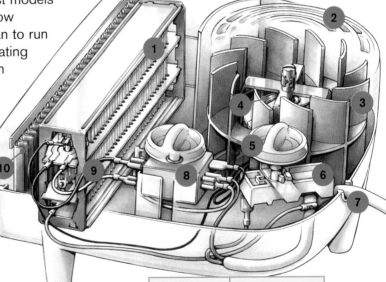

1 Stitched-wire element
2 Air-inlet vent
3 Centrifugal impeller
4 Electric motor
5 Temperature-control knob
6 Thermostat
7 Flex
8 Rotary selector switch
9 TOC
10 Air-outlet vent

Polish the reflector with a duster

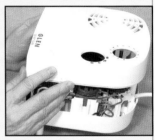

Brush dust off a cool element

with fixing screws. Wipe the reflective surface with a barely damp cloth and then polish it dry with a clean duster – don't use metal polish or abrasive cleaners.

Before you switch on a heater that has been in store over the summer months, carefully brush dust off the elements with a soft paintbrush.

Cleaning convectors
Regularly check the inlet vent on the base of a convector heater to make sure it doesn't become obstructed with fluff. If necessary, use a vacuum cleaner and soft paintbrush to remove debris and dust from the vents and heating elements.

Cleaning fan heaters
Most modern fan heaters are made with heat-resistant plastic casings, which can be wiped clean with a slightly damp cloth. Don't allow moisture to get into the heater.

If there's a smell of burning when you use the heater, dust and fluff may have accumulated on and around the heating elements. Clean them carefully with a soft paintbrush, after unplugging the heater and leaving it to cool down.

Remove dust from a convector

Wipe a fan heater's casing

Removing covers and casings
Always unplug a heater before removing access panels or casings.

Most radiant heaters and convectors have removable access panels held in place with self-tapping screw fixings.

The plastic casing of a fan heater usually consists of two halves, held together with recessed screws. Some fixings may require special screwdrivers. If the screws are of different lengths, label them to make reassembly easier. Having removed the screws, stand the fan heater on a

table and carefully separate the two halves of the casing, so that you can make a mental note of how the various internal components relate to one another and how they fit into the casing. If necessary, draw a diagram. As with all double-insulated appliances (see page 18), it is important to replace all components and wiring in their original positions.

Start with a high temperature

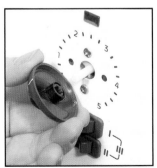

Turn down until you hear a click

1 Test the thermostat

2 Ease off the control knob

CANNOT CONTROL TEMPERATURE.

Thermostat set too high

If the room keeps getting too warm for comfort, start by setting the temperature control to 'high'. As soon as the room feels warm enough, slowly turn down the control until you hear an audible click or the indicator light goes out. Your heater will now cycle on and off to maintain the required temperature.

Thermostat set too low

Most room heaters will not switch on if they detect the ambient temperature is higher than the thermostat setting. This is not a fault. However, because the temperature range may vary throughout a large room, you may need to turn up the temperature control to compensate for 'cold spots'. Alternatively, try moving the heater to a different part of the room.

Faulty thermostat

A faulty thermostat will either neglect to turn off the heater, making the room uncomfortably warm, or it may not switch the appliance on. (Check first for a low setting – see above.).

Unplug the heater and remove the back panel or casing to find the thermostat, which is mounted directly behind the temperature-control knob.

1 Ease the spade connector off one or both of the thermostat terminals. While you hold a probe of a continuity tester on each terminal, have someone operate the temperature-control knob for you. Starting with the control knob on the lowest setting, have your helper gradually rotate the knob until you hear a click, at which point the tester's indicator should be activated. The thermostat is faulty if the indicator is either continuously active or continuously inactive throughout this test.

2 If the thermostat proves to be faulty, ease the control knob off its shaft, with a straight pull.

3 Undo the fixing screws concealed behind the control knob in order to detach the thermostat.

4 Then take out the thermostat and fit an exact replacement.

SAFETY FIRST

Don't use room heaters for drying or airing clothes. Never cover grilles or vents.

Don't restrict the airflow around fan heaters or convectors.

Don't place room heaters too close to furniture and furnishings. Make sure curtains cannot accidentally cover vents and grilles.

Make sure all grilles, covers and casings are in place and in good condition before plugging a room heater in.

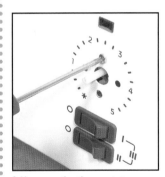

3 Unscrew the thermostat

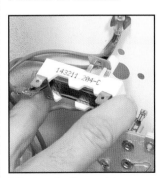

4 Replace the thermostat

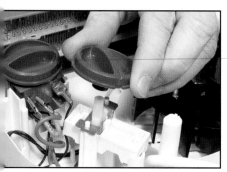

1 Take off the control knob

2 Lift out the thermostat

3 Place a probe on each terminal

You can replace a faulty thermostat in a fan heater in a similar way, but since the components are likely to be packed closely together it is often easier to take the thermostat out of the appliance to test it.

1 Having removed the casing (see page 190), select the lowest temperature setting before you ease the control knob off its shaft.

2 Lift the thermostat out of the appliance so that you can ease off the spade connectors.

3 Lay the thermostat on a bench and test it as described on page 191, rotating the control-knob shaft until you hear a click. If necessary, you can refit the knob temporarily.

Faulty TOC

The thermal-overload cutout is designed to switch off the appliance before it reaches a dangerously high temperature. A service engineer may be able to replace a TOC that trips at normal operating temperatures, but since most TOCs are an integral part of the heating element this would probably be uneconomical.

Unable to turn on all the elements

This symptom is common to room heaters that have two or more elements designed to be switched on sequentially. The complicated wiring to a bank of linked heat-setting switches or a rotary switch makes testing difficult and it is best left to a service engineer.

With basic radiant heaters, however, one element comes on as soon as you plug in the appliance. Operating a simple rocker switch turns on a second element, increasing the heat output. It is relatively easy to test and replace this type of switch yourself.

1 Move the rocker back and forth to make sure the switch is operating mechanically – the switch should click as you move the rocker.

2 To test the switch electrically, label the wires for identification and ease the spade connectors from both terminals, using long-nose pliers or the tip of a screwdriver. Then squeeze the moulded catch on each end of the switch so

SAFETY FIRST

Never leave a room heater unattended where it is accessible to children or where elderly people could fall onto it.

Check the flex regularly for signs of damage. Don't allow it to trail across the grille of an electric fire or over the vents in convector and fan heaters.

If your heater has a flex-storage facility, remember to fully unwind the flex before switching on.

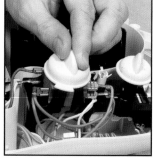

Get a rotary switch tested

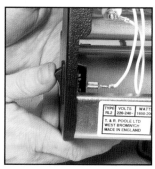

1 The switch should click audibly

• Handle a disc by its edges to avoid contaminating the playing surface.
• Always return your CDs to their plastic cases or a purpose-made wallet.
• Don't store your discs near radiators or in direct sunlight, or near other sources of heat. This is especially important if CDs are used or stored in your car.

How an audio cassette recorder works

The audio cassette – which took over from reel-to-reel tapes in the 1960s – is convenient, portable and capable of providing high-quality sound recordings.

The tape itself comprises a narrow strip of plastic material coated with ferric oxide.

1 Accidental-erasure tab
2 Cassette
3 Tape spool
4 Tape
5 Capstan
6 Pinch roller
7 Recording/playback head
8 Erase head

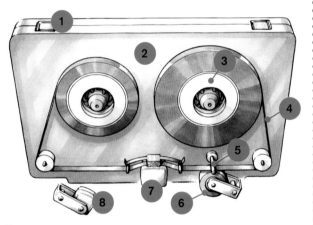

Passing the tape through a magnetic field modifies the properties of the oxide. The recorder's microphone reproduces sound waves as electrical impulses, which cause an electromagnet within the tape machine to imprint the signal onto the tape by magnetizing the ferric-oxide coating in a particular pattern. During playback, the magnetized tape reverses the procedure by replicating the electrical impulses as it passes over the electromagnet. This minute current is amplified and passed on to the speakers, where the drivers (see page 209) reproduce the sound waves picked up by the microphone.

The recording/playback head inside the tape machine comprises a pair of electromagnets (one for each stereo channel), and both channels occupy just one half of the tape. When you turn the tape around, you align the other half of the tape with the pair of magnets, which means you can record twice as much music or dialogue on a single tape. Prior to rerecording, another electromagnet – the erase head – wipes the tape clean by remagnetizing the oxide coating in a random pattern.

A revolving capstan aided by a pinch roller moves the tape across the recording/playback head.

Audio tape cassettes

The standard ferric-oxide tape is perfectly adequate for most purposes and is the standard for pre-recorded tapes. If you want to make better-quality recordings yourself, look for super-ferric and 'chrome' tapes. There are also special metal-particle tapes for use with digital recorders.

In the long run it pays to buy good-quality brand-name tapes. Although these may be more expensive, they reduce the incidence of tape failure and head contamination.

The standard tape cassette measures 100 x 65mm (4 x 2½ in), but tape recorders designed primarily for dictation take microcassettes measuring just 50 x 33mm (2 x 1¼ in).

High-capacity tapes with a running time of up to 120 minutes are usually made from relatively thin material in order to pack more tape into a standard-size cassette. This thinner tape has a greater tendency to stretch and get caught up in the transport mechanism of the machine. Unless you need uninterrupted recordings for long periods, it is safer to choose shorter tapes.

Looking after your cassettes
Although tape cassettes are fairly rugged, irreplaceable recordings can be lost if you don't store and use your cassettes with a modicum of care.

● Don't place cassettes on top of a TV set or hi-fi speakers. This type of equipment creates magnetic fields, which could scramble the recording.
● When they are not in use, keep your cassettes in their plastic cases and store them in a cool, dry environment.
● Don't store your cassettes near radiators or other heaters. And don't leave tapes on the dashboard of your car, where they could get too hot.
● Handle the tape itself as little as possible. Rotate one of the spools with a pen or pencil to rewind a tape that's been accidentally pulled out of its cassette.

How a radio works

In its simplest form, each radio station broadcasts its output as a signal from a powerful transmitter. The aerial connected to a radio receiver is able to pick up this signal. Since there are thousands of radio signals being transmitted simultaneously, the receiver must be capable of tuning in to the signal transmitted from a specific broadcaster. The signal is amplified by the receiver and put out through the speakers as audible sound waves.

Radio frequencies

So that a receiver can differentiate between all the various transmissions, each radio station is allocated a particular frequency, depending on whether the station is transmitting FM (frequency modulated) signals or AM (amplitude modulated) signals.

In this country, FM radio signals are transmitted in the frequency range 88–108MHz, providing high-quality stereo sound. AM signals – medium wave (MW) and long wave (LW) bands – are broadcast in the frequency range 153–1602KHz. AM broadcasts are monophonic, and are more susceptible to interference. Both AM and FM radio signals are transmitted in an analogue format, where radio waves directly represent the original sound.

Digital broadcasting

Digital Audio Broadcasting (DAB) converts sound into binary code, which can be transmitted and then decoded by special radio receivers. The benefits of DAB over FM and AM radio transmissions are:

● Almost CD-quality sound.
● Automatic data-error correction.
● No need to retune when on the move, as the same frequency is used nationwide (single frequency network).
● Interference-free reception on any digital radio receiver.

Radio aerials

All radio receivers require some kind of aerial in order to receive transmissions. Good reception depends on the type of aerial and the strength of the original transmission.

Built-in aerials

Portable radio receivers are invariably fitted with adjustable (usually telescopic) aerials to receive FM transmissions. In addition, most radios will also have an internal ferrite aerial to pick up AM signals.

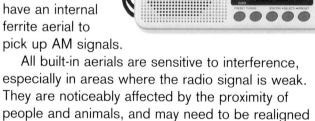

All built-in aerials are sensitive to interference, especially in areas where the radio signal is weak. They are noticeably affected by the proximity of people and animals, and may need to be realigned when you retune the radio.

Hi-fi tuners are sometimes supplied with nothing more than a short length of flexible wire, which serves as an FM radio aerial. This is the least effective type of aerial, and reception can nearly always be improved by replacing it with a good-quality indoor aerial.

Indoor FM aerials

The simplest T-shape or dipole aerial is made from plastic-coated wire. Experiment with the position and orientation of the aerial until you get the best possible reception, then pin or screw the crosspiece to a wall or the back of a hi-fi cabinet. The other end of the aerial is attached to the aerial socket or terminals on the back of the receiver.

Good-quality omnidirectional aerials, similar to set-top TV aerials, can be placed anywhere in the room in order to optimize FM radio reception.

If radio signals are weak in your area, either fit a signal booster to the aerial (see page 214) or have an outdoor aerial installed by a professional.

1 Dipole aerial
2 Fixing screw
2 Coaxial plug

DAB aerials

To receive digital broadcasts, you require a digital receiver and aerial. A VHF aerial, which covers Band 3 between 211.5 and 230MHz, is usually recommended. Get advice before you spend a lot of money on equipment – with digital radio you either get an error-free signal or nothing at all!

Audio cable and connectors

With combined all-in-one audio systems the connections between components are wired internally, alleviating the hassle of having to connect up an amplifier, CD player, tuner and cassette recorder correctly. However, for hi-fi enthusiasts, being able to assemble a made-to-measure system more than compensates for troublesome connectors and the inevitable rat's nest of cables.

Whether you make do with the cables and connectors supplied with the equipment or upgrade them to improve the performance of your system, all cables suffer from stretching, kinking and unsightly knotting unless you impose some sort of order at an early stage. Furthermore, if you take the opportunity to label the various cables, you will find it easier to reconnect your system after moving home or redecorating.

Cable-tidy kits

It does not take a great deal of imagination to improvise a labelling system, but a proprietary cable-tidy kit does it for

you. Each kit contains dozens of preprinted coloured labels, which you can shrink onto your cables, using an ordinary hairdryer. There are also reusable self-adhesive cable clips for attaching the different groups of cables to the back of your hi-fi cabinet or to shelving.

Outdoor FM aerials

Your installer will suggest whether you would be best served by a directional aerial aimed at a particular transmitter or whether you would benefit from an omnidirectional aerial that will receive transmissions from 360 degrees.

Reception is better with a directional aerial, but provided the signals are strong enough an omni-directional aerial can access every transmitter within range. Outdoor aerials can be attached to a wall or chimney stack, or you can have one installed in your loft.

Spray deoxidizing fluid onto all the connections

Or remove oxide with a fibreglass electric-contact cleaner

Cleaning connectors

Signals can be seriously impaired when audio connections become oxidized. Sprayable deoxidizing fluids (sometimes called switch-cleaning lubricants) are available from specialist hi-fi outlets.

With the audio equipment unplugged, spray the fluid sparingly onto all your connections. Wipe up any excess fluid with a paper towel, and leave the remainder to evaporate before you reconnect the cables.

Alternatively, use an electric-contact cleaner. Similar to a retractable pen, this tool has a fibreglass tip that will remove accumulations of oxide from phono and video connectors.

Portable equipment

Portable radios, tape recorders, stereo systems and personal CD players are all subject to many of the problems that affect complete audio systems. But being portable makes them even more vulnerable to physical damage and accidental breakage.

● Keep portable equipment out of the rain. Apart from the damage caused by wetting internal components, rainwater contains minerals that can corrode electronic circuits.

● Don't use harsh chemical cleaners, solvents or detergents to clean portable music players. Wipe their cases occasionally with a barely damp cloth, to keep them looking new.

● Don't use or store this type of equipment in abnormally high temperatures. Portable radios and other personal music players are often left on window sills and car dashboards, where heat from the sun can shorten the life of electronic components, damage batteries and warp or soften plastic cases.

● Remove the batteries if you plan to put a radio, tape recorder or CD player away for an extended period.

● Protect your portable equipment from airborne dust and sand, which can prematurely wear moving parts.

Cleaning audio systems

Dust is the enemy of all electronic appliances, but rotary or slide controls on audio equipment are especially vulnerable. Cigarette smoke is also extremely detrimental to switches, controls and tape heads.

Dust your equipment regularly with an anti-static cloth, which attracts fluff and dust to itself. Use a clean, dry paintbrush to get between press buttons and control knobs. See also, the miniature vacuum cleaner on page 229.

If adjusting slide or rotary controls causes a 'crackling' sound, use an aerosol containing compressed air to blow dust from the vicinity of the controls. This is also the ideal method for removing dust from around your cables and connectors.

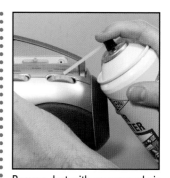

Remove dust with compressed air

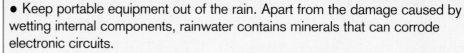

First things first

Before you get a technician to service your audio equipment, check the following:

● Is the system plugged in? And is the socket switched on?

● Have you selected the required mode – CD, radio or tape?

● Is the system playing through remote speakers?

● Are headphones plugged in?

● Are all your cables connected properly?

● Is the CD or cassette inserted correctly? And have you accidentally inserted a blank CD or tape?

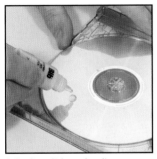

1 Apply polish to the disc

2 Rub surface with straight strokes

CD COMPARTMENT WON'T CLOSE

Never use force to close or open the hinged lid or sliding tray.

Disc not positioned accurately

Check that the disc is loaded correctly, then try opening and closing the compartment to make sure it is operating smoothly.

Faulty drive mechanism

The mechanism (or drive belt) that operates the sliding CD tray may be faulty. This type of mechanism is inaccessible and must be repaired by a technician, which is likely to be cost-effective.

CD SKIPS

Dirty disc

Fingerprints deflect the laser beam, causing it to misread the information stored on the disc – see page 198.

1 Place the disc label-side down on a flat surface or in its storage case. Apply a drop of proprietary CD polish (or clean water) to the shiny side of the disc and wipe the surface clean with a lint-free cloth.

2 To avoid leaving scratches that could mask the spiral data track within the disc, clean and polish, using straight strokes from the centre outwards, towards the circumference of the disc.

Damaged disc

Applying a proprietary CD polish as described above will remove minor scratches, along with greasy fingerprints. However, if the disc continues to skip after cleaning, try restoring the polycarbonate surface, using a repair kit. The kit shown here contains a simple hand-operated resurfacing device.

1 Insert the disc label-side down into the device and spray the damaged surface with the resurfacing liquid provided.

A badly loaded disc may jam a sliding CD tray

1 Spray the disc with the liquid

2 Crank the handle to rotate disc

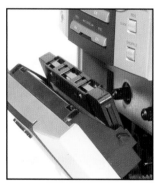

3 Buff the repaired surface

The compartment won't close if the cassette is upside down

Replace both batteries

2 Close the device and crank the handle until the disc makes one complete revolution. Then repeat the operation, reversing the direction of rotation.

3 Remove the CD and dry the surface thoroughly. Finally, buff the disk to restore the shine, using the felt pad supplied with the kit. The label side could be damaged if laid on a dusty or gritty surface – so, if necessary, place the disc on a folded cloth or in its storage case.

Dirty lens

If your CDs keep on skipping or stalling, the player's internal lens may be dirty. Special lens-cleaning discs are available from hi-fi dealers. Cleaning discs usually include recorded instructions. After cleaning, some will check that the system is working efficiently.

Apply the special cleaning fluid sparingly to the tiny synthetic-fibre brush attached to the underside of the CD.

Insert the CD in the player, select the track recommended on the disc and press 'play'. Stop and eject the disc after about 20 seconds, and wait 2 or 3 minutes for the fluid to evaporate before playing another disc.

Player not level

Make sure your CD player is standing on a level surface. This is especially critical with portable equipment.

CAN'T CLOSE TAPE COMPARTMENT

Tape cassette upside down

Turn the cassette over, top to tail, and it should drop snugly into the compartment.

WON'T RECORD TO TAPE

Battery power low

With portable tape players, a low battery may have enough energy to turn on the indicators (it may even play the radio), but the charge is not sufficient to physically move the tape. Insert fresh batteries and try again.

CD WON'T PLAY

CD inserted upside down
Make sure the disc is loaded with the printed label facing upwards.

Blank CD
Has the wrong compact disc been put in the storage case? Check the printed label.

Rewritable CD
Currently, a self-recorded rewritable disc will not be recognized by most CD players.

Pause button engaged
Check to see if the CD player's 'pause' button has been engaged accidentally.

CD mode not selected
Check your amplifier controls to see whether you have selected tape player, instead of the CD player.

Condensation on the lens
This is most likely to occur if you have brought a portable CD player indoors on a cold day. Open the disc compartment and remove the CD, then leave the player to dry out naturally in a moderately warm environment.

Is the pause button engaged?

Break off accidental-erasure tab

Replace the tab with adhesive tape

Pause button engaged
Check to see if the cassette player's 'pause' button has been engaged accidentally.

Voice-activated recording (VOR) engaged
Some tape recorders, especially dictation machines, have a tape-saving facility, which only activates the recording when the microphone is picking up sound. When the voice-activated recording switch is engaged, the machine may switch off if the recording level is too low for the microphone to detect ambient sound. Either turn up the recording level or switch off VOR.

Accidental-erasure tab removed
When you load a cassette into a tape machine, it engages a mechanism that allows recording to take place. In order to prevent a recording being accidentally erased, it is possible to disengage this mechanism by breaking off a small plastic tab situated at either end of the cassette.

If you change your mind at some stage and want to reuse the tape, replace the tab with a small piece of self-adhesive tape.

POOR SOUND ON TAPE PLAYBACK

Dirty heads
Dust, grease and oxide deposits gradually build up on the heads inside the tape machine. Dirty heads can distort the sound on playback and impair recording. The answer is to use a special cassette that cleans the tape path and demagnetizes the heads. Depending on the design, the cassette may contain an absorbent tape to which you add cleaning fluid, or it may have replaceable felt pads that apply the fluid to the head and capstan. Regular cleaning will prevent poor performance in the future.

Apply two or three drops of fluid to the tape or pads, then insert the cassette and run the machine for 20 seconds. Allow the fluid to evaporate for a couple of minutes before you use the tape player again.

Recording level too high
Select the appropriate recording level and record again.

TAPE WON'T PLAY

Tape spool jammed
An old cassette may have been wound back and forth countless times – and if it has been borrowed from a library, possibly on dozens of different tape players. Eventually this can stretch the tape and cause it to run off centre, which prevents the spools from turning. Attempting to rewind a jammed or tight cassette at speed may cause the tape to snap. Instead, try rewinding the tape by hand (see page 200) until the spools turn freely again.

End of recorded tape
Many prerecorded tapes have more music or dialogue on one side than on the other. This invariably results in the shorter side having a relatively long section of blank tape at the end. The cassette continues to run silently, possibly giving the impression that the tape or player is faulty.

Pause button engaged
Check to see if the cassette player's 'pause' button has been engaged accidentally.

Battery power low
See opposite.

Apply cleaning fluid to the pads

SAFETY FIRST

Always switch off and unplug a mains-powered tape player before attempting to remove a jammed tape.

Modern audio systems are made with delicate electronic and mechanical components. Except for cleaning and maintaining easily accessible components, it pays to leave internal servicing to a skilled specialist.

The laser beam in a CD player is potentially harmful if it is directed into the eyes. For this reason, don't dismantle a CD player's casing.

Some audio equipment is fitted with a fan to dissipate heat. Ensure that ventilation grilles are not obstructed or clogged with dust.

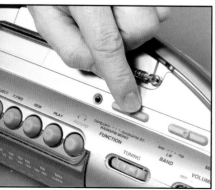

Switching to mono may improve FM reception

Damaged or worn tape

Play another (preferably prerecorded) tape in the same machine. If the sound is satisfactory, try playing the suspect cassette in another machine to find out whether the tape itself is faulty. Unfortunately, there is no way to restore a badly worn tape. As a precaution, it pays to make a backup recording of an irreplaceable tape.

PORTION OF RECORDING MISSING

Voice-activated recording (VOR) engaged

If you were unaware that VOR was switched on during recording, the machine may have switched itself off during a pause and then failed to switch on at critical moments.

PREVIOUS RECORDING AUDIBLE

Dirty erase head

Although it is not used as frequently as the recording/playback head, the erase head may eventually be contaminated with oxide particles shed from the tapes.

Insert an absorbent-tape cleaning cassette (see page 205) and let it run through the machine, which should be set to 'record'. Alternatively, use a foam bud or a chamois-leather swab moistened with head-cleaning fluid to clean the surface of the erase head.

POOR RADIO RECEPTION

Faint sound, hissing, the FM indicator flickers but does not illuminate completely – any or all of these symptoms indicate a weak signal.

Weak FM stereo signal

If you are experiencing a problem with a weak signal when listening to FM stereo, try switching your radio to mono as a temporary solution.

Internal aerial misaligned

There is no point in adjusting the telescopic aerial on a portable radio in order to improve AM reception. Try rotating the radio itself or move it to another location, but not too close to other electrical appliances – such as a TV set, washing machine or microwave oven.

TAPE JAMMED

Dirty pinch roller or capstan

Sticky deposits on the pinch roller or capstan can cause the tape to wrap round them. With care the damaged tape can usually be teased out of the machine, using a plastic or wooden toothpick, but will probably be unplayable afterwards. If the tape snaps in the process, make sure you retrieve every piece from the tape player.

The problem will recur unless you clean the tape-transport mechanism thoroughly – see page 205.

Tape can wrap around mechanism

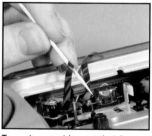

Tease it out with a toothpick

Worn or damaged pinch roller

If the roller is worn or damaged, it will need to be replaced by a technician. You can usually tell whether this is necessary by opening the tape compartment and inspecting the drive mechanism. A pinch roller in good condition should have a matt black surface. A worn roller may be rust-coloured as a result of oxide deposits and will be shiny in parts. If cleaning does not improve the condition of the pinch roller, take the machine to a service centre.

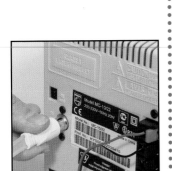

Retune to a stronger signal

Check the aerial connection

Your system may be switched to remote speakers

Receiver not tuned properly

Make sure you are tuned to the strongest available signal. Some nationwide radio stations broadcast on a different frequency in different parts of the country. By retuning you may be able to pick up the same station with much better reception.

If retuning your radio does not produce a stronger signal, you either need a better aerial (see page 201) or you could try fitting a signal booster – see pages 214 and 216.

If you switch off at the mains for more than a day or two, any automatic settings may be cancelled – in which case, you will need to retune and store the relevant frequencies.

Aerial not plugged in

Make sure the aerial cable is connected to the correct socket on the back of your tuner. It may be worth cleaning the contacts – see page 202.

Distorted FM signal

The radio transmission could be bouncing off an obstruction such as a tall building, so that the reflected signal is received by your radio fractionally later than the original signal. This is known as 'multi-path distortion'. Have a directional aerial installed – see page 201.

LIGHTS UP BUT NO SOUND

Headphones plugged in

When earphones are plugged into an audio system, the speakers no longer emit sound.

System connected to remote speakers

Check that the amplifier has not been switched to drive remote speakers in another part of the house.

Loose connections

Check all cable connectors for poor contact.

NO LIGHTS AND NO SOUND

Low or flat battery

Try changing the batteries in a portable appliance.

ELECTRICAL INTERFERENCE

Poor plug-and-socket connection

If there's a poor connection between the plug pins and the mains socket contacts, electrical activity caused by internal arcing could be picked up by the radio aerial, or the interference could even be transmitted directly through the mains connection.

Replace the 13amp plug and try again. If that doesn't work, have the socket tested and, if need be, replaced by an electrician.

Suppressor failure

Manufacturers are obliged by law to fit suppressors to all domestic appliances. If a suppressor fails, electrical interference could be picked up by your audio system. Switching suspect appliances on and off should enable you to locate the source of the interference, and you can then have the appliance tested by a service engineer. If it is a relatively new appliance, it should be returned to the manufacturer for servicing.

Is the power lead disconnected?

Test a figure-of-eight connector and lead for continuity

Power lead disconnected
Make sure the plug is inserted in the wall socket, and that the socket is switched on. If applicable, check that the power lead is plugged securely into the back of the equipment.

Power failure
If other appliances on the circuit have stopped working, inspect your consumer unit for a blown fuse or tripped MCB or RCD – see pages 11 and 12.

Faulty plug or fuse
Check that the plug is wired correctly (see pages 18 and 19), and replace a blown plug fuse (see page 17). If the fuse blows again as soon as you plug in and switch on, have the appliance checked at a service centre.

Broken flex conductor
The power lead to many portable music players and radio receivers is fitted with a moulded-on 13amp plug at one end and a figure-of-eight connector at the other.

To test this lead for continuity (see page 20), place one probe of a continuity tester on the neutral pin of the plug and insert the other probe into each of the figure-of-eight contacts in turn. One contact should activate the tester, but not the other. Then repeat the test with the live pin of the plug. You should get a similar but opposite result.

However, to make sure there's not an intermittent fault, perform both tests again while someone bends the flex gently back and forth, moving gradually along the lead.

If during either test the continuity tester shows no activity whatsoever, buy a replacement lead.

SAFETY FIRST

Don't stand audio equipment on a carpeted floor. Carpet pile can block air intakes, and fibres may be drawn into the equipment.

If you intend to stack your audio equipment, consult your user's handbook first to make sure the lower items are capable of taking the weight and the upper items won't be damaged by rising hot air.

Don't run cables under carpets, and make sure that your cables are not trapped under heavy equipment.

Don't use an adapter to accommodate a number of 13amp plugs. A trailing socket (see page 21) offers a safer alternative.

Switch off and unplug audio equipment before making or changing connections.

Never use headphones while driving or cycling. Even playing loud music through headphones while walking is potentially hazardous – especially when using a pedestrian crossing – because it can prevent you from hearing oncoming traffic.

SPEAKERS

Record companies and broadcasters spend vast amounts of time and money ensuring that the sound you receive is as near perfect as possible, and you may have one of the best made-to-measure audio systems on the market. But none of this matters, if the speakers – the final link in the electronic chain – have been set up incorrectly or are in poor condition.

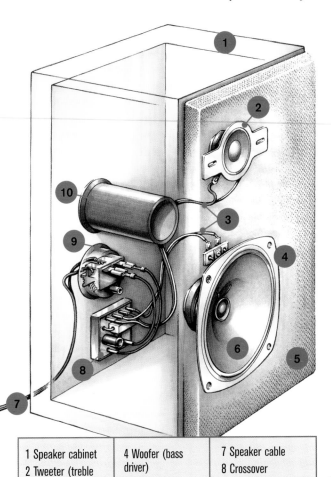

1 Speaker cabinet	4 Woofer (bass driver)	7 Speaker cable
2 Tweeter (treble driver)	5 Speaker grille	8 Crossover
3 Driver wires	6 Diaphragm	9 Terminal block
		10 Rear aperture

How it works

Electrical impulses from the amplifier are converted by the speakers into sound waves. Traditional speakers produce these waves by physically moving conical diaphragms made from paper, plastic or metal. The base of each cone rests within a coil of wire – the voice coil. The coil reacts to the electrical impulses from the amplifier, creating a varying magnetic field that drives the base of the cone-shaped diaphragm back and forth. This movement disturbs the air and makes sound waves.

Inside the speaker cabinet

Technically, the combination of diaphragm and voice coil is a known as a driver. Small drivers, called tweeters, are best at handling high-frequency sound. Woofers, the largest drivers, reproduce low-frequency bass sound. If speaker designers want to create even better separation, they include a third driver to handle the mid-range frequencies.

A sealed speaker cabinet, made from dense chipboard or MDF, directs the majority of sound waves forward into the room. Any backward-moving waves are contained by the cabinet. Nowadays, an aperture is very often cut in the back of the speaker cabinet through which backward-moving waves escape, boosting the overall sound level. Some cabinets are made with a backward-facing driver, which makes for a deeper all-round sound.

Positioning speakers

In reality, few people want to be limited to sitting in exactly the right part of a room when listening to music, and many modern speakers are capable of producing expansive sound even when they are not ideally positioned. Nevertheless, it is generally accepted that for near-perfect stereo performance the speakers and the listener should form an equilateral triangle, with both speakers aimed at the third point of the triangle. Ideally, the tweeters (normally placed near the top of the speaker cabinet) should be at head height. Purpose-made speaker stands may be the best solution.

In most rooms it is difficult to be that precise, but placing your speakers a few metres apart and not too close to the corners of the room usually produces acceptable results. Some speakers produce a rich bass sound when their backs are close to a wall – but this is not a general rule.

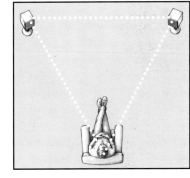

SPEAKER CABLE
There are literally dozens of different cables made for connecting hi-fi speakers to an amplifier. If you want to progress towards the upper end of the market, then you will need to get advice from a knowledgeable hi-fi stockist or explore the numerous articles on the subject printed in specialist magazines.

Basic speaker cable, as supplied with the majority of audio systems, is twin two-core flex. Each core is colour-coded in some way to ensure that the speakers are connected in phase – with the positive output terminal on the amplifier connected to the positive input terminal on the speaker. Similarly, the negative terminals need to be connected in the appropriate way. Getting them the wrong way round produces poor-quality stereo sound.

It's also best to keep both speaker cables the same length and as short as practicable.

ONLY ONE SPEAKER WORKING

Balance control poorly adjusted
Check that the balance control on your amplifier has not been accidentally adjusted to one side. If you find the control is centred, plug a set of headphones into the amplifier to ascertain whether the fault lies with the audio system or the speakers. If only one of the headphones is working, get your system serviced by a technician. Otherwise, try the following:

One wire loose or disconnected
See if the speaker cable is disconnected, either from the amplifier or from the speaker itself.

Broken cable conductor
It is easy to check whether there's a broken conductor within ordinary two-core speaker cable, provided you can disconnect the cable from both the amplifier and speaker. Place one probe of a continuity tester on each end of one of the colour-coded conductors. Then do the same with the other conductor. In each case the tester's indicator will be activated if the wire is intact – but to make sure there's not an intermittent fault, check both wires again while someone bends the flex gently back and forth, moving gradually along the speaker cable. If you detect that either of the conductors is broken, buy a new length of speaker cable.

If the cable is connected permanently to the back of your speaker, try the following test. Disconnect the cable from the amplifier and touch one core of the cable to either end of a 1.5 volt battery. A burst of sound tells you the cable is intact and that the speaker is working. If there's no sound, take the speaker to a service centre.

NO SOUND FROM EITHER SPEAKER

Headphones plugged in
Plugging in headphones disconnects the speakers.

Amplifier switched to remote speakers
Check that your amplifier has not been switched to drive remote speakers in another part of the house.

Check the balance control first

Look for loose or broken cables

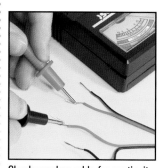

Check speaker cable for continuity

Use a battery to test the speaker

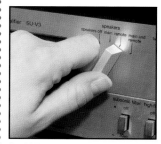

Could be driving remote speakers

DISTORTED SOUND

Wrong cable used
Using the wrong type of flex to connect your speakers may result in distorted sound or unusually low volume. Use purpose-made speaker cable only.

Volume too high
With high volume settings most amplifiers can exceed their rated power output, especially if the tone control is set to near its maximum for long periods of time. Such a combination may overload the speakers, even if they are correctly matched to the amplifier. Try reducing the volume. If this doesn't help, have your speakers checked by a technician.

Loose or punctured cone
Overloading speakers (see above) can eventually damage the drivers. Also, if you permanently remove the speakers' protective grilles, the driver cones are more vulnerable to physical damage.

Check your cones for punctures and tears near the rims. Replacing a driver is normally a task for a technician and may not be cost-effective.

Check for splits and tears near the rim of the speaker cones

RADIO INTERFERENCE
Your speaker cable may be acting as an aerial and picking up radio transmissions from emergency services. Try altering the length of your cables, or swap them for shielded speaker cables.

STEREO SOUND REVERSED

Speakers wired incorrectly
The left-hand and right-hand channels may have been reversed. Try swapping the speaker-cable connections on the back of the amplifier.

INSUFFICIENT BASS/POOR STEREO

Speakers out of phase
The colour-coded speaker cable may be wired incorrectly – see opposite. Check both ends of each speaker cable to make sure that the connections are consistent.

Channels may be reversed

These speakers are out of phase

TELEVISION SETS

Television sets are without doubt the most widely used electronic appliances in the home, with most households boasting two or more large-screen or portable appliances. Despite their obvious popularity, it is not the aim of this book to encourage DIY maintenance of TV sets. Not only are they too complex for the untrained person to test and service but all sets retain high voltages, even when the TV has been switched off and unplugged. For this reason, you should never remove the back panel of a TV set. Nevertheless, there is a lot you can do to improve reception and make viewing more convenient.

How it works

In the UK, our TV pictures and sound are broadcast in analogue format from about 1000 transmitters. Only a small percentage are high-power main transmitters, the majority being smaller low-power transmitters designed to relay the signals to homes outside the scope of the main transmitters. To avoid interference, neighbouring main transmitters broadcast on different frequencies. The whole of the UK's TV network broadcasts on an Ultra High Frequency (UHF) range of between 470 and 860MHz. In order to receive these signals, a TV set must be connected to a suitable aerial.

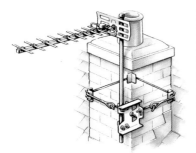

Aerials can be fixed to the stack

Or you can install one in the loft

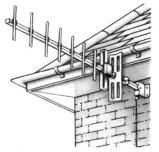

Mounted with elements vertical

Outdoor aerials

Aerials mounted on the roof or a tall mast afford the best possible reception. An outdoor aerial can be installed in the loft, but – depending on the strength of the broadcast signal – picture quality may be reduced.

This type of aerial has a number of elements (crosspieces) and, as a rule, the more elements there are the better the reception. If you happen to live in an area where the incoming signal is weak, you may benefit from using a high-gain aerial, with an even greater number of elements designed to gather more of the available signal.

When directed towards a mains transmitter, an aerial should be mounted with its elements parallel to the ground. If it is receiving a signal from a relay transmitter, then the elements should be vertical.

UHF TV aerial

High-gain aerial

Indoor aerials

Where it is not possible to connect your TV set to an outdoor aerial, a good-quality set-top aerial is preferable to using the built-in telescopic or loop aerial already attached to the set. Built-in aerials are much more susceptible to interference, and you don't have the same freedom to move the aerial around in order to pick up a better signal.

There are directional indoor aerials, which work best when aimed at the transmitter. Omnidirectional aerials are designed to receive signals from any angle, but in practice you may still have to try the aerial in different positions to get the best reception.

Digital terrestrial broadcasting

By converting TV pictures and sound into binary code, digital broadcasters can transmit much more information than is possible with the analogue format. As a result, there are several advantages to be gained from a digital system:

- Sharp, clear pictures with CD-quality sound.
- Greater choice of programmes (you can receive both digital and analogue broadcasts).
- Greatly enhanced Teletext service.
- Interactive TV.

Because the majority of terrestrial broadcasting operates on the same frequencies as analogue TV, many households can continue using their existing outdoor aerials. However, the aerial may have to be realigned and, in some areas, a new wideband UHF aerial may be required.

What is certain is that to receive digital broadcasts you will either have to install a set-top box to decode the signals or buy a digital TV set with an integral decoder.

Satellite broadcasting

Satellite broadcasters transmit low-power signals to a satellite in a geostationary orbit 35,615km (22,130 miles) above the earth. The satellite amplifies the signals, converts them to a different frequency and transmits them back to earth. The area covered by the beam transmitted from the satellite is called the 'footprint'. Signals are strongest in the centre of the footprint and get progressively weaker towards its edges. Signal strength is also affected by weather conditions, with cloud cover, rain and snow all tending to degrade quality of reception.

To receive a satellite signal, you need a dish of a suitable size and shape. As a rule, the weaker the  signal the larger the dish required in order to receive acceptable pictures and sound. Large dishes, which have relatively narrow angles of reception, concentrate the signal and reduce interference but require more accurate alignment.

The dish then focuses the signal onto the low-noise block (LNB) suspended in front of it. The LNB reduces the signals to a lower frequency and sends them via a coaxial cable to the satellite receiver – this is the unit that converts the signals into a format that can be displayed on the TV screen.

Digital satellite broadcasting

A digital satellite broadcaster can transmit literally hundreds of channels, with a mixture of subscription and pay-as-you-view services. To receive digital satellite broadcasts, you need the appropriate set-top decoder or a TV set with an integral decoder, and you will probably have to get a smaller digital dish aerial. If you want to receive both analogue and digital transmissions, you will need two satellite dishes.

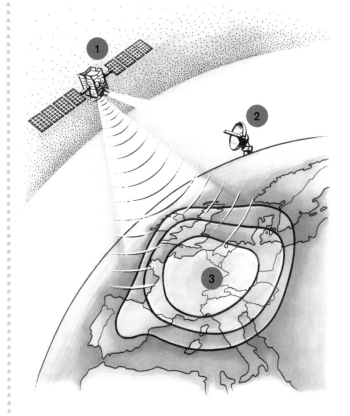

1 Satellite in geostationary orbit
2 Ground-based transmitter
3 Footprint

Cable TV

TV signals delivered by underground cables are not as susceptible to the sorts of interference that affect ordinary satellite reception. Analogue and digital services are on offer. To receive them, you need the appropriate set-top or integral decoders – similar but different from those required for satellite broadcasting.

Signal boosters

In locations where the TV or FM radio signals are weak, a signal booster (amplifier) will improve reception appreciably. With the appropriate booster, you can distribute the signals to a number of TV sets and audio systems without loss of quality.

Masthead amplifiers

In areas where reception is particularly poor, it would be worth having a high-gain outdoor aerial (see page 212) connected to a masthead signal amplifier. Clamped to an external aerial mast, or screwed to a chimney stack or screwed to a wall, the amplifier is powered by a special power-supply unit, which is plugged into an indoor wall socket. If you ask the installer to fit a 'diplexer' alongside the amplifier, you can gather and distribute signals from both a TV aerial and an FM radio aerial.

Plug-in signal boosters

For best-quality reception a signal booster should be placed as close to the aerial as possible – but for sheer convenience nothing beats a booster that you simply plug into a socket next to the television set. Having plugged the incoming aerial cable into the booster, you can then connect up as many appliances as the booster is designed to accommodate.

Other signal boosters are fitted with a 13amp plug on the end of a short length of flex. This type can be left freestanding on a shelf close to your TV set and hi-fi system, or you can mount it on the wall. Some of these are 'fixed-gain' boosters, and some are made with a dial or switch that allows you to increase and decrease the signal gain as required.

1 High-gain outdoor aerial
2 Masthead signal amplifier
3 Wall socket
4 Power-supply unit
5 Coaxial cable
6 TV set

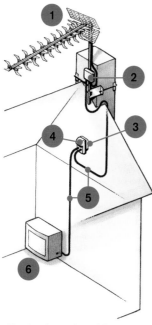

Masthead signal amplifier

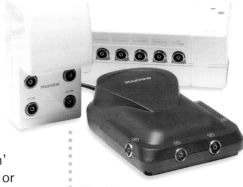

Signal boosters

First things first

The obvious is often overlooked. Check the following before calling out a technician to service your television set:

● Is the set plugged in? And is the socket switched on?

● In the case of a portable TV, is the mains lead plugged into the back of the set?

● Is the aerial cable connected?

● Is the set switched to the auxiliary channel?

● Has the 'mute' switch been engaged to turn off the sound?

● Are the remote controller's batteries flat (see page 221)?

INDISTINCT GRAINY PICTURE

This is caused by generally poor reception or weak signal.

Adverse weather conditions

Bad weather can temporarily affect reception, especially from a satellite.

Temporary transmitter fault

Switch to other channels to see if the quality of reception is better.

Set needs tuning

Retune the set to make sure the original tuning has not wandered.

Poor aerial-cable connection

Check that the aerial cable is securely plugged into the back of the TV set. Then check the other end. Is it inserted properly into the aerial socket, signal booster or VCR?

Faulty aerial cable

Before you do anything else, try plugging the aerial cable into a different TV set: if the picture is perfect on all channels, the fault lies with the original television set.

If the fault persists, gently flex the cable, working from one end to the other. If this causes the fault to come and go, buy or make a replacement aerial cable.

A special insulated and shielded (coaxial) cable is required. There are several types, but most electrical outlets stock the common 6mm (¼in) low-loss cable, which is ideal for the job. For a simple replacement you will also need a pair of special single-pin coaxial plugs. The ones shown here are solderless fittings made with simple screw fixings.

1 Cut the cable to length and slide the plug's locking ring onto one end.

2 Strip off about 30mm (1¼in) of the outer PVC sheathing, taking care not to sever the fine copper strands in the process.

3 Unravel the copper strands and fold them back over the sheathing. Wind the strands in a clockwise direction until they neatly cover the first 6mm (¼in) of the sheathing.

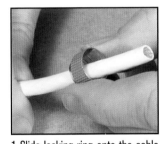

Is the aerial cable plugged in?

1 Slide locking ring onto the cable

2 Strip off the outer sheathing

3 Wind the strands clockwise

SAFETY FIRST

Never remove the back panel of a TV set. Doing so will expose you to components that store a very high voltage.

To avoid accidents, always route cables carefully. Never run cable under carpets or rugs, and don't route them where they could be crushed by furniture.

Solderless coaxial plugs

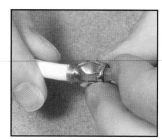

4 Cover strands with the gripper

5 Strip the polythene insulation

6 Trim off excess conductor

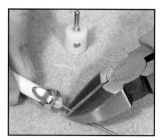

7 Tighten the fixing screw

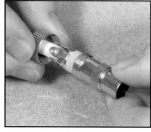

8 Assemble the plug

4 Slide the cable gripper onto the end of the sheathing so that it covers the copper strands. Pinch the gripper onto the sheathing to make sure all the fine copper strands are contained.

5 Strip all but about 3mm (⅛in) of the polythene insulation to reveal the solid copper conductor inside.

6 Trim off excess conductor, leaving about 5mm (¼in) protruding from the insulation.

7 Loosen the fixing screw and insert the conductor into the plug's pin. Tighten the screw, and check the conductor is held securely.

8 Assemble the plug, making sure that none of the copper strands touch the inner conductor, then secure the fitting with the locking ring. Fit a similar plug to the other end of the cable.

Aerial misaligned
Your TV aerial may be misaligned for a number of reasons.

First, go outside to see if a strong wind has dislodged it.

Another possibility is that the aerial may be pointing at a transmitter that has been superseded recently by a more convenient relay transmitter. If you have been away for some time, check the direction of your neighbours' aerials or seek the advice of a local installer.

Or the aerial may have been installed incorrectly. Once again, look at nearby aerials to see if the elements should be vertical or horizontal – see page 212

Different aerial required
Ask a local installer whether it would be worth swapping your existing aerial for a high-gain aerial – see page 212.

Signal needs boosting
Buy and fit a signal booster, or have a professional install a masthead amplifier (see page 214).

The following sequence describes the fitting of a typical fixed-gain signal booster, which in this case can supply up to four devices.

SAFETY FIRST

Don't run coaxial aerial cables beside mains-electricity cables.

Don't overload wall sockets with plug-in adapters. Either use a good-quality extension lead or, preferably, have more sockets installed to power your appliances.

Switch off and unplug a TV set before making or changing connections.

Leave the erection of outdoor aerials to professional installers. They have the necessary equipment to work safely on the roof and will know how to achieve the best-possible TV reception in your area.

1 TV aerial
2 Signal booster
3 Audio system
4 Coaxial (RF) cables
5 Mains power cable
6 Television set

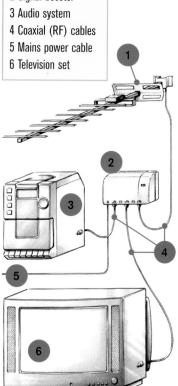

Installing a signal booster

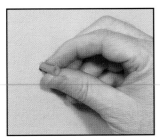

1 Mark fixing holes on the wall

2 Bore holes and insert wallplugs

3 Screw mounting box to the wall

4 Connect coaxial cables

5 Screw the booster to the box

1 Either use the manufacturer's template or the mounting box supplied with the booster to mark fixing holes on the wall or skirting board.

2 Bore the holes, and insert wallplugs if you are attaching the booster to masonry.

3 Screw the mounting box to the wall securely and check that it is level.

4 Connect the coaxial cables from your television sets (and audio system), and also the aerial cable.

5 Screw the booster to the mounting box, then plug it into a 13amp wall socket and switch on.

GHOSTING

Ghosting usually appears as a double image on the TV screen.

Reflected signal

Ghosting occurs when tall buildings, hills or sometimes large trees reflect the TV signal back towards the receiving aerial. On the screen it appears as a less-distinct replica of the image received directly.

Try having the outdoor aerial raised on a mast, or ask the installer whether it is possible to swap the existing aerial for a directional aerial or one with a larger reflector.

Fitting a booster is not a solution. All that will do is enhance the ghosting effect.

ELECTRICAL INTERFERENCE

Uneven bands of white spots and dashes accompanied by crackling or buzzing are caused by electrical discharge from a power tool or vacuum cleaner or some other electrical appliance. This type of interference is rare these days, as manufacturers are obliged by law to fit suppressors to all domestic appliances.

Try to locate the source of the problem and ask for the appliance to be switched off. If it is a relatively new appliance, it should be returned to the manufacturer for servicing.

SPARKLIES (WHITE DASHES)

Similar to the grainy picture described on page 215, but this is experienced with satellite broadcasting only.

Adverse weather conditions
Dense cloud cover, rain and snow can adversely affect reception. If you experience this type of interference regularly, consider having a larger dish installed – see page 213.

Dish misaligned or obscured
Check that your dish aerial has not been blown out of alignment, and make sure that plant growth has not gradually overtaken the dish itself or is blocking direct line of sight with the satellite.

Water penetration
Have your dish-aerial LNB and external cable connections checked for ingress of rainwater.

Faulty dish aerial
The LNB could be faulty. Have it checked and serviced by a technician.

CHANNEL INTERFERENCE

When you receive two channels simultaneously, horizontal bars can be seen on your screen. This may be a temporary effect that will cure itself. If this occurs with a satellite broadcast, your dish aerial may be slightly misaligned or you may need a larger dish that will reduce the angle of reception – see page 213.

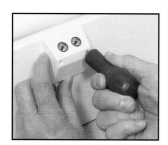

1 Make fixing holes for splitter box

2 Do the same for the outlet box

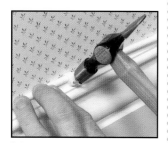

3 Run the coaxial cable

4 Prepare the cable for connection

5 Connect cable to outlet box

POOR RECEPTION ON SOME SETS

If you can't get reasonable reception on every television set in your home, you probably need to hook all of them up to the main outdoor aerial. There are several ways to do this, including using the type of signal booster described on pages 216–17. The following sequence shows one simple solution, using surface-mounted aerial sockets to connect two TV sets to the same aerial.

1 Using a bradawl, make holes for screwing a splitter box to the skirting close to your main TV set.

2 Do the same for a single outlet box in a similar position in the room where you use your second set.

3 Cut a suitable length of coaxial cable (see page 215) to run from one socket to the other. You can attach this cable to skirting boards and architraves, using plastic cable clips. Alternatively, run the coaxial cable under the floor or inside hollow walls – but not next to mains electricity cables.

4 At the single outlet box, strip about 20mm (³⁄₄ in) of sheathing from the coaxial cable, fold back the copper strands and then remove about 15mm (⁵⁄₈ in) of insulation to reveal the inner conductor. Using the outlet box as a guide, trim the solid conductor to length.

5 Connect the conductor to the terminal in the outlet box and trap the braided copper and sheathing under the cable clamp. Tighten both screws, then screw the box to the skirting. Fit a coaxial plug (see page 215) to the other end of the cable, ready for plugging into the splitter.

6 Remove the coaxial plug from the end of the existing incoming aerial cable and then connect the cable to the splitter box, as described above. Screw the box securely to the skirting.

7 Plug in the new cable running from the single outlet box.

1 TV aerial
2 Incoming aerial cable
3 Coaxial (RF) lead
4 Splitter box
5 New cable run
6 Main TV set
7 Single outlet box
8 Second TV set

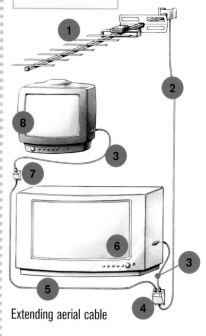

Extending aerial cable

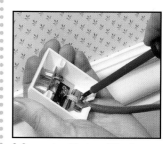

6 Connect cable to splitter box

7 Plug in the new cable

8 Plug in the coaxial leads

SAFETY FIRST

Use a correctly rated fuse in the plug connected to your TV set – see page 17.

Don't use a makeshift support for your television set. Place it on a strong table or shelf or, preferably, on a purpose-made TV stand.

Leave sufficient space around a TV set to promote ventilation.

Read the manufacturer's recommendations to find out whether it is safe to leave your television set plugged in and switched to standby.

8 Buy two ready-made coaxial (RF) leads for your TV sets and connect them, one from each box, to the 'antenna in' (ANT) socket on the back of each set.

WON'T SWITCH ON

Power failure
If other appliances on the circuit have stopped working, inspect your consumer unit for a blown fuse or tripped MCB or RCD – see pages 11 and 12.

TV not plugged in
Make sure the plug is inserted in the socket, and that the socket is switched on. On some portables the mains lead is plugged into the back of the set – check this connection, too.

Plug fuse has blown
Replace the fuse in the plug, making sure the new fuse is the correct amperage, as recommended by the TV manufacturer – see page 17.
  If the fuse blows again as soon as you turn the appliance on, have the TV checked by a service engineer.

Faulty wiring in plug
If possible, take the back off the plug and check that it is wired correctly – see pages 18 and19.

Broken flex conductor
If your mains lead is connected to the back of a portable TV set with a plug-in figure-of-eight connector, you can check the lead for continuity – see page 208.

REMOTE CONTROLLER FAULTY
See pages 220–21.

TELETEXT BREAKS UP

This is often the first sign of a relatively weak signal. Fit a signal booster (see pages 216–17) or an aerial that will improve reception (see page 212).

BLUE SCREEN

A blue screen tells you that the set is detecting a 'no-signal' condition. First, check that the set is not simply switched to a spare channel that has not been tuned to a TV station. If all the channels display a similar symptom, check your aerial connections and adjust the fine tuning on your set.

NO SOUND

Make sure the volume has not been turned down accidentally, then check whether there is sound on other channels.

TV set 'muted'
Check to see if the sound has been turned off at the set itself or on the remote controller.

Headphones plugged in
If you have neglected to unplug headphones, the sound to the TV speakers will be cut off.

REMOTE CONTROLLERS

A staggering number of electronic appliances – ranging from your TV set, VCR and audio system to camcorders, cameras and CCTV installations – are now capable of being operated by remote control, using small hand-held devices.

How it works

Pressing buttons on a remote controller sends out a beam of infrared signals, which is picked up by a diode sensor built into the equipment you are operating. The signal is decoded and amplified, then sent to a microprocessor, which passes control voltages to the various parts of the appliance in order to adjust the volume, switch channels, move tapes, or perform other functions.

Universal controllers

The dedicated controller supplied with a TV set, VCR or audio system operates just the one particular model, because each model has its own specific logic coding.

However, there are also 'universal' controllers, which you can program yourself to operate various types of equipment. Some can be programmed to operate several appliances – which reduces clutter and confusion.

These devices are so inexpensive that, once you have determined that your dedicated controller has broken down irretrievably, it invariably pays to go out and buy a universal controller rather than attempt to have the original one repaired.

Remote-control extenders

Remote-control extenders allow you to operate audiovisual appliances from anywhere in the house. This means that from your bedroom you can watch and control a videotape or DVD being played in your lounge, or you can adjust the volume of a hi-fi amplifier from your workshop.

Infrared signals from your remote controller are converted into radio frequencies by a small transmitter in the room. In another part of the house, a second transmitter picks up those frequencies, converts them back again into infrared and sends them to the equipment you are controlling.

Remote-control extenders

Getting the best from your controller

A remote controller won't let you down very often, provided you treat it with reasonable care.

● Dropping a remote controller is about the easiest way to write it off – so don't throw your controller around.

● Be careful not to spill liquids over a controller – certain liquids will corrode electronic components. Mop up spillages quickly and dry the controller immediately, using a hairdryer on a cool setting. Never overheat a controller.

● Wipe your controller occasionally with a damp cloth to remove greasy fingerprints. Never use strong solvents.

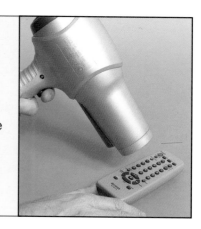

CONTROLLER FAILS TO WORK

Appliance switched off
Check that the equipment you are controlling is plugged in and switched on. If the appliance has a selector switch, make sure the master on/off switch is set to 'remote'.

To eliminate other problems, first try operating the equipment manually and then use another (universal) controller to make sure the equipment can receive infrared signals.

Wrong controller
Have you picked up the wrong remote controller by mistake?

Wrong function set on controller
Are you trying to control a TV set with a multi-function controller that has been switched to the wrong function – to the VCR mode, for example?

Flat batteries
Before you insert fresh batteries, clean any corrosion from the battery contacts. Use a foam bud moistened with any video or audio head cleaner. Be aware that most universal controllers will be deprogrammed within about a minute of removing the batteries. It therefore pays to keep the necessary codes in a safe place.

Wrong code
A universal controller may have become deprogrammed, or it may have been set up to operate a different model. Check which code you should be using and reinitialize the controller – codes and instructions are supplied with the controller.

Dirty button contacts
Use an aerosol can of compressed air to blow dust from around the buttons on your remote controller.

Clean internal battery contacts

Use compressed air to remove dust from controller buttons

Not transmitting infrared signals
Controllers are usually fitted with a small indicator light that flashes each time you press a button. In theory this tells you the controller is working, but how do you know it is actually sending the invisible infrared signals? Aim the controller at a digital camera or camcorder and press any

button on the controller. Look at the camera's LCD screen; and if the infrared transmitter is working, you will see it flashing on the screen as the button is pressed. (This test doesn't work with ordinary optical cameras or camcorders.)

Alternatively, aim your controller at an infrared-detector card. The test area on the card illuminates when it is receiving infrared signals. These cards are available from dealers who specialize in audiovisual equipment.

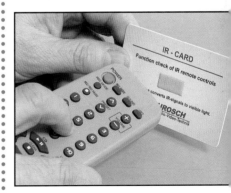

VIDEO CASSETTE RECORDERS

The video cassette recorder is the picture-and-sound equivalent of the audio tape recorder and works in a similar way. VCRs also suffer from some of the same problems – such as a deterioration of sound, and also of picture quality. However, because this is invariably a gradual process, the lack of quality becomes accepted as the norm until something more serious occurs. It pays to get into the habit of maintaining your VCR on a regular basis to keep it in tiptop condition and prevent wear and tear on expensive components.

How it works

Just like audio tape, video-cassette tape comprises a thin plastic backing strip coated with ferric oxide, which can retain the magnetic 'imprint' of pictures and sound. The main difference between the two systems is the way the picture-recording/playback heads write and read the information on the tape. A video tape contains vastly more information than an audio tape, so it has to move past the heads at a greater speed. This is achieved by mounting electromagnets onto a large rotating drum – the video head.

When you insert a cassette into your VCR and press 'play' or 'record', the tape is drawn into the mechanism by rollers that wrap it around the video head, which scans the tape at high speed. The tape's audio track is accessed by a separate stationary head (or heads). There is also an erase head, which removes previously recorded material.

A large pinch roller keeps the tape pressed up against a revolving 'capstan' that moves the tape through the VCR at the required speed. A tracking control synchronizes tape speed with video-head rotation and angle. Finally, a sensor detects the transparent strip or 'leader' at the beginning and end of each tape and switches off the machine.

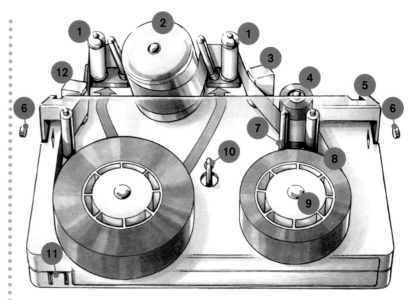

1 Roller	7 Capstan
2 Video head	8 Tape
3 Audio head	9 Tape spool
4 Pinch roller	10 Light
5 Spring-loaded cover	11 Accidental-erasure tab
6 Tape-end sensor	12 Erase head

Cassette tapes

Buy only good-quality branded cassettes. This will minimize any tendency for the tape to stretch and shed the ferric-oxide coating, which is so damaging to the heads and other moving parts of a VCR.

Hired cassettes, in particular, should be inspected for wear and damage before inserting them in your VCR. Don't touch the tape itself, but open the spring-loaded tape cover and inspect the entry points for brown powdery residue of oxide. This indicates that the tape coating is shedding and it would be unwise to run the tape through your VCR.

If you bring home a cassette when it's cold outside, let the tape acclimatize to the warmer environment before playing it. This should prevent the cassette getting caught up in your VCR due to moisture condensing on the cold tape.

Storing tape cassettes

Storing recorded and blank cassettes carefully helps to minimize tape damage and wear on your VCR.

- Keep out dust by storing cassettes in their protective sleeves. If possible, keep your cassettes in a cupboard.
- Store cassettes upright to prevent the wound tape slumping and stretching.
- Don't leave your recorded cassettes near a source of magnetism, such as a TV set or speakers.
- Keep them out of direct sunlight and away from other sources of heat.

Cables and connectors

Various cables and connectors are used to link a VCR with a TV set and possibly an audio system, too. However, they all have one thing in common – the need to pass interference-free signals between the appliances.

Poor connections are a common problem. Stretching cables tends to put a strain on connections; always leave some slack, and try to prevent kinks and knots that might damage the cables themselves.

Fine pins can be bent all too easily – so don't force connections, and take care to ensure they are inserted the right way round.

If possible, buy only good-quality cables and connectors. Bargain-price equipment may prove a false economy in the long run.

1 Aerial
2 Coaxial cable
3 Coaxial plug
4 VCR
5 Scart lead
6 TV set

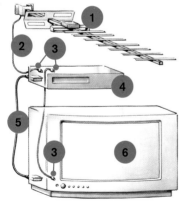

Simple VCR hook-up

Hooking up a VCR to a TV set

A simple system for connecting a VCR and a TV set may comprise the following. The incoming aerial cable is connected to the VCR, using a coaxial plug. A similar cable with a coaxial plug at each end (RF lead) runs from the VCR to the TV set. In addition, there may be a scart-to-scart lead between the VCR and TV set. Scart connectors provide superior picture and sound quality – ideal when playing recorded tapes.

Many people need a more sophisticated setup to accommodate additional equipment. Again there are numerous combinations to suit individual needs, but the following is typical. A satellite dish aerial is connected to the satellite receiver/decoder, using a screw-on F-connector. The cable from the normal terrestrial TV aerial plugs into the same receiver, using its coaxial plug. A scart-to-scart lead runs from the receiver to the VCR, and a similar lead connects the receiver with the TV set. An RF lead fitted with coaxial plugs runs from the receiver to the VCR and a similar lead connects the VCR to the TV set.

For better sound quality, it is possible to connect a hi-fi system to the receiver, using an audio lead that has a pair of single-pin phono plugs at each end.

1 Dish aerial
2 F-connector
3 Terrestrial TV aerial
4 Coaxial plug
5 Satellite receiver/decoder
6 Scart lead
7 RF lead
8 VCR
9 TV set
10 Audio lead to hi-fi system

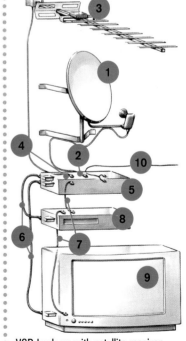

VCR hook-up with satellite receiver

First things first

Before you start looking for serious faults or decide to take your video cassette recorder to a service centre, check the following:

- Is the VCR plugged in? And is the socket switched on?

- Is the power lead plugged into the back of the VCR?

- Is the VCR connected to the TV set?

- Is the TV set switched to the required channel?

- Are the correct time and date set on the VCR?

- Have you inserted a cassette?

- Has the VCR been set to record automatically?

Check all leads, including those with scart connectors

CAN'T INSERT CASSETTE

Cassette wrong way round
Load the cassette with the label facing you. If a cassette is not loaded firmly enough, the VCR may eject it.

Faulty microprocessor
If the cassette goes in partway but then jams, switch off and unplug the VCR, then leave it for a few seconds before plugging in and switching on. Hopefully, the VCR's microprocessor will have reset and the tape will eject.

Cassette slot blocked
Make sure there is not another cassette already loaded in the VCR. Then switch off and unplug the VCR. Open the slot cover to see if there is something blocking the opening – children have a habit of posting toys and small objects into VCRs. If you can't retrieve the object through the slot, carefully remove the VCR casing – see page 226.

NO PICTURE

Switched to wrong channel
If the tape is running but you cannot see the recorded picture on your television set, check that the TV set is switched to the video channel.

Cable disconnected
Check that the cables connecting the TV to the VCR are plugged in at both ends. With some setups you will need to check the scart leads running to and from a satellite receiver.

POOR PICTURE ON PLAYBACK

Faulty tape
Before doing anything else, try playing a different tape in the VCR. This will ascertain whether the tape itself is the source of the problem.

Poor TV reception
If the tape is one you have recorded yourself, check your TV reception by switching to another channel. Then check your aerial, cables and connections – see pages 212–13 and 223.

Insert a cassette firmly

1 Coaxial plug
2 F-connector
3 Scart connector
4 Phono plugs

1 Moisten tape with cleaning fluid

2 Play the tape for 20 seconds

SAFETY FIRST

Ensure that ventilation grilles are not obstructed.

Don't stand a VCR on a carpeted floor. Carpet pile can block air intakes and fibres may be drawn into the equipment.

Check your user's handbook before you place a TV set on top of a VCR – it may not be capable of taking the weight.

Dirty video head

The most likely cause of poor recording and playback is an accumulation of dirt and oxide along the tape path, especially on the revolving video head. Buy a good-quality head-cleaning cassette. This is similar to a normal video cassette except that it contains an absorbent tape, which you moisten with a special head-cleaning fluid supplied as part of the kit.

1 Put three or four drops of fluid into the hole in the cassette.

2 Insert the cassette in the VCR and let the tape play for about 20 seconds. Rewind the tape and eject the cassette.

Allow 2 to 3 minutes for the fluid to evaporate before you play a recorded tape. Cleaning the heads regularly after every 20 hours of playing time will help prevent similar symptoms occurring in the future.

Tracking needs adjusting

If black-and-white streaks appear when playing a hired cassette, play a tape you have recorded yourself. If performance improves, the VCR's tracking control (see page 222) may need adjusting temporarily in order to watch the prerecorded tape. Your user's handbook will tell you which control to use – very often, this is incorporated in the remote controller. Make slight adjustments while watching the playback on screen until the symptoms disappear.

Some video cassette recorders are designed to reset themselves automatically. Otherwise, remember to reset the tracking to its original setting.

If there is no facility for adjusting the tracking manually, wind the tape forwards to the end and then rewind it. This may adjust the tape to match your VCR tracking.

Worn heads

Overusing the pause control can accelerate head wear, because the video head continues to revolve while the tape is stationary. Ask a service engineer to check the condition of your heads. Repairs are likely to be fairly expensive.

FLUCTUATING SOUND

Tape slipping
With wear, the pinch roller becomes smooth and shiny. This causes the tape to slip and the sound to change pitch. Eventually, the picture will be affected, too. The tape itself may show signs of damage – usually herringbone-shape crush marks along the edge.

Try running a proprietary video-head cleaner through the VCR. If that doesn't help, have your VCR checked by a technician.

SQUEALING NOISES

On earlier models, high-pitched squealing may be caused by a worn drive belt. Alternatively the capstan or motor bearings may need lubricating. Get a technician to look at your VCR before the repairs become expensive.

Adjust the tracking

CAN'T EJECT TAPE CASSETTE

First try unplugging the VCR for a few seconds, then plug in and try ejecting the tape again. If that fails, look for the following:

Tape caught up in the mechanism

The tape could be caught up in the drive mechanism. Although you may be able to remove the tape, it will be unplayable. If the tape contains a treasured or irreplaceable recording, get advice from a service centre before attempting to extract the cassette.

1 Switch off and unplug the VCR, then remove visible screws that are holding the casing in place. Look also for catches that have to be released before you lift the casing off the VCR. Remember that removing the casing exposes components that can easily get damaged unless you take care. If you can't see the tape path clearly, replace the casing and take the VCR to a service centre.

2 Use a wooden or plastic cocktail stick to tease out the tape. Avoid touching the video head and other delicate components. Don't poke metal implements into the VCR.

3 The resulting loop of tape could get caught up again when you try to extract the cassette. Since the tape is already unplayable, carefully cut the tape to leave a short tail at each end. Make sure you remove the remainder of the tape from the VCR.

4 Replace the casing, plug in, and eject the cassette. Before you use the VCR, insert a proprietary cleaning cassette to remove oxide dust from the tape path.

Mechanism jammed

The tape itself may have been withdrawn into the cassette, but something could be preventing the mechanism from ejecting the cassette. Very often this is a child's toy or book that has been posted into the slot and is jammed behind the slot cover.

Switch off and unplug the VCR, then remove the casing (see above) and carefully extract the blockage. Replace the casing, then plug in, switch on, and eject the cassette.

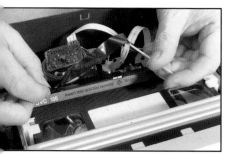

1 Remove the VCR casing

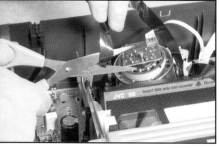

2 Tease out the jammed tape

3 Trim off excess tape before you eject the cassette

TAPE STOPS UNEXPECTEDLY

If the tape stops unexpectedly during fast-forward or rewind, check to see if the tape counter (normally used to locate the starting point of a particular recording) is reading zero.

If so, fully wind the tape backwards or forwards; when the VCR stops again, reset the counter to zero then switch off the counter memory – see your user's handbook.

CAN'T WATCH TV

You should be able to watch broadcast television on the VCR channel. However, it is not possible to receive transmissions if the VCR has been set up to record automatically.

Either turn off the timer or switch the TV set to another channel.

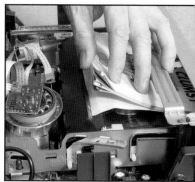

Something may be jammed behind the slot cover

VCR WON'T WORK AT ALL

Condensation

Some VCRs are fitted with 'dew protection' sensors, which prevent the appliance from operating when moisture has condensed on the video head. This can occur, for example, if you have brought a VCR from a cold environment into a warm one. Leave the VCR turned on and let it dry out naturally for two or three hours.

VCR not switched on

The clock display may be functioning even when the VCR is switched off. Press the manual on/off switch.

Timer switched on

With some models, the automatic timer has to be switched off manually before you can use the VCR. Switch off the automatic timer.

VCR not plugged in

Make sure the plug is inserted in the socket, and that the socket is switched on.

Power failure

If other appliances on the circuit have stopped working, inspect your consumer unit for a blown fuse or tripped MCB or RCD – see pages 11 and 12.

Plug fuse has blown

Replace the fuse in the plug – see page 17. If the fuse blows again as soon as you turn the appliance on, have the VCR checked by a technician.

Faulty wiring in plug

If possible, take the back off the plug and check that it is wired correctly – see pages 18 and 19.

Broken flex conductor

If your mains lead is connected to the back of the VCR with a plug-in figure-of-eight connector, you can check the lead for continuity – see page 208.

WON'T RECORD

Safety tab removed
The safety tab has been removed from the cassette to prevent accidental erasure – see page 222. Stick tape over the hole in the cassette.

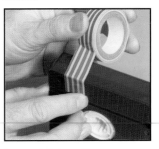

Incorrect date or time
If a preset timed recording has not started automatically, check that you have programmed the correct date and time.

Pause button engaged
Check your VCR display panel to see if 'pause' is displayed. Disengage the pause button – see your user's manual.

Wrong channel selected
Check that your VCR is set to record the required channel. Remember that what you are watching on your TV set is not necessarily what your VCR is recording.

SAFETY FIRST

Ensure the plug is wired correctly and that the appropriate fuse is fitted.

Always unplug a video cassette recorder before servicing it.

When reassembling a cassette recorder, make sure the components and wiring are returned to their original locations.

Before putting a VCR back into service, plug it into a circuit protected by an RCD – see page 11. Switch on, and if the RCD trips, have the VCR tested by a service engineer.

Most VCRs are designed to operate automatically, but check your user's handbook to make sure it is safe to leave your VCR switched on in standby mode.

Switch off and unplug your VCR set before making or changing connections.

COMPUTERS

Microprocessors are now built into so many products that we habitually use computers without even being aware we are doing so. The computer systems we are concerned with here are generally known as PCs (personal computers). They consist of a base unit, a monitor, and a keyboard and mouse. Most individuals or families have at least one of these general-purpose computers, which may be expected to handle word processing, accounts, email and Internet browsing, as well as leisure activities ranging from games playing to digital photography and home-movie editing.

Of all the electronic appliances we use in our homes, personal computers appear to be the most technically difficult to service – which is why it pays to enlist the help of knowledgeable technicians when your computer or peripherals (items connected to it) need repairing or upgrading. However, there are a great many seemingly insoluble problems that can be resolved in moments, even by inexperienced computer users. The aim of this section is to provide those answers that will get you out of trouble quickly and easily, without having to call in expert help.

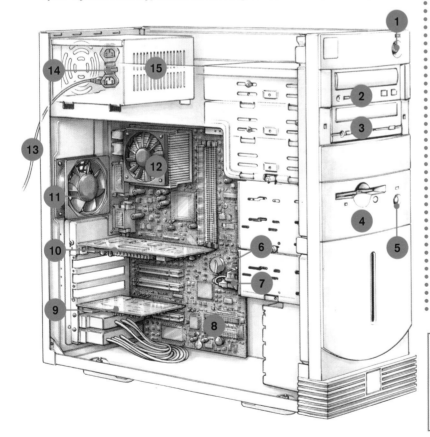

What is a PC?

The term PC has become the generic term for any computer that uses the Windows operating system. An 'Apple Mac', which is also a personal computer, employs a different operating system and is therefore rarely referred to as a PC. Because most home computers are PCs, the advice given here refers primarily to this type of computer. However, as identical problems are often experienced by Mac users, the relevant solutions for Macs are included where possible.

Screen prompts and labels may differ from those described here, depending on which version of Windows is running on your computer.

How a computer works

In simplistic terms a computer is nothing more than a collection of electronic components that, when used in conjunction with appropriate software programs, allows the storing and processing of information.

Programs, including the computer's operating system, are stored on the hard disk. When you run a program, it employs the central processing unit (CPU) to carry out a series of instructions. Many modern computer processors work at such a speed that the hard disk can't supply the required information quickly enough, so completed instructions are stored in the computer's memory (RAM) until the program is ready to use them. In effect, the RAM serves as a temporary holding area, which can store data and programs ready for the CPU to use, as well as the instructions supplied by the CPU. The hard disk is the long-term storage device – data remains on the hard disk even after you have switched off.

1 Power button	6 Backup battery	11 Main cooling fan
2 DVD drive	7 Hard disk	12 CPU cooling fan
3 CD drive	8 Motherboard	13 Power lead
4 Floppy-disk drive	9 Sound card	14 Rocker switch
5 Reset button	10 Graphics card	15 Power supply

REMOVING THE OUTER CASING

Removing the casing from a computer is usually straightforward. There may be visible screw fixings that release individual panels. Or pressing a pair of buttons will enable you to lift off the entire casing. For more specific instructions, consult your user's handbook. Never attempt to dismantle a combined computer/monitor.

Release screws to remove casing

Or depress buttons to release latch

Dispersing static electricity

Our bodies carry sufficient static electricity to damage delicate components inside a computer. You should therefore wear an anti-static wrist strap whenever you remove a computer's casing. Inexpensive disposable straps can be acquired from computer stockists.

Switch off your computer, but leave it plugged into the wall socket. Switch off the wall socket, too. Unplug all other cables from your computer.

Before touching anything inside the computer, wrap the strap around your wrist and then stick the other end of the strap to the computer's metal chassis. Now unplug your computer.

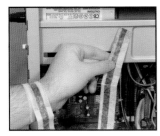

Attach anti-static wrist strap

Taking care of your computer

Despite their complexity, computers are fairly rugged pieces of equipment that rarely come to harm provided they are not abused. Overheating and dust are two of the main causes of physical breakdown.

Keeping the computer cool

Don't place your computer near any source of heat, and keep it out of direct sunlight. One or more electric fans draw air through the computer in order to cool internal components. In some computers, individual components such as the CPU are also fitted with their own cooling fans.

Don't allow books, piles of paper or curtains to cover the inlet and outlet grilles in the casing, and make sure there is enough room around your computer to allow the heat to dissipate.

Remember to remove overnight dust covers from your equipment before switching it on.

Cleaning the casing

To clean greasy fingerprints from the plastic casing, use special cleaning cloths impregnated with isopropyl alcohol. Sometimes known as alcohol wipes, these cleaning cloths are available from most computer stockists. You can also buy isopropyl alcohol separately, for spraying onto a lint-free cloth.

Switch off and unplug your computer before cleaning the casing. You shouldn't spray liquids directly onto the computer – it could contaminate internal circuitry.

Cleaning the grilles

Standing your computer on a desk or work station will keep the ingress of dust and fluff to a minimum, but you should clean the grilles regularly to promote good ventilation. The ideal tool is a miniature battery-powered vacuum cleaner fitted with a brush attachment, which comes as part of a proprietary PC cleaning kit. Having switched off the computer, use the same tool to remove dust from around the various ports in the back of the casing.

Cleaning dust from inside your computer

Once or twice a year, remove the dust that builds up on internal components. Having removed the casing (see left), use an aerosol containing compressed air to blow the dust towards one of the vents. Take care not to blow dust over any of your peripherals.

Clean casing with alcohol wipes

Clear grilles with a vacuum cleaner

Remove dust with compressed air

SHOULD A COMPUTER BE LEFT ON?

SHOULD A COMPUTER BE LEFT ON?
There is no simple answer. Some authorities are of the opinion that frequently turning your computer on and off puts unnecessary stress on some internal components. However, just as many people advocate shutting down every evening to conserve energy, and their computers exhibit few if any ill effects.

A good compromise is to leave your computer switched on overnight once a week for essential maintenance, such as defragmenting the hard disk and scanning for viruses. And you may want to let the computer download large files from the Internet at night, when call charges are lower. The rest of the time you can switch off your computer to save wear and tear on the fan bearings and hard drive.

If you do decide to leave your computer running for extended periods, make sure it is plugged into a reliable surge protector – see pages 16 and 21. In any event, it is not wise to leave a computer running if you intend to be away for more than a day or two.

Cleaning the CD lens
Special lens-cleaning disks are available for your computer. They are similar to the ones used for cleaning an audio-CD lens (see page 204).

Insert the disk into your CD drive and follow the instructions that appear on the screen. Before you buy a cleaning disk, check that it will work with your operating system.

Cleaning a floppy-drive head
The read/write heads in your floppy drive can be cleaned with a special diskette that contains an absorbent pad in place of the usual flexible disk. If you use your floppy drive frequently, it pays to clean the head once a month.

Slide back the metal dust cover on the diskette and apply several drops of cleaning fluid to both sides of the cleaning pad. Insert the diskette in the slot and operate the drive for about 30 seconds. Eject the diskette and allow the fluid to evaporate before you insert another floppy disk.

Clean your floppy-drive head monthly, using a special diskette

How a monitor works
With your home computer, you will probably be using either a CRT (cathode-ray tube) monitor – which looks similar to a portable TV set – or a slim LCD (liquid-crystal display) monitor, similar to the sort of screen that is built into laptops.

CRT monitors utilize an electron beam fired from the back of the tube towards the screen, where it strikes a layer of red, blue and green phosphorous dots, causing them to emit light. This is how the monitor creates a full-colour image on the screen, and it does it anything from 50 to 200 times per second, depending on your 'refresh rate'. On the screen, we perceive this rapidly changing series of images as sharp static or moving pictures.

LCD monitors are made with a liquid-crystal solution sandwiched between two polarized transparent layers. An electric current passing through the crystals varies the level of backlighting that is allowed to pass through the solution, creating the image on the screen. This process is repeated many times a second.

Adjusting monitor settings
Brightness and contrast are set at the factory for optimum conditions, but you can adjust these settings to suit yourself (see the user's handbook or instruction CD that came with the monitor).

Similarly, there will be a setting that allows you to maximize usable screen area. When you switch on a new monitor, there is often a sizeable black strip all round the visible area on the screen. By selecting 'Size' from your monitor's screen-settings menu, you will be able to increase the usable area and centre it accurately, using the buttons on the front of your monitor. See pages 243 and 244 for how to adjust resolution and refresh rate.

Taking care of your monitor

CRT monitors emit a lot of heat, so it is important to provide good all-round ventilation. Remember to switch off a monitor before putting a dust cover over it at night, and never pile up books against the vents at the back and sides.

Cleaning the screen

Static electricity attracts dust and cigarette smoke to the monitor screen. Greasy fingerprints make matters worse.

Switch off your monitor and unplug it, then wipe the glass clean with a proprietary alcohol-free 'wipe' or dust it lightly with a dry cloth. Apply the minimum of pressure when cleaning an LCD monitor.

Beware of magnets

The close proximity of magnets can affect the image on a CRT monitor screen (magnets have no effect on an LCD screen). Speakers designed for use with a computer are shielded to confine magnetic fields, but there's no guarantee that other speakers won't affect your monitor if placed too close. The base unit of a cordless phone may have a similar detrimental effect.

Relatively modern monitors are automatically degaussed (demagnetized) when the power is turned off. However, if your screen is exhibiting unusual dark, light or coloured patches, check your user's handbook or disk to see how to degauss your screen manually, using the on-screen menu. If in doubt, ask a service technician for advice on degaussing the monitor.

Mobile phones may cause interference on a CRT monitor – so when your phone is switched on, keep it a safe distance from the computer.

Don't switch on a mobile phone and leave it next to your computer

Avoiding screen burn

Modern computers are made with a power-saving facility that turns off the monitor after a set period. This not only conserves electricity but also prevents a fixed image from burning itself permanently onto the screen.

If you have an older computer, it pays to load a screen-saver program that plays an ever-changing image on the monitor to prevent screen burn.

How a keyboard works

There are two main types of keyboard – switch-based and capacitive. Both work in a similar fashion – by transmitting signals that correspond to individual keystrokes to the computer, which interprets the signals and modifies the image on the monitor accordingly. Pressing the keys of a switch-based keyboard operates individual switches, whereas a capacitive keyboard incorporates a single touch-sensitive membrane that lies beneath all the keys. Capacitive keyboards, which are relatively quiet and have a smoother keystroke action, are commonly referred to as soft-touch keyboards.

Taking care of your keyboard

Keyboards readily collect dust, pet hairs, crumbs and other debris, which is not only unhygienic but may eventually prevent the keyboard from functioning properly. It is worth buying a dust cover to protect your keyboard when not in use – and it's also worth cleaning your keyboard from time to time.

Cleaning the keyboard

Switch off your computer and disconnect the keyboard. Then remove loose debris from between the keypads, either using the miniature vacuum cleaner described on page 229 or by blowing it away with an aerosol of compressed air. Wipe grubby marks from the keypads, using alcohol-impregnated wipes (see page 229).

Clean marks from your keyboard, using alcohol wipes

Wiping up a spillage

Avoid accidents by not eating or drinking while using your computer. If you do spill water or a beverage over the keyboard, use the mouse to save your work, then shut down and disconnect the keyboard immediately. This type of mishap often ruins a keyboard, but cleaning it before the liquid dries might just save the day. The procedure described below is not suitable for a laptop computer – get expert advice if you spill liquid onto its built-in keyboard.

1 Mop up as much liquid as possible, using a soft cloth or paper towel to get between the keypads.

2 Gently ease off the keypads one or two at a time, using the flat tip of a screwdriver. Wipe beneath each keypad, using a moist cloth and small foam-tipped swabs to clean off sticky deposits.

3 When you replace one of the larger keys, make sure you clip it back onto the bent-wire retainer that holds it in place.

Let the keyboard dry thoroughly before you try using it again.

1 Mop up spilled liquid

2 Then ease off the keypads

3 Clip large keys onto wire retainers

you the option to compress the contents of your hard disk, but this may slow the computer down unacceptably. Alternatively, copy old files onto backup disks and delete the original files.

Hard disk too small for current needs

Another solution is to buy a second hard disk. You can either choose an external disk, which you plug into the computer, or get a technician to install an internal disk.

COMPUTER CRASHES

Every computer will 'freeze' or 'crash' from time to time, leaving you unable to access or control anything displayed on the screen.

Software malfunction

Crashing is often caused by a temporary software malfunction. If you are running the later versions of Windows, you have the facility to locate and switch off the offending software. Pressing 'Ctrl', 'Alt' and 'Del' opens 'Task Manager', which lists the programs that are running. The program that is causing the crash will be identified as 'Not Responding'. Selecting and turning off that program will return control – without having to restart the computer, possibly losing data in the process.

Alternatively, pressing 'Ctrl', 'Alt' and 'Del' may offer you the option to shut down – but at the expense of losing any work not saved before the crash. If you have an Apple Mac, look at your handbook to find out how to 'Force Quit'.

If you are still unable to restore control, check to see if your computer has a reset button, which will restart it. Alternatively, try pressing the power button (the one you use to start your computer) for five seconds.

As a last resort, switch off at the wall socket, wait a few seconds, and then restart the computer. This procedure carries a small risk of damaging the hard disk.

Loose connections

If the computer appears to have stopped working for no apparent reason, check to see if the cable connecting the mouse or keyboard to the computer is unplugged. Push the connection back in and restart the computer.

Hold down Ctrl, Alt, Del

Press the computer's reset button

Hold in the power button for a full five seconds

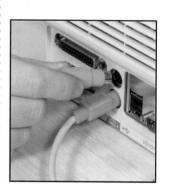
Check the mouse is connected

And also your keyboard

UPGRADE NOT SATISFACTORY

Upgrading existing software or installing new programs may not always result in the improvement you have been expecting. Either your computer doesn't run as well as it used to, or it crashes every time you try to run new software.

You will probably find that other users have been experiencing similar problems, and software manufacturers often offer a repair 'patch' that you can download from the Internet.

Uninstalling troublesome software

To uninstall (remove) troublesome software, go to 'My Computer', open 'Control Panel', and then select 'Add/Remove Programs'. Selecting the software you have recently installed and clicking 'Remove' will delete all trace of that program from the hard disk.

To reinstall software on an Apple Mac, insert the original installation CD and follow the on-screen instructions.

Incompatibility

Older programs won't always work when new hardware is installed; and the latest versions of a program may not run using your present system.

Before you buy new products, always check the minimum system requirement printed on the packaging. If your computer is not up to the job, loading the program or installing the device is bound to cause problems.

CAN'T ACCESS DISK

Protected floppy disk

To prevent information on a floppy disk being over-written or erased accidentally, a small tab in the corner can be slid sideways to protect the disk. To reuse a protected disk, slide the tab back again.

Dirty compact disk

Clean the CD (see page 203), and try reloading it. Also, try cleaning the CD lens – page 230.

Damaged or corrupted disk

If a disk is corrupted or damaged, there may be nothing you can do to access the information. However, you may be able to polish a scratched CD to restore the surface – see pages 203–4.

Select 'Add/Remove Programs'

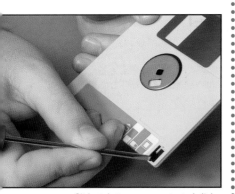

Slide tab to reuse protected disk

Restore the surface of a CD

DISC WON'T EJECT

If you can't eject a disk using an on-screen command, remove the disk by pressing the eject button beside the drive slot or tray.

If that doesn't work, look to see if there is a small hole beside the slot or tray. Turn off the computer and insert a straightened paperclip into the hole to release the latch and eject the disk.

Press button to eject disk

Or release latch with a paperclip

NOISY FAN

Internal cooling fans get very noisy when their bearings begin to wear. You can often prevent costly repairs by replacing a worn fan before it seizes up completely. Before you start, see Dispersing static electricity on page 229.

There may be several fans inside your computer. There will be one just behind the air-outlet grille, and possibly one behind the inlet grille too. There is also a fan inside the sealed power supply, where the power cord plugs into the computer. Don't attempt to dismantle the power supply to service this fan – leave it to a technician.

You can replace accessible fans similar to the ones shown here – but if in doubt, replace the casing and take your computer to be serviced.

1 To check which one is noisy, unplug each fan in turn, then replace the casing temporarily and turn on your computer for a second or two.

2 Remove the fixing screws that hold the noisy fan in place.

3 Take out the fan and make a note of the direction arrows moulded into the fan casing. Install your new fan with the arrows facing in the same direction.

FUZZY PICTURE

Before doing anything else, check the brightness and contrast settings – see page 230.

Resolution needs adjusting

With the later versions of Windows software you can increase picture sharpness on a PC monitor. Use your mouse to right-click on the computer desktop – which will open 'Display Properties' – and then select 'Settings'. Use the sliding scale to increase the resolution to your satisfaction – but not higher than the maximum recommended by the manufacturer (check your user's handbook or disk). Then click 'Apply'. You have 15 seconds to verify the new setting before the computer automatically reverts to the original resolution.

To adjust the resolution on an Apple Mac, open the 'Control Panels' folder and select 'Monitor'. Then select the 'Recommended' resolution/refresh rate.

1 Unplug each fan in turn

2 Unscrew the noisy fan

3 And replace it with a new fan

NO IMAGE ON MONITOR

Computer in power-save mode
The power-save facility turns off the monitor when it detects that there has been no activity for a period of time. Press any keypad to 'wake up' the monitor.

No power supply
If the power indicator is not illuminated, make sure the monitor is switched on and plugged in at both ends of the power lead. The power lead to some monitors plugs into the back of the computer base unit, not into a wall socket. Make sure this power lead is pushed in securely at both ends.

Monitor controls turned down
Check that the brightness, contrast and colour controls have not been set to zero – a common practical joke!

Your monitor controls may have been set to zero

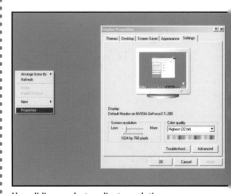

Use sliding scale to adjust resolution

SCREEN FLICKERS

Refresh rate needs adjusting

The refresh rate is a measurement of how many times per second a monitor redraws the image on the screen. A relatively low refresh rate tends to make the screen flicker, especially if there's fluorescent lighting in the room.

For a PC monitor, open 'Display Properties' and 'Settings' as described on page 243 – and then click 'Advanced'. Select 'Monitor' and try setting the refresh rate at 75Hz – then press 'Enter'. Adjusting the refresh rate may not be possible with earlier versions of Windows.

For an Apple Mac, see *Resolution needs adjusting*, page 243.

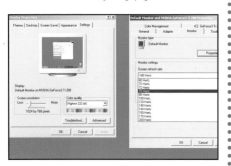

Mobile phone interference

Move your mobile phone away from the computer.

Is the printer plugged in?

MOUSE DOESN'T WORK

Mouse not connected

If your mouse is not functioning, check that it is plugged in securely. You may have to restart your computer before the operating system can recognize that the mouse has been reconnected.

Flat batteries

Try changing the batteries in a cordless mouse.

Mouse needs cleaning

If the cursor behaves erratically or the mouse is not moving smoothly, the internal rollers are probably coated with dirt or grease.

1 Rotate the retaining ring on the underside of the mouse to remove the ball.

2 Use a wooden or plastic cocktail stick to scrape the internal rollers clean. Then use compressed air from an aerosol to clean loose debris from inside the mouse.

3 Clean the ball with a paper towel moistened with water, then reassemble the mouse.

CAN'T LOCATE (OPEN) PRINTER

If your computer tells you it can't locate the printer, try the following.

Printer not switched on

Make sure the printer is plugged in and switched on.

Printer not connected

Check the connections between the computer and printer.

Computer switched to another port

On an Apple Mac computer, the output port into which your printer is plugged may not have been selected. Go to 'Chooser' (under the Apple menu), click on the relevant printer-driver icon, and select the required port from the list supplied. With some computers you will then have to click on 'Setup' before you try printing again.

If you have a switch box connected to a pair of peripherals, make sure you have selected printer.

Check mouse is connected

Change batteries in cordless mouse

1 Remove the ball's retaining ring

2 Scrape rollers clean

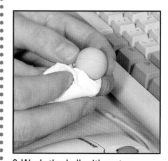
3 Wash the ball with water

WON'T PRINT

No power
Make sure the printer is plugged in and switched on.

Printer not connected
Check the connections between computer and printer. If you are using a USB hub, try plugging the printer cable into a different port. Make sure the hub is plugged in and receiving power.

Computer needs reconfiguring
Restart the computer. If that is unsuccessful, shut down and try switching on your computer and printer in a different order – computer first then printer or vice versa.

Corrupted print driver
For some reason the print driver loaded into the computer may have stopped working properly. Uninstall the driver (see page 242) and reload it from the disk supplied with your printer.

Print queue on hold
If someone switches off the printer, interrupting a print run before it has finished, the print queue may still be paused or on hold.

Usually, selecting the printer icon situated in one corner of the screen will display the print queue, which will give you the option to resume printing.

Broken chain
With some computer setups, two peripherals share the same port. For example, a scanner is plugged into the computer, and the printer is plugged into the scanner. Both peripherals must be turned on in order for the computer to locate the printer.

PAPER JAM
Your printer is equipped with a warning light to tell you when a sheet of paper jams in the mechanism. Open the printer cover (you will also have to remove the paper-delivery tray on some printers) in order to remove the jammed sheet, making sure you don't leave torn fragments behind. Avoid touching hot components when removing paper from a laser printer.

Sometimes, removing the sheet of paper does not cancel the warning light – in which case, switch the printer off and on again to reset the parameters.

Out of paper
The mechanism may have become jammed because the last few sheets of paper in the cassette or sheet feeder were drawn into the printer together. To prevent this happening, load up with paper before it runs out.

Paper loaded incorrectly
If you have experienced a paper jam, riffle the remaining sheets to separate them. Do the same when you reload with fresh paper.

Check that the paper-edge guides are adjusted correctly to prevent paper slewing as it is drawn into the printer.

Paper too thick
Most printers will accommodate relatively thick paper or thin card, but there is a limit.

1 When loading envelopes, make sure they are folded flat when stacked. If your printer is fitted with a thickness-adjustment lever, remember to set it to maximum for envelopes.

2 If necessary, feed envelopes one at a time and crease the leading edge of each one with your thumbnail.

Carefully remove jammed paper

Riffle paper before loading it

Adjust paper-edge guide

1 Set thickness-adjustment lever

2 Crease the leading edge

SAFETY FIRST

Use a surge-protection device to prevent high-voltage 'spikes' damaging internal components. Look for a device that will accommodate your modem connection.

Keep cups and glasses of liquid well away from the keyboard and mouse.

Never use a sharp object to tap on or point at a monitor screen.

Keep printer-ink cartridges out of the reach of children

Wash printer-ink stains off the skin immediately. If you get laser-printer toner on your skin or clothing, wash it immediately in cold water – hot water will fuse the toner.

Condensation
Paper tends to jam more frequently when it is damp. Replace the stack of paper in your printer and try printing again. Store your paper in its original packaging, preferably in a cupboard or drawer.

Dirty paper-feed rollers
Most printers will indicate a paper jam when the feed rollers have simply failed to pick up a sheet of paper. Turning the printer on and off will cancel the warning, and printing will usually resume.

However, if this happens frequently, the feed rollers probably need cleaning. Top-loading printers usually have inaccessible rollers – in which case, have the printer serviced.

You can often clean the rollers in a front-loading printer after removing the paper-delivery tray. However, if your printer looks substantially different from the one shown here, have the rollers cleaned by a technician.

While pressing the paper-feed button, apply light pressure to the underside of each roller, using a chamois-leather-tipped swab, sold for cleaning video heads. Moisten the swab with warm soapy water and hold the swab firmly, so it doesn't get drawn into the machine. Don't apply pressure to the bed of the paper-lift mechanism directly below the rollers. Keep your fingers away from the rollers and other moving parts.

POOR COLOUR PRINTOUT

Paper wrong side up
Some special printing papers are one-sided and must be fed into the printer with the coated surface uppermost.

Print head needs cleaning
If colours look unnatural or there are fine pale lines across the printout, one or more of your print-head nozzles may be clogged.

Depending on the printer, you may be able to print out a test sheet to see if all the colours are printing at full strength – see your user's handbook. If they are not, the same handbook will tell you how to program the printer to clean the nozzles automatically.

Clean paper-feed rollers with a moist chamois-leather swab

1 Clean cartridge nozzles

2 Wipe service-station cups, using a moist swab

1 With other printers, the nozzles are part of the ink cartridge – in which case, clean each nozzle with an alcohol-impregnated wipe (see page 229). Check your user's handbook for details.

If the nozzles clog up again soon after you fit the cartridges, the service station that is designed to clean and seal the nozzles is probably smeared with ink. Turn the printer on and open the printer's cover, letting the ink-cartridge cradle move away from the service station. Then unplug the printer.

2 Wipe the rim of both service-station cups, using a foam-tipped swab moistened with warm soapy water.

Leave the cups to dry out, then plug in the printer and close the cover. The ink cartridges will then move back onto the service station.

Ink cartridge needs changing
Your printer is equipped with warning lights to tell you when to change empty ink cartridges. However, if you have not used your printer for some time, one or both of the cartridges may be clogged with solidified ink. Your printer sensors won't detect this. Replace a cartridge that has become clogged.

To prevent a similar occurrence, make a test print run from time to time in order to keep the inks flowing. Be aware that printing with black ink only could prove a false economy if you allow your colour cartridge to dry up.

Seal still on ink cartridge
Ink cannot flow if you forget to peel the protective strip from either of the ink cartridges.

Wrong media-type setting
It is vital to match ink output to the type of paper you are using. Having opened the 'Print' window, select 'Media Type' and choose the category closest to the type of paper you are using. It may be necessary to experiment a little in order to get optimum results. Also, see Wrong print settings, page 248.

SAFETY FIRST

When any appliance is earthed, you should use a continuity tester to verify that there is a continuous earth path – see page 22.

Before putting a repaired computer or peripheral back into service, plug it into a circuit protected by an RCD – see page 11. Switch on, and if the RCD trips, have the appliance tested by a qualified service engineer.

Replace clogged ink cartridges

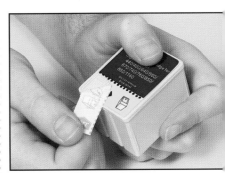

Remember to remove the protective strip seal

Wrong print settings

The printer's automatic settings are designed to make printing simple, but they may not always give the best results. Selecting 'Custom' or 'Advanced' settings gives you the option to adjust colour balance, output speed, resolution – dots per inch (dpi) – and various photo corrections. It is worth spending some time experimenting with the various settings to see what can be achieved.

PRINTS SLOWLY

Check your print settings

Is the printer set for fast output or quality? Quality printing takes longer.

Also, check 'Custom Settings'. The higher the resolution – more dots per inch (dpi) – the slower the rate of printing.

To prevent smearing, some printers can be adjusted to allow more time for the ink to dry. Changing this setting affects output speed.

CAN'T LOCATE SCANNER

If your computer tells you it can't locate the scanner, switch off both scanner and computer and try restarting in a different order – usually starting with the scanner.

Poor connections

Check that the scanner is plugged in and switched on. Make sure all the cables are connected securely.

Wrong port

If you are using a USB hub, try swapping the scanner lead to another port.

If you have an external switch box connected to a pair of peripherals, make sure you have the scanner selected.

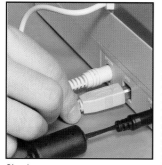

Check scanner connections

Plug the scanner into a different port on a USB hub

WHEN ALL ELSE FAILS

If after all your efforts the computer is still not working satisfactorily, there are a number of excellent technical-support agencies that provide expert advice over the phone. It helps if you can give them a clear description of the symptoms your computer is exhibiting. And don't forget to mention the solutions you have tried already. Telephone numbers for technical support are included in your user's handbooks, and you can usually find contact numbers on manufacturers' websites.

When all else fails, get a professional technician to service your computer. Be aware that, even though your computer is still under warranty, you may be liable to pay the cost of calling out a technician if the problem turns out to be software-related.

If your computer has to be taken away for repair, it is well worth making a backup of everything on your hard disk.

ALARM
SYSTEMS

Home security has become big business. So much so that today's householders are able to buy the type of sophisticated equipment that was once only available to protect commercial premises. The majority of systems, whether they are professionally installed or come as a DIY kit, are extremely reliable and require little if any maintenance on the part of the owners. Nevertheless, problems are bound to occur from time to time with any complex system that relies on each component working faultlessly 100 per cent of the time.

There's no suggestion that the information provided in this chapter will save you from ever having to call out your installer, and on occasion you may need to seek specialist advice from the supplier. Indeed, some insurance companies insist that an alarm system has to be monitored and maintained professionally, and you should check your policy to make sure that adapting or maintaining the system yourself won't invalidate your insurance. However, a lot of false alarms and apparent malfunctions are the result of something trivial that you can put right without expert help. If it proves otherwise, you can at least point a technician in the right direction by being able to rule out some of the more likely possibilities.

INTRUDER ALARMS

It's inconvenient when domestic appliances fail to work properly – but when an alarm system malfunctions, the consequences could be much more serious. It is therefore vital to identify and rectify potential problems before you have to rely on the system working efficiently.

If your alarm goes off, always take the situation seriously – and never assume it's a false alarm until you are able to rule out a genuine emergency. However, you must prevent frequent false alarms or your neighbours, and eventually the police too, will fail to respond. If you cannot identify the cause of a false alarm yourself, obtain expert advice without delay.

1 Exterior siren
2 Smoke detector
3 Glassbreak detector
4 PIR detector
5 Magnetic-contact detector
6 Control unit
7 Remote controllers with panic buttons

How it works

Alarm systems differ greatly, but there are two basic kinds: hard-wired systems, where all the various detectors and sensors are connected to a central control unit by fine cable, and wireless alarm systems that utilize radio signals to perform a similar function. Both types include passive systems that detect the presence of an intruder inside the house, and perimeter systems that guard likely means of entry. The best systems incorporate a combination of features in case perimeter detectors are by-passed.

Control unit

The heart of the system is the control unit, which triggers a siren when it receives an alarm signal from a detector. The control unit has to be programmed to allow sufficient time for legitimate entry and exit. If it has a zone-monitoring option, you can activate door contacts or sensors in part of the house – to permit freedom of movement upstairs at night, for example, while entry doors and downstairs areas are fully guarded.

The control unit must be tamper-proof, so that it will trigger the alarm if disarming is attempted by any means other than a key or the correct digital code. It is usually connected to mains power, but it should also have a rechargeable battery in case of power failure.

Scanning devices

Infrared sensors can be strategically positioned to scan a wide area and will detect the presence of an intruder by measuring body heat. If necessary, you can opt for sensors able to distinguish between household pets and human beings. Passive infrared (PIR) detectors are usually connected to the central control unit, but you can buy independent battery-operated sensors for protecting a single room.

There are also sensors that utilize microwaves to detect movement, but this type of sensor is rarely found in domestic situations.

Magnetic-contact detectors

Entrances can be fitted with small devices that trigger the alarm when a magnetic contact is broken by someone opening a door or window.

Glassbreak detectors

Another type of detector senses vibrations caused by breaking glass. A good detector must be capable of distinguishing between a forced entry and vibration from other sources.

Maintaining the system

Intruder alarm systems are virtually maintenance free, but they should be tested regularly to make sure every device is functioning properly. Your user's manual will tell you how to conduct a 'walk test' that allows you to check the entire system without disturbing your neighbours or raising a false alarm.

Keeping the siren clean

Cut back climbing plants to make sure they don't grow over the exterior siren. If your siren is solar-powered, be sure to wipe the solar panel with a damp cloth at least once a year.

Smoke detectors

Nearly all alarm systems can incorporate smoke detectors, which trigger the alarm in case of fire.

Exterior siren

Most alarms have a siren mounted on an outside wall. These switch off automatically after a set period, but some alarms are designed to continue signalling with a flashing light and some will automatically rearm themselves. It is important that the alarm will be triggered by any attempt to tamper with the siren by dismantling or by cutting wires.

The majority of sirens take their power from the control unit, but some are solar-powered. Ideally, a solar-powered siren should be mounted on a south-facing wall and not too close to overhanging eaves.

Many systems transmit a warning directly to a monitoring centre for a swift and reliable response to a break-in.

Personal-attack devices

With most systems you can have a 'panic button' installed beside entry doors or elsewhere in the house to press in the event of an attack.

There are also portable wireless devices that can be carried on the person to summon help in the case of an emergency around your home or even in the garden. Pressing a personal-attack button triggers the alarm even when the system is disarmed.

SAFETY FIRST

An alarm system should not be your first line of defence. At best, alarm systems are deterrents, and you need to fit reliable locks and catches to all accessible doors and windows.

Lock your workshop, garden shed and garage. They are potential sources for housebreaking tools.

If you can't put a ladder away in a garage or somewhere in the house, use a strong padlock and chain to prevent the ladder being used to gain entry.

FALSE ALARM

Your alarm system could have been triggered for a number of reasons. Once you have ascertained there hasn't been a genuine break-in, investigate the following.

Door or window left ajar

Check that all entry points have been secured before arming the alarm system.

Low battery in detector

A very low battery in just one wireless detector can trigger the alarm. When a detector's low-battery indicator lights up, change the batteries in other wireless detectors too, to avoid false alarms as a result of failing batteries.

Loose battery connections

If you have recently replaced the batteries, the contacts could be loose. Some batteries have very slightly tapering terminals, which means the snap-fastening contacts inside the detector may not make a snug fit. Examine replacement batteries carefully to ensure the terminals are perfectly cylindrical.

Make sure the contacts themselves have not become misshapen, and check for broken wires.

Check for misshapen contacts

PIR detector near heat source

A passive infrared detector must not be mounted directly above a source of heat, such as a radiator, boiler or room heater.

Similarly, most PIR detectors will malfunction if mounted in direct sunlight – they are not usually suitable for installing in conservatories.

Tamper switch activated

Check that all the access covers on your detectors have been replaced securely. If you find that one of the moulded-plastic catches is broken, temporarily tape the cover closed and order a replacement.

An anti-tamper device is usually fitted on the back of the control panel and the exterior siren box to detect any attempt to lever them off the wall. Make sure that both devices are fixed securely and not held away from the wall by a lump of mortar or uneven plaster.

Temporarily tape a broken cover

Pet-initiated alarm

If your pets are to wander freely around the home when the alarm system is armed, you need detectors that are designed to ignore animals. Some devices scan at an angle that detects movement only above a certain height. Other detectors can differentiate between the body weight of a small animal and a human being. Replacing standard PIR detectors with pet-immune detectors is perfectly straightforward.

Giving an animal the run of the house is not quite so simple if you have magnetic-contact detectors on internal doors – you will have to either restrict your pet's movements or disconnect problematic detectors and install pet-immune PIR sensors instead.

Poor magnetic contact

Examine all the magnetic-contact detectors on your doors and windows. The gap between magnet and detector must be within limits, usually no more than about 5mm ($\frac{3}{16}$in) – but check your installer's handbook. If necessary, make adjustments to reduce the gap or resite the device to ensure you can achieve good magnetic contact.

Broken wire

To prevent an intruder disarming a hard-wired system, the alarm will be triggered if any of the cables serving the system are severed. Examine your wiring to make sure that a cable has not been broken or cut (rodents sometimes gnaw through cables).

Control unit unplugged

The siren will be activated if your control unit is not plugged into a mains socket. Also check that the socket is switched on.

Power failure

Inspect your consumer unit for a blown fuse or tripped MCB or RCD – see pages 11 and 12.

Personal-attack button pressed

The alarm will be activated if a personal-attack button is pressed, even when the alarm system is not armed. An elderly person may have pressed a portable device by accident; or someone may have touched a panic button mounted beside the front door while on the way out.

Such incidents merely indicate that your system is working efficiently and – apart from making sure members of your household and people staying with you understand how the equipment operates – there is nothing you need do.

WON'T ACCEPT CODE

If you think you may have entered the wrong access code into the control unit or keypad, wait a few seconds and try again. Check with other members of your family that the code has not been changed.

Adjust a magnetic-contact detector

SAFETY FIRST

Give the impression someone is at home by having an automatic timer switch a light on and off at intervals. It is also a good idea to leave a radio on when you are out.

When you go on holiday, cancel paper and milk deliveries, and ask a trusted friend to collect mail if it can be seen from outside.

Install a door viewer to help you identify callers before opening the front door.

Wait a few seconds and try again

Hesitation
Your control unit or keypad may not accept your user code if you hesitate while entering it. Try again, making sure there are no lengthy pauses between pressing keys.

Device has defaulted
The control unit may have reverted to the factory setting. Try reprogramming the device; and if that is unsuccessful, call out a technician.

DETECTOR NOT REACTING
It is important to test your system when it has been installed and at regular intervals afterwards. If one of your detectors appears not to be activating the alarm, check the following.

Detector upside down
Depending on the design, a PIR detector mounted upside down may be scanning the ceiling instead of the floor area. Look at the illustrations in your installer's manual.

Detector too high
A PIR detector may not be entirely effective if it is too far away from the floor. Check what height is recommended in your installer's manual.

Wrong code
With a wireless system, the same code must be programmed into the control unit and all the detectors before they can communicate with each other. Check the code in each device.

Wireless signal deflected
Radio signals can be deflected by a large metal object, such as a radiator or freezer, situated between a detector and the control unit. Check that there are no large metallic objects within 1 metre (3 to 4ft) of either device.

Too far away
A wireless detector must be within range of the control unit for it to receive radio signals. To monitor a garage or workshop that falls outside the limit, double the range by fitting a repeater unit between the two devices.

Check the code settings in all your detectors

Wireless repeater unit

REMOTE CONTROLLER STOPS WORKING

Many systems can be armed and disarmed using a small hand-held remote-control device. There is usually a small indicator, which flashes when the device is sending signals. If you can't activate your alarm system and there's no flashing to suggest the remote controller is working, try the following.

Battery wrong way round
Make sure the battery inside the control is fitted the right way round, so that the polarity is correct.

Flat battery
Fit a fresh battery in the remote controller.

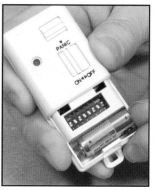

Is the battery fitted correctly?

SMOKE DETECTORS

A smoke detector identifies the presence of smoke and fumes – possibly before flames break out – and sounds a shrill warning. Although detectors can be incorporated into an intruder-alarm system, self-contained battery-operated units are probably more common.

In the event of an alarm, even when there is no obvious sign of smoke or heat, always get your family to a place of safety before investigating further.

How it works

There are two basic types of smoke detector. Photoelectric (optical) devices detect smoke from slow-burning fires, such as smouldering foam-filled upholstery. Ionization detectors are more attuned to hot, blazing fires – such as a burning chip pan – and will react before the smoke gets too thick. There are also detectors that combine both systems to give good all-round performance. For maximum security, you could fit both types.

Photoelectric detectors

A photoelectric detector incorporates a light source and a sensor. Under normal circumstances the light is not aimed directly at the sensor; but when smoke enters the chamber, the smoke particles scatter the light, some of which falls on the sensor.

Ionization detectors

This type of detector has a chamber containing a tiny amount of radioactive material, which ionizes the oxygen and nitrogen atoms in the air, creating a weak electric current. Smoke penetrating the chamber disrupts the flow of current, which activates the siren.

CLEANING A SMOKE DETECTOR
A smoke detector's efficiency is seriously impaired if fluff or cobwebs are allowed to clog the grilles. Clear the slots in the casing, using a soft paintbrush.

Wipe the casing with a damp cloth, and dry it thoroughly. Having replaced it on the wall or ceiling, test the detector is working (see left).

Testing your smoke detector

Testing a smoke detector regularly (perhaps once a week), to check that it is working properly, is a vital safety precaution. Detectors are fitted with a conspicuous test button that, when pressed, simulates the effect of smoke penetrating the unit. There's never any need to generate real smoke. Hold down the button for a few seconds and the detector should emit a shrill alarm, which stops when you release the button.

If no alarm is sounded, check that internal contacts are firmly attached to the battery terminals. Then, if necessary, change the battery and test the smoke detector again.

You should change the battery once a year regardless of how the detector reacts to testing. If your detector is fitted with a battery-powered bulb to indicate an escape route in the event of fire, change both batteries at the same time.

Testing linked detectors

Some homes have a series of smoke detectors linked by bell wire, so they are all triggered as soon as any one of them senses smoke in the air. Pressing the test button on any one detector should activate all the others at the same time.

SAFETY FIRST

Never paint over a smoke detector.

It pays to have spare batteries on hand.

Don't use a rechargeable battery in a smoke detector.

Ask your local authority about how to dispose of unwanted ionization detectors.

Smoke detectors are no substitute for adequate fire insurance.

Familiarize yourself with fire-safety advice, and plan a sensible escape route for the whole family to use in the event of fire.

Don't rely on smoke detectors alone to protect your home from fire. Mount a fire blanket near your cooker and install an all-purpose fire extinguisher in a prominent position, preferably on an escape route.

The alarm will probably sound when you connect a new battery

FALSE ALARMS

If an alarm has been triggered by a harmless event, such as toasting bread, fan the detector vigorously with a newspaper or magazine until the alarm is silenced. Never remove the battery to silence an alarm, in case you forget to replace it.

Some detectors are fitted with a 'silencer' or 'hush' button to temporarily reduce the detector's sensitivity. Most detectors will automatically revert to normal sensitivity after a few minutes, but you can reset the device manually by pressing the test button.

If you are subjected to frequent false alarms, consider relocating the detector. The best place for a smoke detector is on the ceiling, at least 300mm (1ft) away from any wall or light fitting. If it has to be wall-mounted, make sure it is 150 to 300mm (6in to 1ft) below the ceiling. Don't install a detector in a kitchen or bathroom, as steam can trigger the alarm; and don't fix one directly above a heater or an air-conditioning vent.

If you live in a bungalow, fit a smoke detector in the hallway between the bedrooms and living areas. For a two-storey home, fit at least one detector in the hallway, directly above the bottom of the stairs; and if possible, fit a second one on the landing.

DETECTOR CHIRPS REGULARLY

Low battery
Smoke detectors are designed to emit audible warnings at one-minute intervals to persuade you to change the battery. This is quite normal, but should not be ignored. Be prepared for the alarm to sound as you attach the contacts to the new battery.

Silencer mode engaged
After installation, a detector may chirp at frequent intervals (about 40 seconds or so) to indicate it is in silencer or hush mode – see above. To reset the device, hold down the test button until the alarm sounds.

Fan the detector with a magazine

Or press the hush button

NO EMERGENCY LIGHT

Bulb has blown
Detectors fitted with an emergency light are normally supplied with a bulb that should last the life of the unit. However, if the bulb does not illuminate when you press the test button, fit an exact replacement. As it's not always easy to find the right replacement bulb, it's advisable to buy a spare bulb before you need it.

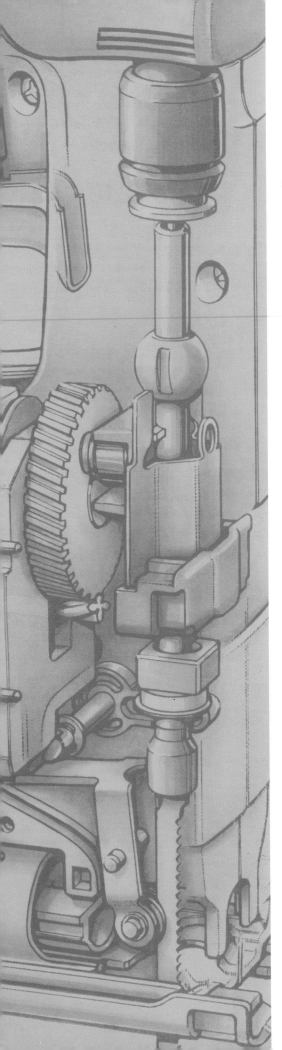

POWER
TOOLS

In the modern home workshop you're likely to find almost as many power tools as hand tools. Nowadays most of these efficient, labour-saving devices can be purchased for quite modest sums – and as well as being faster than their old-fashioned hand-operated counterparts, they usually get jobs done more accurately, too.

The trouble is that now we no longer have to spend a fortune on power tools we invariably take them for granted. We leave lawn mowers and strimmers neglected in the garden shed, and push workshop tools to their limit without taking time to carry out even the most cursory maintenance.

In a book of this length, it isn't possible to include every type of power tool. In any case, being equipped with similar electric motors, gears, cooling systems and trigger switches, many power tools have a great deal in common and so tend to suffer from similar problems.

Like all electric appliances, power tools vary in detail from model to model, but the tools illustrated on these pages are typical examples that will help you service and maintain comparable equipment.

POWER DRILLS

Being indispensable for DIY and woodwork, the electric drill is the most widely sold and used power tool on the market. Manufacturers try to satisfy the huge demand for power drills by producing all sorts of models, ranging from cheap short-life drills to powerful professional models with a variety of sophisticated features.

As they are usually well-made rugged tools, very little goes wrong with electric drills provided they are not abused.

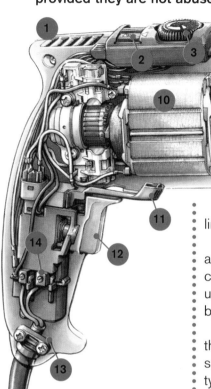

How it works

The heart of a power drill is the electric motor, which delivers rotational force to the drill bit held in the chuck at the business end of the tool. Because the maximum motor speed would be too fast for normal drilling, there is a gearbox, which reduces rotational speed, thereby increasing the torque (twisting force) of the drill.

Most power drills have an adjustable torque control that sets an upper limit to the twisting force in order to prevent screws being overdriven.

The shaft from the gearbox is attached to the chuck – a device designed to accommodate drill bits and other attachments. Most chucks have three self-centring jaws that grip the shank of the bit. With some models, a toothed key is used to open and close the jaws. Other drills have a 'keyless' chuck, operated by turning a cylindrical collar that surrounds the mechanism.

What is termed the 'trigger' on power drills is in fact a switch that controls the flow of electricity to the motor. On very basic drills this is simply an on/off switch, but nearly all modern drills have variable-speed trigger control. With this type of control, the speed varies from zero to maximum according to the amount of pressure applied to the trigger.

On some drills, selecting an optimum speed on a dial limits the movement of the trigger. This is a useful feature for inserting woodscrews, which is best done at a slow, controlled speed.

1 Air vents
2 Screw-function selector switch
3 Speed selector/ torque limiter
4 Hammer-action switch
5 Keyless chuck
6 Self-centring jaws
7 Setscrew
8 Gears
9 Cooling fan
10 Electric motor
11 Reverse-action lever
12 Trigger
13 Cord clamp
14 Flex terminals

Electronic speed selection

Many power drills are controlled electronically. The best electronic speed-control systems maintain the selected speed even when load is applied to the drill bit and have internal torque compensators to prevent the motor being damaged if the bit jams in the work.

Reverse action

Most power drills have a lever conveniently located near the trigger for changing the direction of rotation in order to remove screws.

Hammer action

Operated by a mechanical switch, the hammer action delivers several hundred blows per second behind the drill bit to break up brick or concrete as the drill bores into masonry. It is essential to use special percussion drill bits, and to make sure they are held firmly in the chuck.

Trigger lock

A small button on the handle of the drill is pushed in to lock the trigger for continuous running. Squeezing the trigger releases the lock.

Cordless drills

Within their limits, cordless drills are excellent tools that conveniently do away with the need for long extension leads in order to reach a work site at a distance from the mains.

Some drills are supplied with a wall-hung storage rack, incorporating a charging unit – so long as the tool is replaced every evening, it will always be charged up. However, most cordless drills have removable battery packs that plug into a charger. With this method, you may want to keep a spare pack charged and ready for use.

It usually takes about an hour to fully recharge a drill's battery pack unless you buy a special rapid charger, which will complete the job in 15 minutes or less. Battery packs for power tools can be recharged several thousand times before they need replacing.

Getting the best from your drill

Drill manufacturers recommend a range of speeds at which their tools will perform best – but as a general guide, select a fast speed for boring holes in wood and a slower speed for drilling into masonry or metal and for driving woodscrews.

Operating the chuck

When fitting drill bits into a key-operated chuck, rotate the chuck by hand until it clamps on the shaft, then use the key to tighten the jaws at all three positions around the chuck.

Tightening a keyless chuck by hand clamps a drill bit securely.

Use sharp drill bits

Don't use worn, damaged or blunt drill bits. Not only will the drill perform unsatisfactorily but excess pressure has to be applied to a blunt bit, which inevitably results in the motor and gears overheating. Electric drill-bit sharpeners are especially easy to use: clamping the bit in the device presents the tip at exactly the right angle to a powered grindstone.

Holding the drill securely

It is important to hold a power drill securely. The body of the drill will try to rotate if a bit or attachment jams, which could damage the workpiece or cause injury. Most drills have a clamp-on secondary handle to help maintain control over the drill.

When drilling, don't cover the air vents in the plastic casing with your hands.

CLEANING A POWER DRILL
Brush dust from the air vents when you have finished working, and wipe the casing clean.

If you are not going to use your drill for a while, smear a light coating of oil on any exposed metal surfaces to prevent rusting.

DISMANTLING THE CASING
The casing of a power drill usually splits into two halves. Unplug the drill and lay it flat on a bench. Remove the recessed screws and lay them aside, then carefully separate the two halves of the casing, so that you can make a mental note of how the various internal components relate to one another and how they fit into the casing. If necessary, draw a diagram. As with all double-insulated appliances (see page 18), it is important to replace all components and wiring in their original positions.

SAFETY FIRST

Never change drill bits or attachments without first unplugging the drill.

Having inserted a drill bit or attachment, check that you have removed the chuck key before you plug in the drill.

Before you use an electric power drill, inspect the casing, chuck, flex and plug for any signs of damage.

Don't wear loose clothing or jewellery that could get caught in the moving parts of the drill. Tie back long hair.

Wear protective eye shields whenever you are doing work that could throw up debris.

DRILL BIT SLIPS

Chuck not tightened correctly
Use a key to tighten the chuck at all three positions – see page 259.

Worn chuck
When the jaws wear, it becomes impossible to clamp drill bits or attachments securely. Replacing both keyless and key-operated chucks is relatively straightforward. On most makes of drill you can fit whichever type of chuck you wish, provided they have the same capacity (maximum jaw size).

The following techniques are for removing the chuck from typical relatively modern drills. There may be a locking button that stops the shaft turning, or you may need to use a spanner – check your user's handbook.

Before you start, always unplug the drill or remove the battery pack, and put on a pair of safety goggles.

1 Open up the jaws as far as possible and look inside the chuck. With most drills (those with reverse action), you will see a screw head. This is a setscrew that prevents the chuck unscrewing under power and therefore has a left-hand thread – so you need to turn the screw clockwise to remove it.

2 With the screw removed, insert and securely clamp a large Allen key in the chuck.

3 Using a block of wood or a soft-face hammer, sharply tap the protruding arm of the Allen key to turn the chuck anticlockwise until it begins to unscrew.

4 Remove the damaged chuck and replace it with a new one.

Sometimes a special thread-locking compound is used to secure the setscrew. Check the threads for signs of a white deposit. If necessary, clean the threads with a wire brush and apply a drop of compound before you insert the screw. Thread-locking compound is available from car-spares outlets and hardware stores.

1 Turn the setscrew clockwise

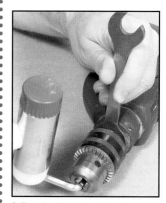
2 Clamp an Allen key in the chuck

3 Tap the Allen key sharply

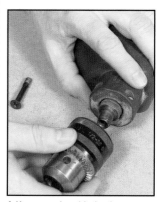
4 Unscrew the old chuck

SAFETY FIRST

Never carry a power drill by its flex, or use the flex to pull the plug out of a socket.

To prevent children getting hold of them, lock your power tools away when you have finished work.

Don't use a mains-powered electric drill in the rain or in very damp conditions.

Keep handles and grips dry and grease-free.

Before putting a power drill back into service, plug it into a circuit protected by an RCD – see page 11. Switch on, and if the RCD trips, have the drill tested at a service centre.

Check for worn chuck bearings

SPARKING INSIDE THE CASING

Poor electrical contact can cause sparks inside the drill casing. There is no cause for alarm – but if sparking seems excessive, either have the motor serviced or replace the brushes yourself and clean the commutator (see pages 289–90).

EXCESSIVE NOISE

Dirty motor or internal fan

You expect power tools to be noisy – but if you hear unusual or excessive noise when using your power drill, dismantle the casing and use a vacuum-cleaner attachment and a brush to remove the accumulation of dust, especially any debris adhering to the electric motor and cooling fan.

Dry or worn gearbox

Carefully dismantle the casing – see page 259.

1 Keeping the drill laid flat on the bench, rotate the chuck so that you can inspect the gears for signs of wear or damage. If you detect broken teeth, ask a service centre whether it is worth replacing the gears.

2 The original lubrication may be adhering to the outer casing, leaving dry gear surfaces. Redistribute the lubrication, using the tip of a screwdriver.

If the gears are completely dry, you may need to apply a high-grade bearing grease, available from car-parts suppliers. Apply it sparingly to the gear drive teeth, then reassemble the casing and run the drill.

Worn chuck bearings

If lubrication does not cure the problem, hold the drill firmly in one hand and waggle the chuck back and forth. If there is excessive movement, ask a service centre whether there is any possibility of replacing the bearings and how much it will cost.

Worn motor bearings

The noise may be due to worn motor bearings. Motors for inexpensive drills are unlikely to be available as spare parts, but it's worth asking at a service centre before buying a new drill.

Remove dust from the cooling fan

1 Inspect the gears for damage

2 Redistribute the original grease

DRILL WON'T WORK AT ALL

For mains-powered drills, check the plug and fuses for faults.

Power failure

If other appliances on the circuit have stopped working, inspect your consumer unit for a blown fuse or tripped MCB or RCD – see pages 11 and 12.

Drill not plugged in

Make sure the plug is inserted in the socket, and that the socket is switched on.

Plug fuse has blown

Replace the fuse in the plug – see page 17. If the fuse blows again as soon as you plug in, have the tool checked at a service centre.

Faulty wiring in plug

If possible, take the back off the plug and check that the plug is wired correctly – see pages 18 and 19.

Faulty trigger switch

Variable-speed switches have complicated wiring and may be connected to circuit boards. Have these switches and those with soldered connections tested and, if need be, replaced at a service centre.

Loose connections

Internal connections can work loose. Check all internal wiring for snugly fitting connectors. Have broken soldered connections repaired at a service centre.

Faulty motor

Worn or sticking brushes may prevent the motor working. See pages 289–90, or have the motor checked at a service centre.

Low or flat battery

When a cordless drill fails to start, try recharging the battery pack.

Don't let a battery drain completely, as in some cases this could lead to permanent damage. It pays to recharge the battery as soon as the drill starts to slow down significantly.

Broken flex conductor

With most drills, the incoming flex will be connected to accessible screw terminals (or simple push-in terminals – see page 270), in which case you will be able to test the flex for continuity and, if need be, replace it (see page 20). Double-insulated drills are wired with two-core flex – see page 18.

If it is not obvious how the flex is connected to the terminals, have a suspect flex replaced at a service centre.

Remove broken flex and replace it

Have a trigger switch replaced at a service centre

Try recharging the battery before looking for other faults

JIGSAWS

Although some manufacturers claim too much for them, jigsaws are undoubtedly versatile tools. They will cut any man-made board and saw through solid timber reasonably well, but the jigsaw's great virtue is its ability to make curved cuts. When fitted with the appropriate blade, it will also cut sheet metal and plastics.

Cordless saws have obvious advantages – avoiding the problem of flex snagging on obstructions or being sawn through by accident.

How it works

Good-quality saws incorporate constant-speed electronics and precisely balanced motors that produce minimum vibration. So long as the blade is sharp, this type of saw is easy to control and relatively quiet.

A basic jigsaw moves the blade straight up and down. Saws with orbital or pendulum action cut faster by advancing the blade into the work on the upstroke and by moving the blade backwards on the down stroke to clear the saw cut. Vertical movement is achieved by a bearing attached off centre to a large cog driven by the motor. At the same time, a separate vertically moving peg rocks the blade-support roller, which drives the blade back and forth.

On most jigsaws the motor-cooling fan blows air along a duct to clear the sawdust from the cutting line. Some saws have a dust-extracting facility: a flexible hose plugs into the back of the saw and sucks dust from the cutting area into a domestic vacuum cleaner.

Single-speed saws operate at high speed the whole time, but most jigsaws have a dial for selecting the optimum stroke rate for the material being cut. On a true variable-speed jigsaw the stroke rate is controlled by the amount of pressure applied to the operating switch or trigger.

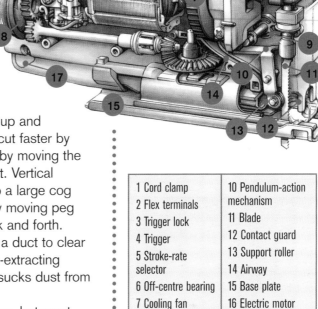

1 Cord clamp	10 Pendulum-action mechanism
2 Flex terminals	
3 Trigger lock	11 Blade
4 Trigger	12 Contact guard
5 Stroke-rate selector	13 Support roller
	14 Airway
6 Off-centre bearing	15 Base plate
7 Cooling fan	16 Electric motor
8 Gears	17 Dust exhaust port
9 Pendulum-action selector	18 Base-plate adjuster

Getting the best from your saw

Jigsaw blades should be replaced as soon as they become blunt or get broken. Blunt blades cut poorly and put excessive strain on both the motor and gearbox.

● There are specially designed blades for cutting various materials; and woodworking blades are available with specific tooth configurations for a finer, faster or cleaner cut. Be sure to fit the right blade for the job in hand.

● Check the saw manufacturer's recommendations for optimum speeds and pendulum action to suit the material you are cutting.

● From time to time, lubricate the blade-support roller with a drop of light machine oil.

CLEANING YOUR JIGSAW

Brush sawdust from the air vents and the dust-extraction port, then wipe the casing clean. If you are unlikely to use your saw for some time, smear a light coating of oil on exposed metal surfaces to prevent rust. Remember to wipe these surfaces clean before using the saw again.

Replace blade as soon as required

Adjust roller to support the blade

Make your guide fence longer

1 Carefully dismantle the casing

2 Lift the roller out of its recess

SAW WANDERS

Blunt or bent blade
Never hesitate to replace a blunt or damaged blade.

Blade-support roller needs adjusting
On some jigsaws the support roller can be adjusted fore and aft until it just touches the back edge of the blade. The roller is sometimes attached to the saw's base plate, which has to be loosened and then slid backwards or forwards to make the adjustment. Be sure to tighten all fixings afterwards.

Poor cutting technique
Forcing the saw through the work can cause the blade to wander off line. Back off and gradually regain the line, maintaining less pressure behind the blade.

An adjustable fence (guide) fitted to the base plate helps keep the saw blade on a path parallel to a straight edge. Make sure the fence clamp is secure and that the fence itself is aligned accurately with the blade.

You can extend a short fence by screwing a longer hardwood strip to it.

BLADE-SUPPORT ROLLER SEIZES
If you forget to lubricate the roller, the bearings may seize up. If lubrication doesn't solve the problem, try replacing the roller. On some saws this may entail fitting an entire base plate. With other models, you will have to dismantle the tool's casing in order to extract the damaged roller.

1 Remove the blade and lay the saw flat on a bench, so you can separate the two halves of the casing. Make a note of the exact position of internal components, and take care not to disturb them unnecessarily.

2 Slide the roller out of its recess and fit the new one. Then replace the casing, making sure that all components and wiring are in their original positions.

WOOD SPLINTERS

As the blade cuts on the upstroke, it tends to lift splinters on both sides of the saw cut on the upper surface of the work.

Turn the work over so that the 'good' surface faces down, or sandwich the workpiece between two sheets of cheap hardboard.

Some saws are supplied with an anti-splinter insert that clips into the base plate, surrounding the blade and supporting the wood fibres on each side of the cut. Other saws are made with an adjustable slotted base plate that performs the same function.

WOOD BURNS

If the wood starts to char and smoke when you are sawing, the blade is probably blunt or twisted. Fit a new blade, and apply less pressure when pushing the saw into the work.

Increasing the blade's pendulum action may prevent sawdust clogging the saw cut – check your user's handbook for advice on optimum settings.

Try increasing the pendulum action

SAW SUDDENLY STOPS WORKING

Severed flex

This is a distinct possibility if you allow the flex to trail in front of the blade or if it gets caught up beneath the workpiece.

The incoming flex may be connected to accessible screw terminals, in which case you will be able to replace it yourself (see page 20). If the existing flex is long enough, prepare the cut end for reconnecting to the terminals. If not, buy new flex with the same specification. All double-insulated tools must be wired with two-core flex – see page 18.

SAFETY FIRST

Unplug the jigsaw before changing blades, and before you clean or maintain it.

Check that the intended path of the blade is clear below the workpiece, and make sure the flex trails behind the saw, never in front of the blade.

Don't curl your fingers around the work near the line of cut.

Switch off and wait until the blade has stopped moving before you put the saw down.

Use a face mask or dust extraction when sawing wood and man-made boards.

SAW WON'T WORK AT ALL

Power failure

If other appliances on the circuit have stopped working, inspect your consumer unit for a blown fuse or tripped MCB or RCD – see pages 11 and 12.

Jigsaw not plugged in

Make sure the plug is inserted in the socket, and that the socket is switched on.

Plug fuse has blown

Replace the fuse in the plug – see page 17. If the fuse blows again as soon as you switch the tool on, have the jigsaw checked at a service centre.

Faulty wiring in plug

If possible, take the back off the plug and check that the plug is wired correctly – see pages 18 and 19.

Broken flex conductor

Provided the incoming flex is connected to accessible screw terminals (or simple push-in terminals – see page 270), you will be able to test the flex for continuity and, if need be, replace it (see page 20). Double-insulated tools are wired with two-core flex – see page 18.

If it is not obvious how the flex is connected to the terminals, have a suspect flex replaced at a service centre.

TOC tripped

Most power tools are fitted with a thermal-overload cutout (TOC) to protect the motor from overheating. If the air inlet vents are covered or blocked, the TOC may trip, cutting off power to the motor.

Clean the grilles (see page 263) and leave the saw to cool down – the TOC will reset automatically.

If you use your saw for a long period on a slow stroke rate, remove the blade and cool the motor by running the saw at maximum stroke rate for about 3 minutes

---

Faulty trigger switch

Variable-speed switches have complicated wiring and may be connected to circuit boards. Have these switches and those with soldered connections tested and, if need be, replaced at a service centre.

Loose connections

Vibration and heavy use can cause internal connections to work loose. Check all internal wiring for snugly fitting connectors.

Older power tools may have solder-tipped wires inserted in screw terminals. These are notorious for working loose.

Low or flat battery

When a cordless saw fails to start, try recharging the battery pack.

Don't let a battery drain completely as in some cases this could lead to permanent damage. Recharge the battery as soon as the tool starts to slow down significantly.

Faulty motor

Worn or sticking brushes may prevent the motor working. See pages 289–90, or have the motor checked at a service centre.

LAWN MOWERS

The traditional push-along lawn mower was transformed many years ago by powering the cutters with an electric motor, which eliminates much of the work. Although this type of mower is still popular, especially with those gardeners who like to create manicured lawns, for sheer convenience and reliability it is hard to beat the relative newcomer, the rotary hover mower, which cuts long grass with ease.

Rotary mowers are invariably mains powered, whilst cylinder mowers can be either mains or battery powered. Petrol-driven motor mowers have been excluded here although much of the basic maintenance is common to the majority of mowers.

How it works

Both types of mower are made in various guises, but apart from obvious differences are very similar in principle. Consequently your mower will probably resemble those described here, except perhaps for model-specific details. Always consult your user's handbook or get professional advice if you are in doubt about any aspect of servicing or maintenance.

Cylinder mowers

This type of mower is made with a set of horizontally mounted helical cutting blades that form the cylinder. A large toothed pulley bolted to one end of the cylinder is driven by a flexible belt (or sometimes a chain), which is looped around another smaller pulley attached to the end of the motor drive shaft. This same motor may also drive a roller that propels the mower forwards.

As the cylinder rotates, it forces the blades of grass against a fixed blade mounted below it, creating a scissor-like cutting action. Any damage, wear or incorrect setting of the blades will reduce the mower's efficiency.

The height of the cut can be varied by adjusting the position of a roller or set of wheels mounted either in front of or behind the cutting cylinder.

Cylinder mower

1 Switch lever
2 Safety/lock-off button
3 Switch
4 Filter
5 Air-inlet grille
6 Blade-clearance adjuster
7 Fixed blade
8 Cylinder (blades)
9 Large toothed pulley
10 Drive belt
11 Drive-shaft pulley
12 Height-adjustment lever
13 Electric motor
14 Roller
15 Flex

Rotary mowers

Rotary mowers usually have a single horizontally mounted metal cutter fixed directly to the shaft of the drive motor. Rotating at high speed, the cutter slices through grass and weeds. Instead of a single cutter, some models have a disc with detachable plastic blades.

Some rotary mowers are mounted on wheels, but the popular rotary hover mower floats on a cushion of air. In this instance, the motor drives a large impeller (fan) that forces air to flow beneath the dome-shaped cowling, creating lift. The metal cutter is mounted below this impeller. With a hover mower, spacers inserted above the blade are used to adjust the height of cut. Alternatively, the cutter disc, including plastic blades, can be turned over to reduce or increase the height of cut.

Plastic blades are easy to replace

Mulch mowers

All types of mower are available with containers for collecting the grass cuttings. Some gardeners prefer to use a mower that chops the grass very finely, returning it to the lawn as mulch.

Safety switches

All modern lawn mowers have safety systems that prevent the equipment working unless a pair of handles or a combination of switch lever and lock-off button are operated simultaneously. The switch should disengage as soon as you release the lever.

Getting the best from your mower

Safety is vitally important when operating electric mowers, and you should avoid using this type of equipment when tired and unable to concentrate.

Check that the flexible cord is in good condition, and make sure all guards, fixings and cutters are secure before you plug in.

Uncoil the full length of the flex and place the surplus just off the lawn nearest to the edge where you intend to start mowing. Before using the mower, inspect the lawn for small objects (such as pebbles or bones) that could damage the cutters or be propelled by them.

Drape the flex over one shoulder and take the mower's handle in both hands, then engage the switch.

As you proceed to cut the grass, keep an eye on the trailing flex, making sure it is always behind and to one side of the mower.

1 Switch lever
2 Safety/lock-off button
3 Switch
4 Electric motor
5 Cowling
6 Drive shaft
7 Hood
8 Impeller
9 Cutter clamp nut
10 Cutter
11 Spacer
12 Air-inlet grille
13 Flex

Hover mower

Adjusting height of cut

As described opposite, lawn mowers can be adjusted to cut grass to a specific height. Various methods may be employed, perhaps the simplest being a pair of levers, one on each side of the mower, that raise or lower a roller. When cutting long grass or mowing an uneven lawn, set the adjustment to 'high'. Unplug the mower before you make any adjustments.

CLEANING YOUR LAWN MOWER

When you have finished mowing the lawn, unplug the mower and brush grass cuttings off the cutters and out of the air-inlet grilles. Wipe down the casing with a dry cloth.

Scrape the mulch from the underside of a hover mower, using a plastic or wooden spatula.

Winter storage

At the end of the season, clean your mower thoroughly and rub over the cutters with an oily rag. Lubricate adjusters and accessible bearings.

Before you store the mower, inspect the cutters and flex for signs of damage and, if necessary, order replacements in time for the following spring.

Unbolt a cutter to sharpen it

SAFETY FIRST

Always plug your mower into a circuit protected by an RCD – see page 11.

Before using a mower, check for damaged casing, cutters and flex.

Check regularly for loose screws, nuts and bolts.

Adjust blade clearance

MOWER WON'T CUT GRASS

Blunt or damaged cutters

For the best results, buy a new cutter for a rotary mower every season. Make sure you buy the right cutter for your particular model. If this type of cutter is blunt, you can sharpen the cutting edges on a powered grindstone (or with a file).

When sharpening cutters, wear goggles and strong protective gloves. The cutter must be ground evenly on both sides to an angle of about 30 degrees. Check the cutter is balanced by threading it onto a screwdriver. If need be, grind off a little more metal from one side.

You can get a cylinder mower sharpened at a service centre, but there are simple clip-on sharpeners that you can buy from a garden centre. Before fitting one, unplug the mower and adjust the cylinder to achieve maximum cutter clearance (see Blades poorly set, below).

1 Stick one strip of self-adhesive abrasive to the face of the sharpener.

2 Following the manufacturer's instructions, clip the sharpener onto the mower's fixed blade, with the abrasive facing the cylinder.

Readjust the clearance until the cylinder just touches the abrasive. Plug in the mower and run it in short 15-second bursts until all the cutting edges are sharp. If you wear through the abrasive, replace it immediately.

Before you use the mower, remove the sharpener and adjust the cutter clearance again – see below.

Blades poorly set

With cylinder mowers, the clearance between the fixed blade and the revolving cylinder must be less than the thickness of a piece of paper. Some models are fitted with integral knurled adjusters, one on each side of the mower. Alternatively, you may need a spanner or screwdriver to make the necessary adjustments – see your user's handbook. Always unplug the mower before making adjustments

Clearance must be even along the entire length of the cylinder. To test the setting, place a

1 Stick abrasive strip on sharpener

2 Clip sharpener to fixed blade

Rotate cylinder to cut paper

Rotate jammed cylinder backwards

1 Remove drive cover

2 Loosen motor screws

3 Ease new belt onto the pulley

sheet of paper between the cylinder and fixed blade and, wearing a protective glove, carefully rotate the cylinder by hand. Make slight adjustments on both sides until the paper cuts cleanly at any point along the fixed blade.

MOWER WON'T WORK

Jammed cutters
Long grass, especially if it is damp, can jam the cutters of a cylinder mower. Unplug the mower and use a piece of wood to rotate the cylinder backwards (away from the fixed blade) until it revolves freely. This is not recommended for a petrol-driven mower.

Broken drive belt
The flexible belt that drives a cylinder mower may be worn or broken. The following procedure for replacing a belt is fairly typical, though it may vary slightly from model to model.

1 Remove the drive cover to see if the drive belt is broken or has slipped off its pulleys.

2 Loosen the motor screws and slide the small motor pulley towards the large cylinder pulley.

3 Slip the new belt over the small pulley and rotate the large pulley as you ease the belt onto it.

4 Slide the motor pulley sideways to tension the belt and then tighten the motor screws.

5 Before you replace the cover, check that the belt is tensioned correctly – it should flex no more than about 4mm ($\frac{1}{8}$in), but this may vary slightly from model to model.

Broken flex conductor
Each time you cut the grass, the flex on your electric mower is uncoiled, moved about the garden and then rewound. It isn't surprising that internal conductors sometimes break.

On many mowers the incoming flex is connected to accessible screw terminals, so you will be able to test the flex for continuity and, if need be, replace it (see page 20). Double-

MOWER DIFFICULT TO MOVE

If you are having trouble propelling your lawn mower, you may be trying to cut grass that is too long. See *Adjusting height of cut*, page 267.

Roller or wheels jammed
Check the rollers or wheels to see whether an accumulation of grass cuttings and other debris is preventing free rotation. You may have to remove the rollers or wheels to clean them thoroughly.

Air intakes blocked
If airflow is impeded for any reason, a hover mower creates less lift, making the mower relatively difficult to manoeuvre. Reduced airflow will eventually cause the motor to overheat. Unplug the mower and brush grass cuttings from the air-inlet grilles.

4 Adjust belt tension

5 Flex the belt to check tension

1 Take off plastic switch cover

2 Unscrew cord clamp

3 Release terminal with Allen key

4 Insert flex wire into terminal

insulated mowers are wired with two-core flex – see page 18.

Other models are wired with push-in terminals designed for easy flex replacement. The type shown here is relatively common.

1 Pull out the plug, then unscrew the switch cover and carefully lay it aside.

2 Before you unscrew the cord clamp, make a note of how the flex is connected to the switch, so you can match it colour for colour if you need to wire in the new flex.

3 To disconnect the flex from the switch, insert a 1mm diameter rod (Allen key) into the same hole (terminal) as each conductor. This releases a catch and the conductor can be pulled out. Test the flex for continuity – see page 20.

4 If necessary, prepare a new flex for connection (see page 19), twisting the strands of wire together. Slide the cord support onto the flex, then insert each twisted end into its terminal. Pull on each conductor to make sure it is firmly connected and that no strands of wire are exposed. Replace the cord clamp complete with cord support, and then screw on the switch cover.

If your mower flex is wired with terminal connections that are different from the ones shown here or on page 20, have it replaced at a service centre. Alternatively, you may be able to buy a replacement flex for your mower, complete with a new plug and push-on connectors.

Faulty switch

Have a suspect control switch tested and replaced at a service centre.

Power failure

If other appliances on the circuit have stopped working, inspect your consumer unit for a blown fuse or tripped MCB or RCD – see pages 11 and 12.

Mower not plugged in

Make sure the plug is inserted in the socket, and that the socket is switched on.

Plug fuse has blown

Replace the fuse in the plug – see page 17. If the fuse blows again as soon as you start your mower, have the mower checked at a service centre.

Faulty wiring in plug

If possible, take the back off the plug and check that the plug is wired correctly – see pages 18 and 19.

TOC tripped

The thermal-overload cutout (TOC) built into some mowers may trip if the motor overheats. Make sure the cutters are not jammed (see page 269), and brush grass cuttings out of the air-inlet grilles. Then leave the motor to cool down and allow the TOC to reset automatically.

SAFETY FIRST

Unplug the mower before inspecting it or carrying out replacements or repairs.

Don't turn a hover mower over until you have unplugged it.

Wear sturdy footwear when using any type of lawn mower.

Never cut the grass while walking backwards, pulling the mower towards you. Be especially carefully to keep your footing on sloping ground or wet grass. Mow across slopes, not up and down them.

Keep pets and children at a safe distance.

Never use mains-powered lawn mowers in the rain.

It is essential that all wiring, covers and components are refitted in their original positions after servicing.

HEDGE TRIMMERS

The electric hedge trimmer probably saves more time and effort than any other powered garden tool. However, to avoid serious accidents, it must be maintained properly and handled with considerable care. You can buy cordless and mains-powered trimmers.

How it works

Essentially an electric hedge trimmer emulates a pair of traditional garden shears, but the scissor action is achieved by having two long metal blades with rows of teeth or notches on each side. An electric motor drives a pair of large-diameter gear wheels that move the blades back and forth. This rapid reciprocation effectively opens and closes the array of notches, creating hundreds of small but powerful cutting strokes per minute.

For safety, all modern hedge trimmers are equipped with two separate switch controls, which have to be operated simultaneously before the trimmer will run. This ensures that both hands are kept well away from the blades behind a sturdy plastic guard or shield.

Getting the best from your trimmer

Before you plug in your trimmer, inspect the hedge for obstructions such as metal posts or wire that could damage the blades. Uncoil the flexible cord and pass it over your shoulder. Never allow the flex to drape across the hedge.

Standing well balanced on both feet, take the tool in both hands and, with the blades pointing away from you, switch on.

Start by trimming the top of the hedge, then shape the sides from the bottom upwards. If necessary, you can use a stretched string line to help you cut straight.

1 Switch controls	7 Blade-support bar	12 Terminal block
2 Return spring	8 Gear wheels	13 Cord clamp
3 Shield	9 Electric motor	14 Cord support
4 Tooth	10 Cooling fan	15 Flex
5 Notch	11 Switch-connector rod	16 Switch unit
6 Reciprocating blades		17 Return spring

Cleaning your hedge trimmer

As soon as you have finished trimming, unplug the tool or remove its battery pack, then brush the blades clean and wipe the casing with a dry cloth.

Any cuttings trapped in the air vents should be removed with a brush.

Clean residual sap from the blades, using a plastic scouring pad dipped in white spirit, and then dry the metal with a cloth.

Finish off by spraying the blades sparingly with light oil, then run the trimmer for a few seconds to spread the oil evenly.

Wipe off excess oil with a cloth before you slip the trimmer's protective guard over the blade assembly.

Check for loose nuts and screws

CUTS POORLY

Blunt or damaged blades
Have blunt or damaged blades replaced at a service centre.

ABNORMAL VIBRATION
Switch off and unplug immediately. Continuing to use the trimmer could be dangerous and may seriously damage the motor.

Loose components
Check all nuts and screws are secure. If vibration continues, take the trimmer to a service centre.

TRIMMER STOPS WORKING

Plug pulled out of socket
This could happen if you are working at the limit of the flex.

Severed flex
This is a common occurrence with mains-powered trimmers. Because the tool is double-insulated and it is plugged into an RCD, it's possible to cut through the flex without even noticing.

Some hedge trimmers may require a new flexible cord with special connectors – have this type of flex replaced at a service centre. On other trimmers the incoming flex is connected to accessible screw terminals, in which case you will be able to replace it yourself.

1 Some trimmers are made with an access panel that makes changing the flex simple.

2 Make sure you know which terminal takes the brown (live) conductor and which takes the blue (neutral), then unscrew the terminals and lift out the severed flex.

3 Prepare the new flex for connection (see page 19). Slip the cord support over the end of the flex and connect the conductors to their relevant terminals.

Check the flex is clamped securely before replacing the access panel.

1 Remove access panel

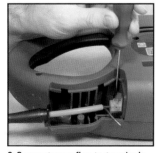

2 Detach the severed flex

3 Connect new flex to terminals

SAFETY FIRST

Always plug a mains-powered hedge trimmer into a circuit protected by an RCD – see page 11.

Don't operate a hedge trimmer when tired and unable to concentrate.

Never trim your hedge in the rain. Work only in good light.

Before using a hedge trimmer, always check for damage to the casing, flex, blades and shield.

Keep pets and children at a safe distance.

Never overreach when working from a stepladder. Always make sure the ladder is standing safely on firm ground.

Don't put a trimmer down until the blades have stopped moving.

If the blades strike an obstruction, switch off immediately, unplug the trimmer and inspect it for damage.

Check regularly for loose screws, nuts and bolts.

Unplug a hedge trimmer or remove the battery pack before you inspect the tool for problems or carry out replacements or repairs.

It is essential that all wiring, guards and other components are refitted in their original positions after servicing a hedge trimmer.

Jammed blades

If the blades jam while the hedge trimmer is in use, switch off immediately and unplug the tool or remove its battery pack.

Snap off any thick stems caught in the notches, then clean and oil the blades – see page 271.

TOC tripped

The thermal-overload cutout (TOC) built into some trimmers may trip if the motor starts to overheat. Brush cuttings out of the air vents, then leave the motor to cool down and allow the TOC to reset itself.

1 Lift out switch-connector rod

2 Operate the switch manually

3 Replace complete switch unit

TRIMMER WON'T WORK AT ALL

Faulty switch

In general, it is best to have a suspect switch tested and replaced at a service centre. However, if your trimmer is similar to the one shown here, it is possible to check the mechanical operation of the switch.

Unplug the tool and lay it flat on a bench, so you can remove the screws that hold the two halves of the casing together. Take great care not to disturb internal components until you have had chance to make a note of how they fit together.

1 Carefully lift out the metal rod that connects the controls to the switch unit.

2 Operate the switch manually. There should be audible clicks from the switch, and the mechanism should move smoothly.

3 The type of switch unit shown here can be unplugged and replaced easily. Any other type of switch should be replaced at a service centre.

Faulty motor

Worn or sticking brushes may prevent the motor working. See pages 289–90, or have the motor checked at a service centre.

Loose connections

Vibration can cause connections to work loose. Check all internal wiring for snugly fitting connectors.

Power failure

If other appliances on the circuit have stopped working, inspect your consumer unit for a blown fuse or tripped MCB or RCD – see pages 11 and 12.

Trimmer not plugged in

Make sure the plug is inserted in the socket, and that the socket is switched on.

Plug fuse has blown

Replace the fuse in the plug – see page 17. If the fuse blows again as soon as you turn the tool on, have the trimmer checked at a service centre.

Faulty wiring in plug

If possible, take the back off the plug and check that the plug is wired correctly – see pages 18 and 19.

Broken flex conductor

If the tool fails to start or works intermittently, one of the flex conductors may have broken. If the incoming flex is connected to screw terminals (or simple push-in terminals – see page 270), test the flex for continuity and then replace it – see pages 20 and 272. Double-insulated trimmers are wired with two-core flex – see page 18.

Low or flat battery

When a cordless trimmer fails to start, try recharging the battery pack. Don't let a battery drain completely, as in some cases this could lead to permanent damage. Recharge the battery as soon as the tool starts to slow down significantly.

Check for loose connections

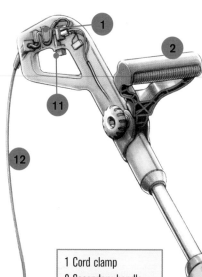

STRIMMERS

The strimmer is a versatile labour-saving tool capable of trimming weeds from around trees, posts, sheds and other garden structures. Most can also be used for lawn edging.

As with most electrical garden tools, strimmers are available in both mains-powered and battery-powered versions.

How it works

For a highly effective tool, the average strimmer is surprisingly simple. When the switch or trigger is depressed, a high-speed electric motor drives a spool wound with nylon cord. The one, or sometimes two, short tails of cord protruding from the spool slice through grass and weeds with ease.

A trimming blade mounted in the strimmer's plastic guard is designed to trim the cord automatically to the optimum length.

Depending on the model, there are four basic ways in which the cutting cord is extended:

- On older models, loosening a nut at the centre of the spool holder allows the cord to be pulled out of the spool and then trimmed to length, using the small blade mounted on the edge of the guard.
- A length of cord is ejected from the spool each time the spool holder's spring-loaded cover is bumped against a firm surface.
- Operating a trigger or button ejects a short length of nylon cord.
- A centrifugal sensing mechanism advances the required amount of cord automatically.

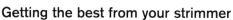

Some models incorporate a semi-ridged strip of plastic instead of the usual spool of nylon cord. Several variations of this kind of strimmer are in use, and most are designed only to accept the strip supplied by the tool's manufacturer (don't attempt to fit any other type).

1 Cord clamp
2 Secondary handle
3 Cooling fan
4 Cutting cord
5 Spool
6 Spool cover
7 Cord-trimming blade
8 Guard
9 Electric motor
10 Air-inlet grille
11 Trigger
12 Flex

Getting the best from your strimmer

If possible, make adjustments to the shaft of the strimmer and its secondary handle until the tool feels balanced – this will reduce the strain on your back.

Drape the flex over your shoulder before switching on, making sure there is sufficient slack so as not to impede movement.

Gently swing the tool from side to side as you advance it into the plant growth. Don't try to force the pace; and when cutting long grass or weeds, work down in stages, removing the tops first.

If the tool starts running slowly, back off and let it run up to speed again. Damp grass and weeds can be difficult to cut, so let them dry out before you start work.

On most models, rotating the head allows you to trim the edge of a lawn.

Cleaning a strimmer

Each time you finish strimming, unplug the strimmer and use a stick or spatula to scrape plant debris from the guard and spool. Brush the tool vigorously with a stiff-bristle brush before you put the tool away.

1 Fit a new or rewound spool

2 Refit the spool cover

3 Trim the cutting cord to length

A poorly wound spool will jam

WON'T CUT GRASS OR WEEDS

Cord needs trimming

An overlong cord is unable to get up to speed and therefore cuts inefficiently. On most strimmers the cord is trimmed to length each time it strikes the small blade mounted in the edge of the guard.

If possible, use long-nose pliers to pull out and replace a blunt or rusty trimming blade. With some models, the strimmer's blade holder is designed to take a short length of a snap-off blade intended for retractable craft knives – check your user's handbook.

If replacement blades are not available for your strimmer (you may have to purchase a new guard), your only option is to trim the cord to length by hand – see below.

Spool needs rewinding or replacing

Wound spools or lengths of cord are available from most garden centres.

1 Fit only the type of spool designed for your particular strimmer.

2 Refit the spool cover, making sure the cord is able to feed smoothly.

3 If the cord protrudes beyond the trimming blade, cut it to length so that it just reaches the blade.

If you rewind a length of cord onto an existing spool, take the time to wind it neatly and evenly. A poorly wound spool will jam and the cord will not feed.

WON'T WORK AT ALL

Power failure

If other appliances on the circuit have stopped working, inspect your consumer unit for a blown fuse or tripped MCB or RCD – see pages 11 and 12.

Strimmer not plugged in

Make sure the plug is inserted in the socket, and that the socket is switched on.

ABNORMAL VIBRATION

Switch off and unplug the strimmer immediately.

Damaged spool cover

A cracked or broken spool cover will throw the tool out of balance. Try to obtain a replacement at a service centre.

STRIMMER RUNS SLOWLY

Jammed spool

You may have to replace a poorly wound spool (see left). But check that a piece of wire or length of garden twine has not become caught up in the mechanism; if so, carefully tease it out from behind the spool housing.

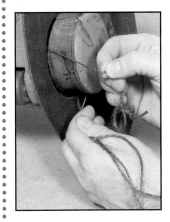

Sometimes flex comes complete with terminal connectors

Cordless strimmers are convenient in large gardens

Plug fuse has blown
Replace the fuse in the plug – see page 17. If the fuse blows again as soon as you turn the tool on, have the strimmer checked at a service centre.

Faulty wiring in plug
If possible, take the back off the plug and check that it is wired correctly – see pages 18 and 19.

Broken flex conductor
If the tool fails to start or works intermittently, one of the flex conductors may have broken. If the incoming flex is connected to screw terminals (or simple push-in terminals – see page 270), test the flex for continuity and replace it – see page 20. Double-insulated strimmers are wired with two-core flex – see page 18.

With some strimmers you may have to buy a replacement flex that comes complete with a new plug and push-on connectors.

TOC tripped
The thermal-overload cutout (TOC) built into some strimmers may trip if the motor starts to overheat. Brush cuttings out of the air vents, then leave the motor to cool down and allow the TOC to reset itself.

Faulty switch
It may be possible to have the on/off switch (trigger) tested and replaced at a service centre – but even if spare parts are available, the cost is likely to be uneconomical.

Faulty motor
Worn or sticking brushes may prevent the motor working. See pages 289–90, or have the motor checked at a service centre.

Low or flat battery
When a cordless strimmer fails to start, try recharging the battery pack.

Don't let a battery drain completely, as in some cases this could lead to permanent damage. Recharge the battery as soon as the tool starts to slow down significantly.

SAFETY FIRST

Always plug a mains-powered strimmer into a circuit protected by an RCD.

Never use electric garden tools in the rain.

Before using a strimmer, check for damage to the casing, flex, spool and guard.

Wear safety goggles when cutting weeds and long grass.

Wear sturdy footwear when using a strimmer.

Keep pets and children at a safe distance.

Don't put a strimmer down until rotating parts have stopped moving.

If you accidentally throw up stones or similar debris, switch off immediately, unplug the strimmer and inspect it for damage. Do the same if the strimmer starts to vibrate excessively or runs more noisily than usual. Be especially careful when working near glass.

Check regularly for loose screws, nuts and bolts.

Unplug a strimmer or remove the battery pack before you inspect the tool for problems or carry out replacements.

It is essential that all wiring, guards and other components are refitted in their original positions after servicing.

SAFETY FIRST

Never throw any type of battery into a fire.

Don't dispose of batteries by putting them in an ordinary household waste bin. Ask your local authority to recommend an alternative method of disposal.

Keep batteries (especially button batteries) out of the reach of small children.

Avoid potential damage from corrosive materials by removing batteries from equipment that is to be stored for any length of time.

Always recharge Ni-Cad batteries in a dry well-ventilated room.

Attempting to recharge ordinary disposable batteries is extremely dangerous.

Don't short-circuit a battery by bridging the electrodes with a metal object – it is not safe to carry unwrapped batteries in your pocket or handbag.

Never try to dismantle a sealed battery pack.

Charging often makes batteries feel warm, but they should never get hot – excessive heat will damage the cells.

If possible, recharge a battery pack before it is completely discharged. Continuing to run tools until they stop working may damage the battery pack.

Rechargeable Li-Ion batteries are more often found in devices such as camcorders, cameras and laptop computers.

Never fit different types of battery together in the same appliance.

Battery packs

Some equipment is supplied with a sealed pack containing two or more interconnected rechargeable batteries. Cordless tools, for example, are fitted with powerful sealed packs that are removed for charging. Never attempt to dismantle a battery pack.

Battery chargers

When plugged into a mains wall socket, a battery charger reduces 230V electricity to the lower voltages used by rechargeable batteries.

General-purpose chargers will accommodate any of the common-size batteries. Charging time varies from 5 to 7 hours, but you can buy rapid chargers that will undertake the task in anything from 3 to 5 hours. Some may even be capable of charging a battery in a couple of hours.

Cordless appliances are packaged with chargers designed specifically for them.

Some tools and appliances are designed to take a continuous 'trickle' charge, but in most cases it is advisable to remove the battery pack from the charger as soon as it is topped up. Check the manufacturer's instructions.

Never attempt to use any chargers other than those designed specifically for use with the battery or battery pack. Car-battery chargers, for example, are totally unsuitable.

Rechargeable battery pack

Rechargeable batteries and charger

Battery memory

Recharging a Ni-Cad battery or battery pack before it is entirely exhausted may result in a lower energy capacity, so it becomes impossible to ever fully recharge the battery again. This is often referred to as 'memory effect'.

Some battery chargers are capable of discharging a partially used battery, then reversing the process and topping the battery up again. Ideally this should be done each time a Ni-Cad battery needs charging, but in practice you should avoid recharging a battery more than five times without fully discharging it. Check the user's manual supplied with the charger.

Memory effect does not occur with either Ni-MH or Li-Ion batteries.

ELECTRIC MOTORS

There are so many things that can go wrong with electric motors that under most circumstances it makes sense to have a faulty motor serviced or replaced by a professional engineer. However, with certain motors it is possible to carry out very basic servicing yourself – namely replacing worn carbon brushes and cleaning the commutator.

In many cases you can undertake these simple tasks without having to take out the motor. With some appliances, however, you would have to disconnect and unbolt the motor in order to gain access to both brushes. Depending on how difficult it is to remove the motor, you might prefer to leave all servicing to an engineer.

Universal motors

Universal motors are fitted in many types of appliance, ranging from washing machines and vacuum cleaners to mains-operated and cordless power tools. The term 'universal' stems from the fact that this type of motor can be configured to operate with an AC (alternating current) or DC (direct current) power supply. Mains current is AC, whereas DC is supplied by batteries and transformer/rectifiers.

A typical universal AC motor turns electrical energy into mechanical energy (motion) by utilizing the properties of magnetism. Passing electric current through two coils of wire creates a magnetic field. In a motor, these particular coils are surrounded by a laminated-steel block that concentrates the magnetic field. Together, the metal block and coils form an electromagnet, which in a motor is called the field windings.

Situated between the two field coils is a cylindrical metal armature, which is the moving part of the motor. Wrapped longitudinally around the armature is a series of separate wire coils (armature windings). Attached to the ends of each coil is a pair of flat strip contacts made from copper. These copper contacts are grouped together at one end of the armature, each linked pair of contacts being on opposite sides of the cylinder. Collectively these contacts are known as the commutator.

Sticks of carbon (carbon brushes) positioned on opposite sides of the commutator are pressed against opposing pairs of contacts. Current introduced to the carbon brushes passes via the commutator through a particular armature winding, creating an individual magnetic field. The basic laws of magnetism cause this magnetic field to react with the surrounding magnetic field created by the field windings – the N pole of one field attracts the S pole of the other – making the armature move in a certain direction. This movement aligns the carbon brushes with the next pair of commutator contacts, creating yet another magnetic field. Each newly created magnetic field reacts in turn to the field windings, creating smooth continuous rotation of the armature.

DC motors

DC and AC universal motors work on similar principles, but DC motors have permanent magnets instead of field windings.

Cordless tools such as drills, jigsaws and hedge trimmers have DC motors powered by batteries with capacities of up to 30V or more. To provide this amount of power, several batteries are usually wired in series.

Reversing the direction of rotation in a DC motor is achieved by simply

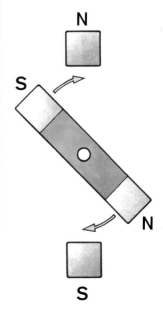

Universal motor

| 1 Field coil |
| 2 Armature |
| 3 Carbon brush |
| 4 Commutator |
| 5 Strip contact |
| 6 Armature winding |

Opposite poles attract

changing polarity to the motor terminals. In power tools, this is done by a changeover switch.

Replacing a DC motor is usually cheaper than repairing it. However, it may be worth trying to obtain replacement brushes and cleaning the commutator (see page 290). Not all DC motor brushes are made from carbon – in some cases they are nothing more than sprung metal arms in contact with the commutator.

Induction motors

Universal motors are found in the majority of electrical appliances, but in certain situations induction motors are preferable. Induction motors are relatively quiet and, because they are not fitted with brushes, there's no carbon dust to contaminate the motor.

A split-phase induction motor has a complex series of windings called the stator (similar to a universal motor's field windings), enclosing a cylindrical rotor made from aluminium and steel. There are no electrical connections to the rotor, and rotation is induced by another set of stator windings called start windings. A capacitor is often placed in series with the start windings to increase the starting torque of the motor.

A shaded-pole induction motor is similar to the split-phase variety but has just the one stator coil, which creates a constant magnetic field. Copper bands within the stator's mild-steel laminations distort the magnetic field in a given direction, inducing the rotor to move.

As there are no brushes to replace in induction motors, it is best to leave all servicing to a professional.

Servicing universal motors

If there is poor contact between the carbon brushes and the commutator, a universal motor will not run efficiently. Poor commutation, as it is known, could be the result of worn or jammed carbon brushes; or the commutator itself could be dirty.

Worn or sticking brushes

Carbon brushes are fitted in various ways, but they are invariably held in contact with the commutator by a spring of some sort. The following sequences show three typical carbon-brush arrangements, all of which make for easy replacement. Always unplug or disconnect an appliance (see page 13) before servicing the motor.

Split-phase induction motor

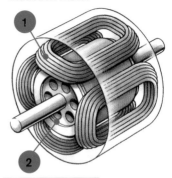

1 Stator windings
2 Rotor

Shaded-pole induction motor

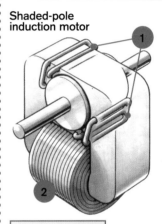

1 Copper bands
2 Stator coil

1 Prise off the metal cap

1 In this motor a metal cap holds the carbon brush in position. Carefully prise off the cap with the tip of a screwdriver.

2 Brushes wear to fit snugly against the surface of the commutator – so before you remove a brush completely, make a small scratch in the carbon. This will help you reinsert the brushes exactly as you found them, should you decide that neither brush has worn sufficiently to require replacement.

2 Make a small mark on the brush

3 Take the brush from its holder

4 Brush dirt from the commutator

5 Buff the copper contacts

3 Take out each brush, along with its captive spring. If the carbon is virtually worn away, fit new brushes.

Cleaning the commutator

Before inserting the brushes, take the opportunity to clean the surface of the commutator.

4 Use an old toothbrush to remove surface dust and grime, and to scrub out dirt that may have accumulated in the narrow gaps between the copper contacts.

5 Then buff the copper with a fibreglass electric-contact cleaner, sold for servicing audio equipment (see page 202). If the commutator shows signs of excessive wear or burning, ask a service engineer whether it is possible to have the motor repaired.

External-spring brushes

In some universal motors, each carbon brush is held in contact with the commutator by an external sprung-wire arm that has to be lifted out of the way before you can remove the brush. Each brush is wired with a braided-copper conductor attached to a spade connector.

Replaceable brush units

It is even easier to service motors that have replaceable carbon-brush units.

1 Start by detaching the spade connector attached to each brush unit. Make a note of the terminal to which it is connected – there are sometimes very similar spare terminals close by.

2 Then take out the screws that hold the plastic brush unit to the body of the motor.

3 Lift out each brush unit and replace it with an identical unit.

Having carried out basic servicing, use a paintbrush and a vacuum-cleaner attachment to remove dust and fluff adhering to the motor. Far from being a cosmetic exercise, cleaning the motor reduces the risk of an accumulation of conductive carbon dust, which could permit current to leak to earth. This could cause an RCD to trip or, eventually, blow a fuse.

Lift the spring to remove the brush

1 Detach the spade connector

2 Unscrew the brush unit

3 Lift out and replace the unit

BUYING SPARE PARTS

Tracking down a source of relevant spare parts is very often the key to getting an appliance up and running again. In many cases, spares are available over the counter from local suppliers, who will probably be able to order a component for you if it is not in stock already. Your Yellow Pages telephone directory and local newspapers will be useful sources of likely stockists.

You will find numerous spares suppliers on the Internet, including many of the major appliance manufacturers who supply parts by mail order.

Patterned and manufacturers' parts

If you apply to the manufacturer, you will get an identical component to the one you have removed from the appliance. Genuine spare parts will be clearly marked as such, either on the packaging or on the item itself.

Retailers can sell you components marked OEM (Original Equipment Manufacturer), which are exactly the same as those fitted by the appliance manufacturer. Independent spares distributors purchase these OEM components directly from the factory and supply them to the retailer for sale to you, the customer. This avoids an appliance-manufacturer's mark-up, which can be quite considerable.

You may also be offered so-called patterned parts, which are essentially copies of the manufacturer's genuine spares. Patterned parts are usually marked 'suitable for' or 'to fit' brand-name appliances, and are usually cheaper than the manufacturer's equivalent. However, this does not imply that a patterned part is inferior – a reputable dealer or service centre will supply only good-quality parts, whatever their source.

In an effort to maintain the sale of 'genuine' spare parts, many appliance manufacturers discount their authorized spares to compete with patterned and OEM spares.

Ordering spares

When ordering spare parts from any supplier, it's essential to supply accurate information. Ideally you should know the name of the component and, more important, its part number. An exploded diagram and a comprehensive list of part numbers are sometimes supplied with smaller appliances, but this vital information often gets discarded along with the packaging. Although this type of information is rarely, if ever, supplied with larger appliances, check the manufacturer's website to see if it is available there. Phone numbers of genuine spare-parts suppliers are often printed in the manufacturer's literature.

You should at least make a note of the product number marked on your appliance, and write down its brand name and model. Then describe the component you wish to purchase in as much detail as possible. Don't forget that some appliances may have two or more similar components (switches or pumps, for example) and your spares supplier will need to know exactly which one you need. If possible, take the faulty component to the supplier, so you can compare the original part with the replacement offered.

SELECTING A REPAIRER

Knowing when not to undertake a repair is as important as knowing how to repair an appliance.

Time and again throughout this book you are advised to either call out an engineer or take a faulty appliance to a service centre. This merely acknowledges that we are not all equally endowed with confidence or experience, and that some tasks are best left to a professional. You will then need to find a competent tradesperson who can do the job for you.

The detailed illustrations and information on how appliances work will help you explain your problem to a technician or engineer. He or she may use technical terms and different names for components, but you will at least be able to communicate your needs and discuss potential solutions.

Finding helpful, knowledgeable professionals in the appliance-repair industry is no different from tracking down qualified tradespeople in other fields.

- Appliance manufacturers invariably have their own service agents or will recommend service centres that undertake repairs. Using authorized service agents is one of the best ways to locate reliable repairers.
- If you prefer to use local independent agents or engineers, make a list of likely companies or individuals before you need them. You can usually rely on personal recommendation.
- If possible, ask local consumer or Trading Standards organizations if they have information on the company or person you are considering.
- Look for professional qualifications, training awards, and membership of reputable trade associations.
- You can expect company staff to be courteous and helpful. Even though in some cases it may be impossible to give you a firm quotation, before embarking on a repair they should be willing to discuss callout charges, hourly rates and methods of payment.

Service and spare-parts agents

You may find this list of major manufacturing companies useful as a source for spares or service agents. Unfortunately, there are too many independent agents and service centres to include here. If there are none in your locality, try using an Internet search engine to track down likely mail-order sources.

No list of this kind can be all-inclusive, and details change constantly as companies merge or move elsewhere. For more up-to-date information, try Directory Enquiries.

DOMESTIC APPLIANCES

AEG
See Electrolux

Amana
Bradshaw Appliances
Bristol BS21 6LH
Tel: 01275 343000

Appliance Tecnik
Red Scar Industrial Estate
Longridge Road
Preston PR2 5NA
Tel: 01772 798282
Fax: 01772 792424

Aqua-Dial
See Culligan

Ariston
See Merloni

Asko
See Servis

Atag
(Asdal, Atag, Pilgrim)
19 Hither Green
Clevedon
Avon BS21 6XU
Tel: 01275 870606
Fax: 01275 871371

Atlant
(Atlant, Exquisit, Favorit)
Atlant House
Abbeymead Industrial Estate
Brooker Road
Waltham Abbey
Essex EN9 1JD
Tel: 01992 712335
Fax: 01992 712336

BaByliss
See Conair Group

Bauknecht
See Whirlpool

Baumatic
6 Bennet Road
Reading
Berkshire RG2 0QX
Tel: 0118 9336900
Fax: 0118 9310035
www.baumatic.com

Beko
Beko House
Caxton Way
Watford Business Park
Watford WD1 8UF
Tel: 01923 654850
Fax: 01923819653

Belling Appliances
Talbot Road
Mexborough
South Yorkshire S64 8AJ
Tel: 01709 579901
Fax: 01709 579905

Brandt
(Brandt, De Dietrich, Ocean)
Wade Road
Basingstoke
Hampshire RG24 8NE
Tel: 01256 308000
Fax: 01256 346877
www.brandt.co.uk

Breville
See Pulse Home Products

BSH Appliance Care
(Bosch, Gaggenau, Neff,
Siemens)
Old Wolverton Road
Wolverton
Milton Keynes MK12 5ZR
Tel: 08705 222777
Fax: 01908 328670

Candy
New Chester Road
Bromborough
Wirral
Merseyside CH52 3PE

Tel: 0151 3342781
Fax: 0151 3340185

Cannon
See GDA

Carmen
See Pifco

Conair Group
(BaByliss, Revlon, Interplak)
PO Box 612
Frimley
Camberley
Surrey GU16 7YU
Tel: 01276 687500
Fax: 01276 687528
ukinfo@conair.com

Consort
Thornton Industrial Estate
Milford Haven
Pembrokeshire SA73 2RT
Tel: 01646 692172
Fax: 01646 695195
Service and spares:
Tel: 01873 854729
Fax: 01873 855821
enquiries@consortelp.com
www.consortepl.com

Coolectric
(Coolectric, Liebherr)
Express Way
Whitwood
Near Wakefield
West Yorkshire WF10 5QJ
Tel: 01977 665665
Fax: 01977 665669

Creda
See GDA

Crosslee
(Whiteknight, Hostess, Odell,
Royal Cozyfires)
Hipperholme
Halifax
West Yorkshire HX3 8DE

Tel: 01422 203585
Fax: 01422 206652
Service: 01422 200600
Fax: 01422 206304
Spares: 01422 203963
spares@crosslee.co.uk
www.crosslee.co.uk

Culligan
(Aqua-Dial, Liff, Waterside)
Culligan International
Culligan House
The Gateway Centre
Coronation Road
High Wycombe HP12 3SU
Tel: 01494 838100
Fax: 01494 838101
www.culligan.co.uk

Daewoo Electronics
640 Wharfedale Road
Reading
Berkshire RG41 5TP
Tel: 0118 9252500
Fax: 0118 9252577

De Dietrich
See Brandt

DeLonghi
15–16 Bridle Close
Finedon Road Industrial Estate
Wellingborough
Northamptonshire NN8 4RJ
Tel: 01933 442040
Fax: 01933 441891

Demena
Unit 20
Ridgewood Industrial Park
Uckfield
Sussex TN22 5QE
Tel: 01825 749498
Fax: 01825 749499

Dimplex
See Glen Dimplex

Dirt Devil
Midlands Distribution Centre
Mill Road
Rugby CV21 1PR
Tel: 01788 547547
Fax: 01788 565159

Dreamland
See Pulse Home Products

Dyson
Tetbury Hill
Malmesbury
Wiltshire SN16 0RP
Tel: 01666 827200
Fax: 01666 827299
Service and spares:
0870 5275204
Fax: 01666 827298
www.dyson.com

Elcold
See Frigidaire Consolidated

Electrolux
(AEG, Electrolux, Moffat,
Parkinson Cowan, Tricity
Bendix, Zanussi)
PO Box 2175
Luton LU4 9GE
Tel: 01582 491234
Service: 08705 929929
Customer care:
08708 055055
Spares – see Yellow Pages

Fagor (Caple, Fagor)
PO Box 1747
South Woodham Ferrers
Essex CM3 5WR
Tel: 01245 320992
Fax: 01245 329483

Finlux
See Prima International

Fridgemaster Corporation
Express Way,
Whitwood

Wakefield WF10 5QJ
Tel: 01977 665577
Fax: 01977 603159

Frigidaire Consolidated
(Frigidaire, Elcold, Norfrost,
Novum)
Express Way
Whitwood
Wakefield WF10 5QJ
Tel: 01977 665590
Fax: 01977 665589

GDA
(Cannon, Creda, Hotpoint)
Morley Way
Woodston
Peterborough PE2 2JB
Tel: 01733 568989
Fax: 01733 341783
www.theservicecentre.co.uk

Glen Dimplex
(Berry, Dimplex, EWT, Glen,
Unidaire)
Millbrook House
Grange Drive
Hedge End
Southampton SO30 2DF
Tel: 08700 777117
Fax: 08707 270109

Goblin
(Aquavac, Goblin)
Talbot Road
Mexborough
South Yorkshire S64 8AJ
Tel: 08457 010340
Fax: 01709 579905

Goldair
See Prima International

Haden
Mount Road
Burntwood
Staffordshire WS7 0AW
Tel: 01543 675222
Fax: 01543 674509

Hitachi
Dukes Meadow
Millboard Road
Bourne End
Buckinghamshire SL8 5XF
Tel: 01628 643000
Fax: 01628 643400

Hoover
Pentrebach
Merthyr Tydfil
Mid Glamorgan CF48 4TU
Tel: 01685 721222
Fax: 01685 382946

Hotpoint
See GDA

Ideal
See Prima International

Ignis
See Whirlpool

Imetec
(Imetec, Slumberland,
Sleeptight)
3 Aston Way
Middlewich
Cheshire CW10 0HS
Tel: 01606 837222
Fax: 01606 837444
service@imetec.co.uk
www.imetec.co.uk

Indesit
See Merloni

Kenwood
New Lane
Havant
Hampshire PO9 2NH
Tel: 02392 478000
Fax: 02392 392395
Service: 02392 392146

KitchenAid Europa
Spares & Service APWRO Ltd,
Unit 21a
Monkspath Business Park,
Highlands Road
Shirley
Solihull B90 4NZ
Tel: 0121 7440968
Fax: 0121 7440974

Krupps
See Moulinex

Lec Refrigeration
Shripney Road
Bognor Regis
West Sussex PO22 9NQ
Tel: 01243 863161
Fax: 01243 868052
info@lec.co.uk
www.lec.co.uk

Leisure
(Flavel, Kohlangaz, Leisure)
Meadow Lane
Long Eaton
Nottingham NG10 2AT
Tel: 0115 9464000
Fax: 0115 9466123
www.leisurecp.co.uk

Liebherr
See Coolectric

Liff
See Culligan

Merloni
(Ariston, Indesit, Philco)
3 Cowley Business Park
High Street
Cowley
Uxbridge UB8 2AD
Tel: 01895 858200
Fax: 01895 858270

Miele
Fairacres
Marcham Road
Abingdon
Oxfordshire OX14 1TW
Tel: 01235 554455
Fax: 01235 554477
Service: 01235 554466
Spares: 01235 233133
Fax: 01235 233139
general@miele.co.uk

Moffat
See Electrolux

Morphy Richards
Talbot Road
Mexborough
South Yorkshire S64 8AJ
Tel: 08450 777700
Fax: 01709 579905

Moulinex
(Krupps, Swan)
Merlin Park
Wood Lane
Erdington
Birmingham B24 9LZ
Tel: 0121 2020500
Fax: 0121 2020501
www.moulinex.com

Mountain Breeze
See Pifco

Naiko
(Iceline, Naiko, Vanilla)
Phoenix House
Roman Terrace
Leeds LS8 2DU
Tel: 0113 2888998
Fax: 0113 2888889
naikouk8@aol.com

National Homecare
Darlaston Road
Kings Hill
Wednesbury
West Midlands WS10 7TE
Tel: 0121 5263199
Fax: 0121 5284194

Neff
Grand Union House
Old Wolverton Road
Milton Keynes MK12 5PT
Tel: 01908 328300
Fax: 01908 328399
www.neff.co.uk
Spares:
Tel: 08705 543210
Fax: 01908 328650

Nicky Clarke Electric
See Pulse

Norfrost
See Frigidaire Consolidated

Novum
See Frigidaire Consolidated

NRC Refrigeration
(Amana)
Finedon Road Industrial Estate
Wellingborough
Northamptonshire NN8 4TG
Tel: 01933 388222
Fax: 01933 392302

Ocean
See Brandt

Oracstar
Weddell Way
Brackmills
Northamptonshire NN4 7HS
Tel: 01604 674444
Fax: 01604 701743

Oster
Oster International
Swindon SN5 7YJ
Tel: 01793 539300

Philco
See Merloni

Philips DAP
420-30 London Road
Croydon CR9 3QR
Tel: 020 86892166
Fax: 020 87818326
Consumer hotline:
0845 6010354
Spares:
Electric Shavers Services
Tel: 01786 475865
Fax: 01786 450533.
Olympic Shavers
Tel: 0115 9506514
Fax: 0115 9414016

Pifco
(Carmen, Mountain Breeze,
Pifco, Russell Hobbs, Salton,
Scholtes, Tower)
Failsworth
Manchester M35 0HS
Tel: 0161 9473000
Fax: 0161 6821708
postmaster@pifco.co.uk

Prima International
(Akai, Finlux, Goldair, Ideal,
Prima, Sewland)
Prima International Group
Prima House
Premier Park
Oulton
Leeds LS26 8ZA
Tel: 0113 2511500
Fax: 0113 2511515
Service and spares:
0113 2511500
mail@prima-international.com

Pulse Home Products
(Breville, Dreamland, Nicky
Clarke Electric, Viva)
Vine Mill
Middleton Road
Roxton
Oldham OL2 5LN
Tel: 0161 6521211
Fax: 0161 6260391
customerliaison@pulse.co.uk

Rowenta
See Tefal

Russell Hobbs
See Pifco

Salton
See Pifco

Scholtes
See Pifco

Servis
(Asko, Servis)
Darlaston Road
Wednesbury
West Midlands WS10 7TJ
Tel: 0121 5688333
Fax: 0121 5688500
Service and spares:
Tel: 08705 168299
Fax: 0121 5263839

Siemens
See BSH Appliance Care

Sodastream
Morley Way
Woodston
Peterborough PE2 7BS
Tel: 01733 366000
Fax: 01733 231234

SMEG
(White Westinghouse)
87a Milton Park
Abingdon
Oxfordshire OX14 4RY
Tel: 01235 828300
Fax: 01235 861120

Stoves
(Creations, New World,
Stoves, Stoves Newhome)
Stoney Lane
Preston L35 2XW
Tel: 0151 4308497
Fax: 0151 4263261

Sunbeam
Delaware Drive
Tongwell
Milton Keynes MK15 8HG
Tel: 01908 206500
Fax: 01908 210641

Swan
See Moulinex

Tefal
(Rowenta, Tefal)
PO Box 15
Slough PDO SL3 8WH
Tel: 01753 713000
Fax: 01753 583938

Teka
177 Milton Park
Milton
Abingdon
Oxfordshire OX14 4SE
Tel: 01235 861916
Fax: 01235 832137

Tower
See Pifco

Tricity Bendix
See Electrolux

Ufesa
Express Way
Whitwood
Near Wakefield WF10 5QJ
Tel: 01977 603222
Fax: 01977 665635

Unidare
(Berry Fire, Unidare)
Church Road
Seago
Portadown
Co Armagh BT63 5HU
Tel: 01763 333131
Fax: 01763 351141

Vacman
(Vacman, Zelmer)
Anderson Electrical
Colombo House
Colombo Street
Derby DT1 1TW
Tel: 01332 343121
Fax: 01332 294736

Valor
Wood Lane
Erdington
Birmingham B24 9QP
Tel: 0121 3738111
Fax: 0121 3738181

Vax
Kingswood Road
Hampton Lovett
Droitwich WR9 0QH
Tel: 01905 795959
Fax: 01905 795963
Service: 0870 6061248

Viva
See Pulse Home Products

Voltaire
6 Vivian Avenue

London NW4 3YA
Tel: 020 82035721
Fax: 020 82035843

Wahl
Herne Bay Trade Park
Sea Street
Herne Bay
Kent CT6 8JZ
Tel: 01227 740066
Fax: 01277 367550
Service: 01277 744331
Spares: 01227 744330

Waterside
See Culligan

Whirlpool
(Bauknecht, Ignis, Philips)
PO Box 45
209 Purley Way
Croydon CR9 4RY
Tel: 020 86495450
Fax: 020 86495461
Service and spares:
Tel: 08706 008989
Fax: 020 86495130

White Westinghouse
See SMEG

Zanussi
See Electrolux

Zelmer
See Vacman

AUDIOVISUAL EQUIPMENT

Aiwa
Unit 5,
Heathrow Summit Centre
Skyport Drive
West Drayton
Middlesex UB7 0LY
Tel: 0208 8977000
Fax: 0208 5649446

Akai
See Prima

Akura
Spectra House
Spring Villa Park
Spring Villa Road
Edgware
Middlesex HA8 7EB
Tel: 0208 9514323
Fax: 0208 9514174

Service for TVs and DVDs:
Tel: 0121 7069900 or
01442 203676
Spares:
Tel: 01484 842761
Fax: 01484 306337
100600.307@compuserve.com
www.akura.com

Alba
(Alba, Bush, Goodmans,
Harvard, Hinari)
Harvard House
14–16 Thames Road
Barking
Essex IG11 0HX
Tel: 020 85945533
Fax: 020 85910962

Amstrad
Brentwood House
169 Kings Road
Brentwood
Essex CM14 4EF
Tel: 01277 228888
Fax: 01277 211350

Audioline
See Doro

Beko
Caxton Way
Watford Business Park
Watford WD1 8UF
Tel: 01923 818121
Fax: 01923 819653

Celtel
PO Box 135,
Basingstoke
Hampshire RG25 2HZ
Tel: 01256 474900
Fax: 01256 818064
celtel@ibm.net

Crown
Express Way
Whitwood
Wakefield WF10 5QJ
Tel: 01977 604111
Fax: 01977 603159

Daewoo
640 Wharfedale Road
Winnersh Triangle
Wokingham RG41 5TP
Tel: 0118 9252626
Fax: 0118 9252532

Deccacolour
See Tatung

Doro
(Audioline, Doro, Moss
Security, Southwestern Bell)
22 Walkers Road
Redditch
Worcestershire B98 9HE
Tel: 01527 583800
Fax: 01527 583801
Service and spares:
For telephones:
Matrix Alexander
5 Rovex Estate
Hay Hall Road
Tyseley
Birmingham B11 2AG
Tel: 0121 6831881
For alarms:
Cranmore Services
190a Bridge Street
West Newtown
Birmingham B19 2YT
Tel: 0121 3597020
For payphones:
Incom Telecommunications
Waterside
Trafford Park
Manchester M17 1WD
Tel: 0161 9351031

Dynatron
See Roberts Radio

Grundig
Elstree Way
Borehamwood
Hertfordshire WD6 1RX
Tel: 020 83249400
Fax: 020 83249401
www.grundig.co.uk

Hitachi
Dukes Meadows
Millboard Road
Bourne End
Buckinghamshire SL8 5XF
Tel: 01628 643000
Fax: 01628 643400
Spares:
Charles Hyde & Son Ltd
Prospect House
Barmby Road
Pocklington
York YO4 2DP
Tel: 01759 303068
Fax: 01759 303620
www.charleshyde.co.uk

JVC
Eldonwall Trading Estate
Priestley Way
London NW2 7BA
Tel: 0208 4503282
Fax: 0208 2083038

LG Electronics
264 Bath Road
Slough
Berkshire SL1 4DT
Tel: 0870 6075544
Fax: 01753 517445
ukhelpdesk@lge.com

Longmill
7 Laxcon Close
London NW10 0TG
Tel: 020 84516461
Fax: 020 84517799

Maxview
Common Lane
Setchey
King's Lynn
Norfolk PE33 0AT
Tel: 01553 811000
Fax: 01553 813301
www.maxview.ltd.uk

Mitsubishi Electric
Travellers Lane
Hatfield AL10 8XB
Tel: 01280 826006
Fax: 01707 278762

Morphy Richards
PO Box 129
Mexborough
South Yorkshire S64 8AJ
Tel: 01709 585525
Fax: 01709 580366

Nokia
Bridgemead Close
Westmead
Swindon
Wiltshire SN5 7TS
Tel: 01793 556000
Fax: 01793 556010
Service:
Tel: 01793 556046
Fax: 01793 556014
Spares:
DigiTec Direct – Manchester
Tel: 0161 6546664
uk-nmt.customer-
service@nokia.com
www.nokia.co.uk

Pace Micro Technology
Victoria Road
Saltaire
West Yorkshire BD18 3LF
Tel: 01274 532000
Fax: 01274 532010
CPC Tel: 01722 654455
Vale Tel: 01734 876444

Panasonic
Willoughby Road
Bracknell
Berkshire RG12 8PF
Tel: 01344 862444
Fax: 01344 853168

Philips
(Philips, Pye)
420–30 London Road
Croydon CR9 3QR
Tel: 0208 6894444
Fax: 0208 6894312

Pioneer
Hollybush Hill
Stoke Poges SL2 4QP
Tel: 01753 789786
Fax: 01753 789534

Powermax
Thornton Industrial Estate
Milford Haven
Pembrokeshire SA73 2RT
Tel: 01646 692172
Fax: 01646 695195
enquiries@consortepl.com
www.consortepl.com

Pye
See Philips

Recoton
(Ross)
Towngate Business Centre,
Lester Road
Walkden
Manchester M38 0PT
Tel: 0161 7025000
Fax: 0161 7025001
www.recoton-europe.com

Remotes Direct
PO Box 6293
Basingstoke
Hampshire RG25 2XP
Tel: 0800 7832874
Fax: 0702 0966458
sales@remotesdirect.com
www.remotesdirect.com

Roberts Radio
(Dynatron, Roberts)
PO Box 130
Mexborough
South Yorkshire 864 8YT
Tel: 01709 571722
Fax: 01709 571255
Service:
RR Technical Services
97–9 Worton Road
Isleworth TW7 6EG
Helpline: 020 87580338

Ross
See Recoton

Samsung
225 Hook Rise South
Surbiton
Surrey KT6 7LD
Tel: 020 83910168
Fax: 020 83979949
www.samsungservice.co.uk

Sanyo
Otterspool Way
Watford
Hertfordshire WD2 8JX
Tel: 01923 246363
Fax: 01923 477450
www.sanyo.co.uk

Sharp
Thorpe Road
Newton Heath
Manchester M40 5BE
Tel: 0161 2052333
Fax: 0161 2052638

Sony
Customer Service Group
Pipers Way
Thatcham
Berkshire RG13 4LZ
Tel: 01635 869500
Fax: 01635 860020

Steepletone
Park End Works
Croughton
Brackley
Northamptonshire NN13 5RD
Tel: 01869 810081
Fax: 01869 810784
service@steepletone.com

Tatung
(Deccacolour, Tatung, Vibrant)
PO Box 230

Telford
Shropshire TF3 3WX
Tel: 01952 290111
Fax: 01952 292096
service@tatung.co.uk
www.tatung.co.uk

Toshiba
European Service Centre
Admiralty Way
Camberley
Surrey GU15 3DT
Tel: 01276 622222
Fax: 01276 692256

Vibrant
See Tatung

Yamaha
200 Rickmansworth Road
Watford WD8 7GQ
Tel: 01923 233166
Fax: 01923 810409

ALARM SYSTEMS

Wireless Alarms
17 Church Road
Great Bookham
Surrey KT23 3PG
Tel: 01372 450960
Fax: 01372 450961
www.protectdirect.tv

POWER TOOLS

Atco
See Qualcast

Black & Decker
(DeWalt)
210 Bath Road
Slough SL1 3YD
Tel: 01753 511234
Fax: 01753 551155
www.blackanddecker.co.uk
www.2helpu.com

Bosch
Robert Bosch Limited
PO Box 98,
Uxbridge
Middlesex UB9 5HJ
Customer service enquiries:
01895 838743
www.bosch-pt.co.uk

DeWalt
See Black & Decker

Flymo
Electrolux Outdoor Products
Aycliffe Industrial Park
Newton Aycliffe
Durham DL5 6UP
Tel: 01325 300303
Fax: 01325 310339
Customer helpline:
01325 300303
www.flymo.co.uk

JCB
JCB Power Products
Harvard House
14–16 Thames Road
Barking
Essex IG11 0HX
Tel: 0845 602381
Jcbcustomercare@albaplc.co.
uk

Makita
Michigan Drive
Tongwell
Milton Keynes MK15 8JD
Tel: 01908 211678
Fax: 01908 211400
www.makitauk.com

Plasplugs
Wetmore Road
Burton-on-Trent
Staffs DE14 1SD
Tel: 0128 3530303
Fax: 0128 3531246
www.plasplugs.com

Qualcast
(Atco)
Suffolk Works
Stowmarket
Suffolk
IP14 1EY
Tel: 01449 742000
Fax: 01449 675444
www.qualcast.co.uk
www.atco.co.uk

DIAGNOSTIC TOOLS

Rapitest
GET plc
Unit 4
Brunswick Industrial Park
London N11 1JH
Tel: 0208 2119211
Fax: 0208 2119222
www.getplc.co.uk

GLOSSARY

A

Accessory

An electrical component permanently connected to a circuit – a switch, socket outlet, fused connection unit, etc.

Amp

Short for ampere – unit of measurement of the flow of electricity through an electrical circuit or appliance.

Analogue

Descriptive of a continuously variable signal.

Armature

Rotating cylinder, wound with wire, at the heart of a universal electric motor.

Appliance

Machine or device powered by electricity.

Arcing

Electrical discharge (spark) that occurs when current bridges the gap between two electrodes or any other two surfaces separated by a small gap and a high potential difference.

B

Backup

Copy made on disk for safekeeping of a computer file.

Bimetallic

Term used to describe a component made from two different metals joined together, usually as part of a heat-sensing device such as a thermostat or thermal-overload cutout. With heat, the metals expand at different rates, making the component bend in a particular direction, which eventually causes the device to operate.

Blow

To burn out a fuse.

Branch pipe

A pipe that runs from the main water supply (rising main) to an appliance, tap or valve.

C

Cable

Insulated solid-copper conductors enclosed by PVC sheathing. Cable is used for permanent circuits carrying mains electricity.

Capacitor

Component used to temporarily store an electric charge. Often referred to as a condenser.

Carbon brushes

Conductive sticks of carbon that pass current to an electric motor's armature windings via the commutator.

Cathode-ray tube (CRT)

A glass tube in which a beam of high-energy electrons is focused onto a fluorescent screen in order to create an image. Cathode-ray tubes are often used in TV sets and computer monitors. See also Liquid-crystal display.

CCTV

Closed-circuit television-security system used to observe and sometimes record potential intruders as they approach a building.

CD-R

Compact-disk drive capable of both recording and playback.

CD-ROM

Compact-disk drive capable of playback only.

CD-RW

Compact-disk drive capable of recording, re-recording and playback.

Central processing unit (CPU)

A computer's main system processor.

Chase

A groove cut in masonry or plaster to accept pipework or an electrical cable.

Circuit

A complete path through which electric current is able to flow.

Cistern

Cold-water storage tank.

Closed circuit

Intact electrical circuit that permits current to flow as intended.

Coaxial cable

Cable comprising a solid-copper conductor surrounded by insulation and stranded-wire braid. Used to transmit radio-frequency signals.

Commutator

Part of the armature of an electric motor. Comprises copper-strip contacts connected to the armature windings.

Compressor

Device for pressurizing a gas.

Condensation

The process of water vapour liquefying on a relatively cold surface.

Conductor

A component, usually a length of wire, along which an electric current will pass.

Consumer unit

Formerly known as the 'fuse box', the consumer unit is a box from which all the household electrical circuits emanate. Within the consumer unit, each circuit is protected by a fuse or miniature circuit breaker. The main isolating switch is also housed in the consumer unit.

Continuity

Completeness – the condition of an unbroken circuit through which electricity can flow unhindered.

Cord clamp

Strap securing flexible cord in an appliance or plug in order to prevent the conductors being pulled out of their terminals.

Cord support

Flexible plastic or rubber sleeve fitted over flexible cord just where it enters an appliance in order to reduce stress on the insulated conductors at that point.

Cordless

Generally, a term used to describe an appliance or tool powered by an internal battery instead of mains electricity. Appliances such as kettles or irons that draw power from a separate base unit that is plugged into the mains supply are also described as cordless.

Core

The innermost wire of an electrical conductor.

CPU

See Central processing unit.

Crashed

Term used to describe the condition of a computer that has ceased to function, leaving an image on the screen that cannot be accessed or controlled.

CRT

See Cathode-ray tube.

Cursor

Small icon – usually in the form of a pointer or a vertical bar – that is used to select and control data on a computer screen.

Cylinder

Hot-water storage tank.

D

Defragment

To reorganize files stored piecemeal on a computer's hard disk.

Desktop

The area of a computer screen visible at startup before any software program has been launched.

Dew protection

Preventative measures designed to alleviate condensation.

Diaphragm

Thin membrane that vibrates in response to sound waves.

Digital

Representing data as a series of numerical values.

Digital readout

Display of information as numbers (on a meter, for example), rather than by a pointer moving round a dial.

Digital versatile disc (DVD)

High-density compact disk for storing large amounts of data, especially high-resolution audiovisual material.

Double-insulated

Term used to describe appliances made with non-conductive (usually plastic) cases or shielding that insulates the user from metal components which could become live. Double-insulated appliances are not earthed.

dpi

Dots per inch – measurement of computer-screen resolution.

Draincock

Valve for draining a pipe, appliance or water-storage tank.

DVD

See Digital versatile disc.

E

Earth

A connection between an electrical circuit and the ground.

ELCB

Earth-leakage circuit breaker – now known as a residual current device.

Element

A resistance wire (and sometimes its outer casing) designed to heat up when carrying electric current.

Emery paper

Abrasive paper coated with crushed emery – a hard grey-black mineral, largely composed of corundum.

GLOSSARY

Extension lead
A length of electrical flex (with a socket on one end and a plug on the other) used for temporarily connecting the short permanent flex of an appliance to a wall socket.

F

F-connector
Coaxial connector used primarily to link satellite-broadcast receivers and cables.

Firewire
Fast-acting interface between computers and peripheral devices – it provides transfer rates of up to 3200 Mbits/sec. Also known as IEEE 1394 standard, i.Link connector and High Performance Serial Bus (HPSB). Firewire connectors are 'hot-swappable'.

Flex
See Flexible cord.

Flexible cord
Commonly called flex. Electrical conductors made from numerous wire filaments enclosed in PVC insulation. Usually, two or more insulated conductors are sheathed within an outer layer of PVC. This type of flexible cord is invariably used to carry electricity from wall sockets or similar outlets to electrical appliances.

Floppy disk
A flexible recordable computer disk, contained within a rigid-plastic protective case.

Footprint
Area on the surface of the earth within which it is possible to receive trans-missions from an orbiting satellite.

Format
To prepare a computer disk electronically for use with a particular operating system.

Fuse
Protective device containing a wire that is designed to melt at a predetermined temperature when current exceeds a certain value.

G

Ghosting
Double-image on a TV screen caused by transmitted signals being reflected back to the TV aerial from tall buildings or hills moments after the aerial receives the signals directly.

Glassbreak detector
Device that triggers an alarm system when it detects the particular frequencies generated by door and window glazing being shattered.

Graphics card
Computer circuitry responsible for the images on the monitor screen.

Grommet
Plastic or rubber plug used to conceal a screw fixing. Alternatively, a ring of rubber or plastic that lines a hole to protect electrical cable from chafing. A blind grommet incorporates a thin web of plastic or rubber that seals the hole until the web is cut to provide access for a cable.

H

Hard disk (HD)
Device for long-term storage of computer data (including the computer's operating system).

Helical
Spiral-shaped.

Hone
To sharpen a cutting edge.

Hose clip
Metal or plastic band that, when tightened, prevents flexible plumbing from becoming disconnected.

Hot-swappable
Capable of being disconnected from one system and plugged into another while the power is switched on and the equipment is operating.

Humidistat
Device that regulates the relative humidity of the surrounding air.

I

Icons
Small graphic images generated on the monitor to enable computer users to open programs and access the operating system.

Immersion heater
Electric heating element inserted into a hot-water storage cylinder.

Impeller
Vaned rotating disc inside pumps, compressors, extractor fans and similar appliances.

Inkjet
Nozzle that squirts ink onto paper being fed through a printer attached to a computer.

Insulating tape
Colour-coded self-adhesive tape, usually made from PVC.

Insulation
Nonconductive material surrounding electrical wires or connections to prevent the passage of electricity.

Isolate
To disconnect from the supply of electricity or water.

J

Junction box
Accessory for joining cables used for mains-electricity circuits.

K

Knurled
Impressed with a series of fine grooves designed to provide a better grip – for instance, a knurled knob or handle.

L

Laptop
Portable computer.

LCD
See Liquid-crystal display.

LED
See Light-emitting diode.

Liquid-crystal display (LCD)
Used for TVs, computers, cameras, control panels, etc. LCD screens consist of a liquid-crystal solution sandwiched between two polarized transparent layers. An electric current passing through the crystals varies the level of backlighting that is allowed to pass through the solution, thus creating the image on the screen.

Light-emitting diode (LED)
Small visual indicator used to confirm operation of testing equipment, alarm systems and other electrical appliances.

Lime scale
Dense off-white coating of calcium and magnesium laid down by the storing or passage of water with a naturally high mineral content.

Lint
Fluff – as intercepted by tumble-dryer filters, for example.

Live
The section of an electrical circuit that carries the flow of current to an appliance. Also known as phase.

M

MCB
See Miniature circuit breaker.

Microwave detector
Part of an alarm system that uses high-frequency radio waves to detect movement.

Miniature circuit breaker (MCB)
Special switch inside a consumer unit that cuts off the supply of electricity to a circuit as soon as a fault or an overload is detected. Performs the same function as a fuse.

Motherboard
A computer's central circuitry, to which all other circuits and devices are connected.

Mouse
Device that controls the movement of the cursor on a computer screen.

Mute
Deliberately silence – usually by pressing a button or operating a switch.

N

Neutral
The section of an electrical circuit that carries the flow of current back to its source.

Non-return valve
Device that prevents contamination by ensuring a liquid is unable to flow back towards its source.

O

Open circuit
Discontinuous electrical circuit through which current is unable to flow.

Oxidize
To form a layer of metal oxide, as in rusting.

P

Panic button
Intruder-alarm device that enables you to activate the alarm in an emergency, regardless of whether the system is set. Also known as a personal-attack button.

Passive infrared detector (PIR detector)
Intruder-alarm sensor that transmits a beam of infrared radiation. When the system is set, anyone passing through the beam triggers the alarm.

Personal-attack button
See Panic button.

GLOSSARY

Phase
See Live.

Phono plug
Type of coaxial connector used for audio equipment.

PIR detector
See Passive infrared detector.

PME
See Protective multiple earth.

Port
External connection on a computer – used to link the computer to another device, such as a modem, printer or scanner.

PVC
Polyvinyl chloride – plastic material used for electrical insulation and sheathing.

R

RAM
See Random access memory.

Random access memory (RAM)
Electronic storage facility for data, which can be accessed in any order.

Ratchet
Device that permits movement in one direction only by restricting the reversal of a toothed wheel or rack.

RCCB
Residual current circuit breaker – now known as an RCD. See Residual current device.

RCD
See Residual current device.

Reciprocation
Repetitive forward and backward motion.

Refresh rate
The number of times per second that a device such as a cathode-ray tube or a dynamic RAM chip is re-energized.

Residual current device (RCD)
Device that monitors the flow of electrical current through the live and neutral wires of a

circuit. When an RCD detects an imbalance caused by earth leakage, it cuts off the supply of electricity.

Resolution
Degree of the definition created on a computer monitor. Resolution is measured in dots per inch (dpi).

RF lead
A length of coaxial cable with a coaxial plug at each end.

Ring circuit
Type of domestic power circuit that forms a continuous loop, emanating from and returning to a single fuseway or miniature circuit breaker in the consumer unit. Also known as a ring main.

Ring main
See Ring circuit.

Rising main
Section of domestic plumbing that carries mains-pressure water to the cold-water storage tank, which is usually situated in the loft.

In mains-fed plumbing systems, the rising main is the first section of pipework through which incoming water flows directly to toilets and cold-water taps.

ROM
See Read only memory.

Read only memory (ROM)
Electronic facility that allows fast access to permanently stored data but prevents any modification to that data.

RSI
Repetitive-strain injury (also called repetitive-stress injury).

S

Scart
Twenty-one pin plug-and-socket system that carries audiovisual signals to and from television sets and video-cassette recorders.

Screen burn
Permanent discoloration or image ghosting on a CRT screen, caused by the continuous displaying of high-contrast imagery. Screen savers are designed to avoid this.

Service pipe
The section of plumbing that runs from the water company's external stopcock to the domestic stopcock situated inside a house or flat.

Sheath
The outer layer of insulation surrounding an electrical cable or flex.

Short circuit
The accidental rerouting of electricity to earth – which increases the flow of current and blows a fuse.

Socket adapter
Electrical connector that enables two or more appliances to be plugged into a single wall socket.

Software
Programs installed on or loaded onto a computer.

Sound card
Part of the circuitry responsible for computer audio signals.

Static electricity
Electric discharge resulting from the accumulation of electric charge on an insulated body.

Stator
Stationary electromagnet in an electric motor.

Stopcock
Valve that turns off the flow of mains-pressure water to a house or flat.

Supplementary bonding
Essential special earthing of electrical appliances and exposed metal pipework in a bathroom or kitchen.

Suppressor
Device – such as a resistor –

used in an electrical or electronic system to reduce unwanted electric currents.

Surge
Large momentary increase in mains voltage. Sometimes referred to as a voltage spike.

T

Terminal
A connection to which the bared ends of electrical cable or flex are fixed.

Thermal fuse
Protective device that permanently breaks an electrical circuit at a predetermined temperature in order to prevent overheating.

Thermal-overload cutout (TOC)
Protective device that breaks an electrical circuit at a predetermined temperature in order to prevent overheating. Once the temperature falls below a certain level, a TOC will either reset itself automatically or can be reset manually.

Thermostat
Device that regulates temperature.

TOC
See Thermal-overload cutout.

Trailing socket
Fitted with its own length of flexible cord and 13amp plug, a trailing socket allows for simultaneous connection of several appliances to a mains-fed wall socket.

Transformer
Device that alters voltage – usually from 230V (mains electricity) a higher or lower voltage.

Trip
To activate, usually in the form of switching off.

Tweeter
Audio-speaker driver that handles high-frequency sound waves.

U

USB
Universal Serial Bus – fast-acting interface between computers and peripheral devices such as printers and scanners.

V

Valve
Device for controlling the flow of a liquid – including shutting it off.

VCR
Video cassette recorder.

Virus
A program intended deliberately to disrupt computer operations. Viruses are usually passed from computer to computer via the Internet or contaminated disks.

Volt
Unit of measurement of pressure (potential) difference provided by electricity generators. In the UK, 230V (formerly 240V) is the standard mains voltage.

W

Watts
Units of electricity consumed by an appliance when working. 1000W equals 1kW.

Winding
Coil of copper wire that, when supplied with electric current, induces a magnetic field.

Wireless alarm system
Intruder-alarm system that uses radio frequencies to communicate between detectors and the control panel.

Woofer
Audio-speaker driver that handles low-frequency sound waves.